From Fra Angelico to Bonnard

Sénat
Musée du Luxembourg

From Fra Angelico to Bonnard

Masterpieces from the Rau Collection

SKIRA

Art Director
Marcello Francone

Editing
Doriana Comerlati

Layout
Cinzia De Zani

First published in Italy in 2000 by
Skira Editore S.p.A.
Palazzo Casati Stampa
via Torino 61
20123 Milano
Italy

Printed and bound in Italy. First edition

ISBN 88-8118-802-3 hardcover edition
ISBN 88-8118-801-5 paperback edition

Distributed in North America and Latin America by Abbeville Publishing Group, 22 Cortlandt Street, New York, NY 10007, USA.
Distributed elsewhere in the world by Thames and Hudson Ltd., 181a High Holborn, London WC1V 7QX, United Kingdom.

SÉNAT
MUSÉE DU LUXEMBOURG

19 rue de Vaugirard, 75006 Paris
tel : 01 42 34 28 64 - fax : 01 46 34 61 62

The exhibition is presented
by the Senate of the French Republic
within the Musée du Luxembourg

Under the Presidency of
Mister Christian Poncelet,
President of the Senate

Representative Artistic Direction:
Patrizia Nitti   Marc Restellini

From Fra Angelico to Bonnard
Masterpieces from the Rau Collection
12 July 2000
4 January 2001
Paris, Musée du Luxembourg

Exhibition:

General Commissioner:
Marc Restellini

The works of this exhibition have been selected by Doctor Rau with assistance of Marc Restellini

Collaborated by
Robert Clémentz
Administrator of the collection and private secretary of Doctor Rau

General organization of the exhibition:
Sylvestre Verger

Catalogue of the exhibition:

Supervised by Marc Restellini

Entries on artists and works:
Grahal under the supervision of Michel Laclotte

List of the authors:
Françoise Kunzi (F. K.)
Véronique Damian (V. D.)
François de Vergnettes (F. de V.)
Jean-Christophe Baudequin (J.-Ch. B.)
Isabelle Mayer (I. M.)
Frédéric Elsig (F. E.)
Olivier Zeder (O. Z.)
Philippe Laux (Ph. L.)
Cécile Bouleau (C. B.)
Odile Delenda (O. D.)
Hélène Toussaint (H. T.)
Christophe Dejaune (Ch. D.)

Entries on periods:
Charlotte Martin

Press:
Observatoire, Véronique Jeanneau

Scenography:
Direction: Patrick Marant
Conception: Laurent Guinamard
Description and design: Gilles Guinamard

Model maker:
Jean-Claude Barotto

The exhibition organizers particularly wish to thank the following personalities for their intervention and support:

For the Senate:
Alain Méar,
Directeur du cabinet du Président du Sénat
Yves Marek,
Conseiller au cabinet du Président chargé de la Culture
Hélène Ponceau,
Secrétaire Général de la Questure
Le Général Paul Moulian,
Commandant militaire du Palais du Luxembourg
Alain Di Stefano,
Directeur de l'Architecture, des Bâtiments et des Jardins
Claude Dufour, *Service de l'Architecture*

And also:
François Debouté,
Directeur de la communication de Paris Match
Jean-François Chaigneau, *Journaliste,* Paris Match
Lorraine Willems,
Directeur du marketing et de la communication, LCI
Laeticia De Luca,
Chargé des relations presse et des relations publiques, LCI
Françoise Rey, *Société Decaux*
David Caméo,
Cabinet du Ministre de la Culture
Christian Mantéi,
Directeur Général de l'office du Tourisme de Paris
Didier Hamon,
Directeur de la stratégie et de la politique commerciale, ADP
Jean-Paul Bailly, *Président de la RATP*
Gérard Gros, *Métrobus*
Jérôme Bellay,
Directeur Général de l'antenne, Europe 1
Jean-Paul Giraud,
Président Directeur Général de la Fnac

We particularly wish to thank all people from Art Life, and especially:
Yoshito Nichida, *Chairman*
Teiichiro Yoshida, *Vice-Président*
Yoïchi Nakao, *Managing Director*

The Musée du Luxembourg, housed in the Palais du Luxembourg and placed under the Senate's responsibility, has a prestigious history.
As early as 1615, Marie de Médicis had wanted the Palais du Luxembourg to contain two galleries designed to exhibit paintings. It was for these galleries that Rubens painted L'Histoire de la Reine, *currently in the Musée du Louvre. From 1750 onwards, the Musée du Luxembourg was the first painting museum open to the public, who could thus admire works by Leonardo da Vinci, Titian, Veronese, Rembrandt, van Dick, Poussin or Caravaggio.*
In 1818, the Musée du Luxembourg became the living artists' museum and, in a way, the very first "Modern Art Museum". It showed David, Gros, Girodet, Vernet, Ingres, Delacroix.
Between 1884 and 1886, the Senate put up the building which now contains the museum. It was left the important Caillebotte legacy. Works by Pissarro, Bonnard, Renoir, Degas and Gauguin were on display there until 1937, when the collections were moved to the new Musée d'Art Moderne.
Devoted to modern art, the museum did not avoid controversy. Picasso announced that it was "the most beautiful space in the world", whereas Gauguin, unhappy with the choice of artists, wrote that the the Luxembourg was "a brothel"!
Since then the Musée du Luxembourg, managed by the ministry of Culture, had become an exhibition space, chiefly devoted to the heritage of the French provinces, which provided the general public with a nostalgic taste for a more glorious era.
This year 2000 is now marked by the renewal of the Musée du Luxembourg, which returns to its original function on the Parisian and international art scene, thanks to the convention I signed with the ministry of Culture and the exhibition of masterpieces from Doctor Rau's collection.
I wish to thank Doctor Rau, who managed to assemble an impressive collection, as well as conduct admirable humanitarian actions, for honouring the Senate by his choice of the Musée du Luxembourg to share some of the exceptional masterpieces from his collection, chosen in conjunction with Marc Restellini.
I also want to thank Ms. Patrizia Nitti and the exhibition's general commissioner, Marc Restellini, for bringing to fruition this ambitious project, and, as delegate artistic directors of the museum, for putting their proficiency and knowledge of the art world in the service of the policies the Senate intends to implement for the renewal of the Musée du Luxembourg.
The choice of the prestigious Skira editions to inaugurate, with this exhibition and this very handsome catalogue, a "Musée du Luxembourg" collection, must also be mentioned, for it shows that, straightaway, with the "Masterpieces from the Rau Collection", the Senate has achieved its objective: to place the Musée du Luxembourg at the forefront of cultural life.

Christian Poncelet
President of the French Senate

It is for me a great pleasure to see realized today a long-cherished wish: to show the general public the collection I have put together over more than thirty years. France is now playing host to this exhibition which is travelling all over the world, and which affords a look at the most representative pieces in the collection.
I am very happy that France is doing me the honour of receiving me, France which has been at the heart of Western art for many centuries and has always played a dominant role in my choices for the collection. This collection that I put together patiently and passionately will, I hope, provide a brief look at five centuries of Western art. It is for me highly symbolical that France welcomes me today in one of its most prestigious public spaces, at a time when the whole world is celebrating the millennium. Perhaps this exhibition can also contribute, in its way, to pay homage to the millennium just past.
First of all I want to thank Mr. Christian Poncelet, President of the French Senate, for his warm welcome, and I wish to express my gratitude to him for having chosen my collection to inaugurate the Senate's new cultural policy as regards the Musée du Luxembourg. This honour bestowed on me by the French state is naturally a consecration not only of my artistic choices through the collection, but also for the humanitarian actions I have carried out over the past thirty years.
I also want to extend thanks to the organizers of the exhibition who have worked unstintingly for several months to put on this show. I want to thank Mr. Méar, chief of staff of the President of the Senate, as well as Mr. Marek, technical counsellor to the President of the Senate. I congratulate Mr. Marc Restellini, as well as Ms. Nitti on their new positions on the board of the Musée du Luxembourg, and address my warmest thanks to Mr. Sylvestre Verger for the organization of the exhibition.
Finally, I particularly wish to thank Mr. Marc Restellini, general commissioner of the exhibition, whom I asked several years ago to undertake the setting up of this project, and to set up a travelling show of my collection throughout the world, and without whom none of this would have happened. May he here receive the friendliest and warmest of thanks.
I now wish the exhibition good luck on its new stage and a great deal of pleasure to all the visitors.

Doctor Gustav Rau

Contents

13 From Fra Angelico to Pierre Bonnard
Masterpieces from the Rau Collection
Marc Restellini

Paintings
21 The Italian School
53 The Flemish and Dutch School
81 The German School
95 The French School
121 The Spanish School
131 The British School
139 The Impressionist Revolution
205 Symbolism and Nabis
235 Fauvism
247 Expressionism
257 After 1940

Appendixes
264 List of Illustrations
266 Timeline

Marc Restellini

From Fra Angelico to Pierre Bonnard
Masterpieces from the Rau Collection

Important collectors are essential figures in the art world. They represent the final link in the economic chain of artistic creation. The finality of every work of art is to hang on a public or private wall. Without the collector, the artist has no genuine reason for creating. Whether they were commissions carried out for such and such a benefactor, civil or religious, from the fifteenth to the eighteenth century, whether they were presented in the Salons during the nineteenth century, or thanks to an art dealer, from the end of nineteenth century each work only achieves legitimacy, and its creator recognition, when its purpose is to belong to an individual or to an institution.
Very soon, in the twentieth century, and more particularly in its second half, the major private collector replaced the institutional patron, and acted as a link with the public by means of museum exhibitions and with the ever more popular system of endowing museums.
In the very small and restricted world of contemporary collectors, one can count on the fingers of one hand collections as important as that of Doctor Rau. Most of the great collectors have focussed on one period (frequently the nineteenth and twentieth centuries), a type, a style (Impressionism, Fauvism, School of Paris), sometimes on a single artist. In each case, there is a reasonable motivation for these choices: because they know the artist, because their parents had started a collection at a precise moment in time, or else, the inherited collection created an opening towards something different, a continuity of the preceding one, or alternatively, by breaking away completely from it. But there are practically no collections which, in themselves, cover five centuries of art history with such a refined taste and such quality.
Furthermore, the very rare collections on Doctor Rau's level are usually public ones. They were part of a bequest or are exhibited within a public foundation, like that of Baron Thyssen in Madrid, the Frick Collection in New York, or else those of Wallace or of Dulwich in London. Doctor Rau's collection is the only one of such quality and, probably, the last one not available to the public. So Doctor Rau gives us a very fine present indeed, today, by agreeing to show a representative part of his collection in public. The initiative is all the more symbolical since it coincides with the change of millennium and allows us to view a remarkable synthesis of half a millennium of Western art.
Indeed, one of the particularities which provides this collection with its exceptional character is precisely the fact it spans five centuries of European art in a didactic spirit equal to that of the greatest museums throughout the world. The works have therefore been classified according to the great schools of art from the Renaissance until the 1950s. Nothing is missing, not one period, not one school, no geographical area from the best Europe had to offer within the last five centuries.
The Italian School is present with such important works as two fragments of one of the most beautiful altarpieces painted by Fra Angelico for the high altar in San Domenico in Fiesole (cat. nos. 1, 2), as well as an impressive panel by Vittore Crivelli – a *Pietà* (cat. no. 3) – and major works such as a delightful *Portrait of a Young Woman* (cat. no. 4) by

Bernardino Luini, which recalls the huge influence of Leonardo da Vinci on this artist. From the Bolognese artist Guido Reni an astonishing *David Decapitating Goliath* (cat. no. 6). We must also note the admirable *Saint John the Evangelist* (cat. no. 8) by Carlo Dolci, which comes from one of the best series by that artist representing the four Evangelists, and which was part of the Riccardi collection in Florence before belonging to Lucien Bonaparte. The later Italian School is represented by such great Venetian painters as Canaletto (cat. no. 11), Bernardo Bellotto (cat. no. 12) and Giandomenico Tiepolo, with a stunningly modern *Allegorical Portrait of a Young Woman with Flowers* (cat. no. 13).

The Flemish School and the Dutch School are also perfectly illustrated by different masterpieces from the most original and most representative masters, starting with the admirable *Saint Veronica* (cat. no. 14) by Colyn de Coter, a brilliant student of Rogier van der Weyden. In the best style of Hieronimus Bosch's "devilishnesses", stands the very imaginative *Temptation of Saint Anthony* (cat. no. 15) by Jan Mandyn. One must also note some splendid men's portraits by Frans Pourbus (cat. no. 16) and Gerard Ter Borch (cat. no. 24), as well as the very Italianate vision of the *Backgammon Players* (cat. no. 17) by Hendrick Ter Brugghen.

Let us overlook the Dutch landscapes such as those by Jan van Goyen (cat. no. 18), Salomon van Ruisdael (cat. no. 19) and Frans Post (cat. no. 21). Flemish painting would not be properly represented without these images of daily life in Flanders. Doctor Rau has chosen to display *Interior of the Oude Kerke, Amsterdam* (cat. no. 23) by Emmanuel de Witte, as well as the formidable *Art Lover's Cabinet* (cat. no. 26) by Jan Siberechts. But two of the most remarkable works from this period are the *Still-life with Herring's Head* (cat. no. 25), by Willem van Aelst, probably one of his most important *Vanities*, in which he shows his mastery in the rendering of the glasses' transparencies and brilliance. The other masterly piece from the collection concerning that period is, of course, *The Cook* (cat. no. 22) by Gerard Dou, one of those little panels which the artist favoured for depicting popular characters in Flanders, often ugly people, worn out by a difficult life and service in the pay of the establishment of the city of Leyden.

From the German School, we must point out two works by Lucas Cranach the Elder, one of which is a *Triptych* (cat. no. 28) whose very original iconography depicts episodes from the life of Christ, particularly *Christ among the Doctors*, surrounded on one hand by the *Multiplication of the Loaves*, and by the *Marriage at Cana* on the other. This work shows how influenced Cranach was at the time by the German Humanists' ideas. The other work by the German master, a little tondo of 1525, shows a very cruel *Judith* (cat. no. 29) most unusually surrounded by two serving maids looking upon her with respect and veneration; she herself wears a headdress which gives her a part well beyond that of a simple heroine saving her people. Doctor Rau's coherence led him, in 1987, to purchase the *Servant in a Kitchen* (cat. no. 31) by Jeremias van Winghe, a superb genre scene which shows the cook's pleased and slightly amused look at the sight of a kitten "stealing" a piece of meat, while in the background the rich owners are quietly feasting. One should also note the superb portrait by Graff (cat. no. 32), which recalls Doctor Rau's fondness for very intense and heavily worked portraits.

The very classic French School starts by providing us with a very flattering glimpse of the seventeenth century with the other superb *Vanity* in the Rau collection, this time by Jacques Linard (cat. no. 33), alongside his very last work, dated the year before his death. This profound work, with its strong religious flavour, gives us an opportunity to appreciate a rare artist. Mainly based in the eighteenth century, the rest of the works in the collection displaying French art is characterized by landscapes. Among the superb paintings by Jean-François Millet (cat. no. 35), Jean-Baptiste Pater (cat. no. 37) and the spectacular Chevalier Volaire (cat. no. 41), we can also admire one of François Boucher's major works, the *Flute Lesson* (cat. no. 38), from the

Baroness de Rotschild's collection, which had previously been in the Wildenstein collection. In the purest *Pastor Fido* tradition, this wonderful pastoral scene depicting two children playing the flute in the midst of a flock of sheep is splendidly harmonious. In the portrait series, it is worth looking closely at the magnificent representations by Nicolas de Largillière (cat. no 36), Maurice-Quentin de La Tour (cat. no. 39), Elisabeth-Louise Vigée-Le Brun (cat. no. 44) and Jean-Baptiste Greuze (cat. no. 40) to come finally to one of the most exceptional pieces in the collection: *Portrait of François-Henri, Duke of Harcourt* (cat. no. 42) by Jean-Honoré Fragonard, one of his fifteen fantasy figures.

With fewer works, the two Spanish and English Schools still count many important pieces, such as El Greco's admirable *Saint Dominic in Prayer* (cat. no. 45), or José de Ribera's *Saint Jerome* (cat. no. 46) for the Spaniards and the very different and representative portraits by John Michael Wright (cat. no. 47), Joshua Reynolds (cat. no. 48) and Thomas Gainsborough (cat. no. 49) for the English.

The modern part of the Rau collection is quite as impressive and important as the ancient one. Naturally, it gives pride of place to Impressionism, from its beginnings to its final developments. And so we can admire, among the important precursors of Impressionism, one of the most beautiful of all Camille Corot's works: the *Algerian Woman* (cat. no. 51). On the same high level of quality, Gustave Courbet's *Bacchante* (cat. no. 52) gives us an inkling of the evolution of women's representations at the end of the nineteenth century. Of the five works by Eugène Boudin in the Rau collection, we have selected here the *Beach at Trouville* (cat. no. 53), probably the most important and certainly one of the most intimate and beautiful *crinoline* scenes painted by the artist from Honfleur. The selection of Impressionist works really starts with Frédéric Bazille's masterpiece *Fisherman with a Net* (cat. no. 54). An emblematic painting, it is one of the defining works marking the transition from classical art and the academic representation of the body to the great Impressionist theories, concerning light, colour and man's relationship with nature.

After that, all the great artists of Impressionism are to be found in the collection. Claude Monet is present with six masterly works which are almost enough by themselves to constitute a little retrospective of the Master. In a style very reminiscent of that of the Barbizon School, the *Woods and Undergrowth* (cat. no. 59), dated 1865, is evidence of the importance Monet attached at that time to Corot, Courbet or Daubigny. Already less classical in style, the *Wooden Bridge* (cat. no. 60) is dated 1872; it comes from Manet's collection and was also previously in the Baret-Decap collection then in that of Henri Canonne. Respectively from 1874 and 1881, the *View of Amsterdam* (cat. no. 61) and *Flood* (cat. no. 62) attest to the painter's move to Impressionism. But from 1886 there is another of the masterpieces in the Rau collection, one of the most remarkable works by Monet, the *Port-Coton Pyramids* (cat. no. 63), one of the series of six which the artist painted in Belle-Ile-en-Mer. The last Monet in the collection is dated 1895 and represents a marvellous snowscape: *Houses in the Snow in Norway* (cat. no. 64). This landscape shows the master's technique for handling light and colour effects since, in this instance, he practically undertook a monochromatic variation on white, almost thirty years before Malevitch.

The collection presents two works by Auguste Renoir, one of which was among the fifteen paintings the artist showed in the second Salon des Impressionnistes in 1876. This major work, entitled *Head of a Woman* or *Woman with a Rose* (cat. no. 65), shows us the young Margot (Marguerite Legrand) who also posed for Renoir in the *Moulin de la Galette* and in the *Cup of Chocolate*. Also by Renoir, the *Portrait of Henry Lerolle* (cat. no. 66) recalls Doctor Rau's preference for powerful men's portraits, such as those seen before in the collection.

We must also draw attention to the superb sketch by Edouard Manet (cat. no. 56) before coming upon one of the masterpieces of the modern collection, the *Sea at L'Estaque* (cat. no. 55) by Paul Cézanne, which marks the start of modernity and prefigures the art of the twentieth century.

By Edgar Degas, we will chiefly point out the last *Self-portrait* (cat. no. 58) painted by the artist (1900), where traces of his tragic infirmity can be seen and which stresses the solitude of the nearly blind painter in the greyness of his studio.

By Camille Pissarro a magnificent series traces some of the most beautiful stages in the oeuvre of one of Doctor Rau's favourite artists. The splendid *View of L'Hermitage, Jallais Hill in Pontoise, 1867* (cat. no. 67), is yet again one of the masterpieces of the collection, but we can also admire the very fine *Road from Saint-Germain to Louveciennes* (cat. no. 68), or else a view of the *Courthouse at Pontoise* (cat. no. 69). By Alfred Sisley, the collection has one of his admirable snowscapes – *Effect of Snow at Marly* (cat. no. 71) – which the artist painted during the winter 1875-1876. Gustave Caillebotte is also well represented in the collection with an important view of *Snow-covered Rooftops* (cat. no. 74), a rare subject for this artist, unlike Sisley.

Among the major masterpieces of Impressionism, the Rau collection owns one of Mary Cassatt's finest pastels: a maternity showing *Louise Feeding Her Child* (cat. no. 75). The painting reminds us that the American artist had a great fondness for this subject with its biblical overtones which she reinvented in the Impressionist period at a moment when feminist thinking and movements were getting under way.

Along with the artists as part of the continuing tradition of Impressionism, the collection owns a major work by Paul Signac, a jewel of Pointillism: this profound and sober work represents the *Sea. Saint-Briac* (cat. no. 77) and shows how at that particular time Signac worked completely according to Seurat's ideas and his series of the Grande Jatte island. By Gino Severini, the large *Landscape at Civray* (cat. no. 81) also attests the implication of the Impressionist movement on the international level and on other artistic movements in the twentieth century. In particular, this work from Severini's first period shows up the influence of Impressionistic landscape in such a specific movement as Futurism in Italy.

Doctor Rau pays homage to Symbolism first of all with Odilon Redon, represented by two major works. One of them is the very impressive *Apollo's Chariot* (cat. no. 83) from the Milton de Groot collection, which was for a long while shown in the Metropolitan Museum of Art in New York. There are also Ferdinand Hodler (cat. no. 84) and Gustav Klimt (cat. no. 85) with two very interesting works.

The Rau collection has large holdings of the Nabi group. Gauguin's presence is very strongly perceived in Sérusier's *Spring at Pouldu* (cat. no. 86); but it is thanks to two essential works – *July* (cat. no. 94) and *Mother and Child on a Yellow Bed* (cat. no. 95) – by the group's theoretician, Maurice Denis, that the Nabis are probably best represented. Then there is a fine work by Félix Vallotton (cat. no. 87), two very representative paintings by Pierre Bonnard, including an important *Saint-Tropez Bay* (cat. no. 88), and a fine series of Edoaurd Vuillard, including two *Self-portraits* (cat. nos. 90, 92), a view of *Chestnut Trees, Rue Truffaut* (cat. no. 91), which is very Nabi, and finally an exceptional large-scale work, painted in tempera, showing a *Portrait of Monsieur André Benac* (cat. no. 93).

Doctor Rau also wants to signify his special fondness for Fauvism and Espressionism. For the first of these two movements, which have many affinities, the main painters in the movement are shown: Maurice de Vlaminck with a rather Fauvist view of the Parisian outskirts – *Fauve Landscape near Chatou* (cat. no. 97); André Derain with some magnificent *Cypresses* (cat. no. 100) from 1907; Albert Marquet (cat. no. 96); Kees van Dongen with a splendid *Little Girl with Sailor Collar* (cat. no. 99), in a square format, showing Dolly van Dongen, his daughter; and above all the *Beach at Sainte-Adresse* (cat. no. 98) by Raoul Dufy, of an exceptional quality, undoubtedly one of the most important by the master from Le Havre. Among the Expressionists are to be found, of course, Edvard Munch (cat. no. 101), but, particularly, a major work by Alexei

Jawlensky (cat. no. 102) and an extraordinary *Clown in a Green Costume* (cat. no. 103) by August Macke. Let us note, finally, an important *Still Life with Bottle and Glasses* (cat. no. 106) by Giorgio Morandi. This exhibition provides a very complete look at the Rau collection and shows up the magnitude of the task undertaken by Doctor Rau over nearly thirty years. An exceptional collection which shows one man's enlightened choices, a man who is a great art lover, rarely seeking advice, and who has managed to endow this collection with a unique specificity and originality. A man of incredible human resources, his collection is like him: powerful, deeply humanistic, solid and independent, never superficial, always profound.

This exhibition is due simply to Doctor Rau's own wishes. All of the organizers join me in espressing here all our gratitude and our friendship. We wish to thank all the members of the Rau Foundation, and particularly Ms. Thost. We also want to express our gratitude to Mr. Clémentz, who looks after the Rau collection and who played a leading role in the setting up and success of this exhibition. We would finally like to thank the team of the Grahal for its active participation in the making of the catalogue, by writing the technical and scientific notes of the works. We wish to extend our warmest thanks to Messrs Borjon and Simonetti, as well as Ms. Gautier.
We wish this exhibition all the success and enthusiastic response it deserves.

Paintings

Remarks

The plates have been grouped into twelve categories by periods and styles.
For each plate the following data are given: catalogue number, artist, title, year of production, material, size, inscriptions.

All of the commentaries have been originally written in French by the following authors who are identified by the uppercase initials at the end:

F. K.	Françoise Kunzi
V. D.	Véronique Damian
F. de V.	François de Vergnettes
J. Ch. B.	Jean-Christophe Baudequin
I. M.	Isabelle Mayer
F. E.	Frédéric Elsig
O. Z.	Olivier Zeder
Ph. L.	Philippe Laux
C. B.	Cécile Bouleau
O. D.	Odile Delenda
H. T.	Hélène Toussaint
Ch. D.	Christophe Dejaune

The entries regarding the works were carried out under the editorship of the Grahal (Groupe de Recherche Art Histoire Architecture et Littérature), who since 1991 has been engaged in carrying out for Doctor Rau the catalogue of the works comprising his collection of paintings (two volumes under the editorship of Michel Laclotte) and of sculptures (one volume under the scientific direction of Bertrand Jestaz). The texts appearing here will be updated on the occasion of the publication of the general catalogue of works scheduled for 2001, in particular the references regarding the "bibliography" and "exhibitions" headings.

Many thanks to all the team at Grahal:
Michel Borjon, Pascal Simonetti,
Claire Gautier, Pierre Legros.

The works marked with an asterisk (*) were a donation and form the patrimony of Doctor Rau's Art Foundation, at Embrach.

The Italian School

Unlike Flemish and French painters, the Italians soon left behind the Gothic style which, in any case, they had adopted with some misgivings.
It should also be noted that Italian art is not absolutely homogenous and that the cities – often rivals – in the peninsula witnessed many different schools and styles.
The birth – or Renaissance – of Italian painting as such was mainly developed in Siena and Florence. Although during the fifteenth century there were still to be found traces of a late Gothic (Gentile da Fabriano, Pisanello), most artists, from the fourteenth century on, attempted to create a new style, less rigid and more expressive. Giotto was undoubtedly the forerunner of this new style. The expression of his figures, the movement of forms, the rendering of forms and space mark a break with the Middle Ages, and in this instance, the first approach to modernity.
In the fifteenth century, with the flowering of humanist philosophy and the spread of patronage, Florence definitely enjoyed the status of a cultural capital. Donatello, Brunelleschi and Masaccio are the incarnation of Florentine spirit and style. At that time, Venice remained aloof and marked by the imprint of northern countries.
During the second half of the fifteenth century, provincial workshops sprang up around Florence. The most noteworthy are those of Orvieto, Perugia and Ferrara, in which one finds, respectively, Luca Signorelli, Perugino and Mantegna.
At the end of the fifteenth century a turnabout took place: Rome, under the impulse of the pontifical power, became the main pole of attraction for artists, especially for two geniuses: Raphael and Michelangelo. The *venustà* of the former and the *terribilità* of the second led to a taste for the bizarre, the fantastic in their successors, contorsions or exaggerated stretching of forms. Thus was born the "Mannerist" style, which could be defined as a form of art which, instead of creating forms, is inspired by existing models and frequently arrives at artificial representations; Vasari, Salviati, Parmigianino, Il Rosso, Romano, Beccafumi and Pontormo are among the main exponents of this movement.
With the Counter-Reformation inaugurated by the Council of Trent, the Italian painters at the end of the sixteen century evolved differently. We have to await the arrival of the Carracci brothers to see a return of a kind of "Classicism". As for Caravaggio he provided a realistic style, considered outrageous by the critics, but followed by a great many of his contemporaries (Reni, Caracciolo); Italy and soon all of Europe in the seventeenth century saw the emergence of a new style which blossomed mainly through architecture and monumental designs. The chief characteristics of Baroque appear in works by Bernini, Pietro da Cortona, Domenichino, Guercino and Guido Reni. The change from Baroque to the Rococo style took place during the eighteenth century in the cities of Genoa and above all in Venice, in which the painters of *vedute* and of great sceneries, such as Tiepolo, Canaletto and Bellotto, all worked.

1-2

Fra Angelico
(Guido di Pietro, known as Fra Angelico, before 1396 ? – 1455)
Saint Nicholas of Bari, 1424–1425
Saint Michael, 1424–1425

Panel, gold background.
H: 35.5 cm; W: 14 cm (each).
On the back of *Saint Nicholas of Bari*, an old ink writing: *Questa figura che rappresenta S. Agostino Vescovo e Dottore, di mano di Giov. Beato Angelico era una delle dieci che adornavano l'Altare del convento di S. Domenico di Fiesole*.
On the back of *Saint Michael*, an old ink writing: *Questa [?] figura che rappresenta [?] S. Michele Arcangelo, di mano di Giov. [?] Beato Angelico: era una delle dieci che adornavano un Altare del convento a [?] S. Domenico di Fiesole*.
GR 1.696 and GR 1.697

The first mention of Fra Angelico (Vicchio di Mugello, Florence, before 1396 ? – Rome, 1455) in a document notes his registration as a painter in the company of San Niccolò at the Carmine church in Florence in 1417; he then entered, around 1418, the San Domenico monastery at Fiesole. His early works, contemporary with those of Masaccio and of Masolino, fall within the sphere of the late Gothic represented in Florence by Starnina, Lorenzo Monaco and Gentile da Fabriano. For San Domenico at Fiesole, he carried out the triptych for the high altar – to which belong the two saints in the Rau collection – the Annunciation *(Madrid, Museo del Prado) and later the* Coronation of the Virgin *(Paris, Musée du Louvre). In 1438, Fra Angelico joined the monastery of San Marco whose decoration he started, with the aid of colleagues, the following year. In 1446, Eugene IV summoned the artist to the Vatican to decorate a chapel which is now destroyed. His successor, Nicholas V, commissioned the painter to decorate a neighbouring chapel with the* Scenes from the Lives of Saint Lawrence and Saint Stephen. *After a stay in Florence (1450–1453) he went back to Rome where he died February 18, 1455.*

J. Pope-Hennessy's proposal in 1952 to associate the two altarpiece sections in the Rau collection – *Saint Nicholas of Bari* and *Saint Michael* – with that executed by Fra Angelico for the high altar at San Domenico at Fiesole has been critically accepted. The vicissitudes which the triptych showing the *Virgin and Child between the Angels, Saint Thomas Aquinas and Saint Barnabas*, and *Saint Dominic and Saint Peter Martyr* has undergone prove that even masterpieces are not immune from the ravages of time and from the hard law of taste.
Vasari corroborated that in 1501 the Florentine painter Lorenzi di Credi assembled the three main panels to form a unified *pala*. He also enlarged it and added painted architecture and a landscape to the gilt background. The small figures of the saints in the frame's pilasters did not escape this updating: a niche of the *pietra serena*, still visible on photographs taken prior to restoration, covered up the gold background. But it was probably at the end of the eighteenth or beginning of the nineteenth century that the altarpiece was dismembered. In fact between 1792 – the year Moreni (*Notizie istoriche dei contorni di Firenze parte terza: della porta a San Gallo alla città di Fiesole*) saw the altarpiece still intact – and 1827 – the date of the sale of the five elements of the predella by a Florentine merchant (now London, National Gallery), other elements coming from a fourteenth century polyptych were substituted for the pilasters; the pieces of the base suffered the same fate. Moreover, the dismantling of the altarpiece corresponds to the period of discovery of, and new interest in, the Primitives, the taste for those artists who preceded Raphael having established itself in the second half of the eighteenth century. The inscription on the back of the Rau panels suggests that "ten figures" – meaning ten elements – made up the triptych with pilasters, predella and gables. The attempt at reconstitution put forward by U. Baldini (1977) proposes the following identities, besides two saints in the Rau collection and the three elements which remain in the San Domenico at Fiesole: *Saint Mark* and *Saint Matthew* (Chantilly, Musée Condé), two tondi, the *Angel* and the *Virgin Annunciate* (previously Vienna, Tucker collection), the reliquary-tabernacle in the Hermitage Museum in Saint Petersburg, the two *Angels* in the Galleria Sabauda in Turin, and *God the Father in Benediction* in the British Royal Collection as well as the two bishop saints, one in the National Gallery in London, and the other formerly in the Moses collection in New York.
Although it can still be argued that some of these elements never belonged to the San Domenico polyptych, there is no doubt that the two saints in the Rau collection did. It is however necessary to review the iconography of one of them and to recognise – at the side of *Saint Michael Slaying the Dragon* – not, as the inscription says, Saint Augustine, but *Saint Nicholas of Bari* who is indicated by the presence of three golden balls, his traditional attribute. The

History:
Fiesole, high altar in the church of the San Domenico convent; Sheffield, Rev. Hawkins-Jones collection; London, Sotheby's, June 26, 1957, no. 151; Bel Air (California), Mr. and Mrs. Deane Johnson's collection; London, Sotheby's, December 6, 1972, no. 6.

Exhibition:
Florence, *Mostra delle opere del Beato Angelico*, 1955, nos. 7–8, pl. VIII (presented as from Fra Angelico's studio).

Bibliography:
G. Vasari, *Le Vite de più eccellenti pittori, scultori ed architetti* [1st ed. Florence, 1568], ed. Milanesi, 1878–1885, vol. II, p. 510; J. Pope-Hennessy, *Fra Angelico*, London, 1952, pp. 166–167; B. Berenson, *Italian Pictures of the Renaissance: Florentine School*, London, 1963, p. 15, pls. 592, 593; J. Pope-Hennessy, *Fra Angelico*, London, new ed. completed 1974, pp. 189–190, figs. 7a, 7b; U. Baldini, "Contributi all'Angelico: il trittico di San Domenico di Fiesole e qualche altra aggiunta", in *Scritti di storia dell'arte in onore di Ugo Procacci*, Milan, 1977, pp. 236–246; U. Baldini, *Beato Angelico*, Florence, 1986, pp. 19–20, 228.

high quality of the panels, brought out by their excellent state of preservation and underlined by some stylistic characteristics such as the luxury of the garments and the impact of the colours, as well as the chiaroscuro modelling of the complexions in the manner of Gentile da Fabriano, prove that they are part of Fra Angelico's altarpiece.
In the second edition of his monograph on the artist, J. Pope-Hennessy (1974) goes back on his previous dating of 1428–1430 and dates the altarpiece – and hence the *Saint Nicholas of Bari* and the *Saint Michael* – to the years 1424–1425. The altarpiece of San Domenico in Fiesole thus becomes the first known work by the artist, completed even before the *Saint Peter Martyr* altarpiece (Florence, Museo di San Marco) dated 1429. Consequently, Masaccio's influence on it can be more directly grasped, while the sculptural aspect of the Rau collection saints is still very similar to Donatello's statues.
V. D.

3

Vittore Crivelli (circa 1440 – 1501)
Christ of Pity or *Pietà*, 1460

Tempera on panel.
H: 106 cm; W: 72 cm.
GR 1.1000

History:
Florence, Brentano collection; London, Priestley collection; London, Christie's, July 5, 1991, no. 75.

Bibliography:
R. van Marle, *The Development of the Italian Schools of Painting*, The Hague, 1936, vol. XVIII, p. 84, note 1; F. Zeri, "Appunti nell'Ermitage e nel museo Puskin", in *Bollettino d'arte*, July-September 1961, p. 236, note 45; S. Di Provvido, *La pittura di Vittore Crivelli*, L'Aquila, 1972, p. 188, pl. 55.

Vittore Crivelli (Venice, circa 1440 – Fermo, 1501) was the famous Carlo Crivelli's younger brother. In 1465 they left their native city, Venice, probably together, for Zara before going to the Marches. Vittore's name is mentioned for the first time in 1481, in the contract for a painting commissioned by a church dedicated to the Virgin in Monteparo. From 1487 to 1501 he lived in Fermo. Like Carlo, he worked for churches in small towns in the Marches. They painted few works together, but Vittore's style echoes his brother's. He shared Carlo's taste for decorative effects, but preferred more rigid and less dramatic compositions.

Following Raimond van Marle and Federico Zeri, Sandra di Provvido has included this *Christ of Pity* or *Pietà* in Vittore Crivelli's oeuvre. The shapes of the faces, eyes and mouths as well as the sense of the setting are unmistakable clues. Moreover, Vittore Crivelli handled this subject in a fairly similar way in several works. Approximately ten have been listed.
In the Rau collection painting, Christ has just been taken down from the cross, which is located behind him. His body is presented frontally and upright by Saint John and the Virgin, who is clasping his son's head against hers with her left hand. Her other hand is holding up his torso. Behind the Virgin, Mary Magdalen is kissing Christ's arm. In the foreground, a stone and marble parapet evokes the tomb where Christ's body will be buried, which the figures may have already entered. Rona Goffen's studies of Giovanni Bellini's works (1430?–1516) on the same subject suggest that the Rau collection painting, which portrays a scene of the Passion, is a timeless devotional image (R. Goffen, *Giovanni Bellini*, Yale University, 1989, pp. 67–68). These images enabled the faithful to contemplate the body of the sacrificed Christ during each Eucharist.
The rich drapery covering the cross behind Christ and the parapet in front of him indicate that his body is an object of veneration. The low wall becomes the symbolic equivalent of an altar. Christ's hand moves towards the space of the viewer, who, in his adoration, may be tempted to kiss it.
Emile Mâle studied the evolution of the Christ of pity, an image which was brought from the East in the twelfth or thirteenth century and interpreted in Rome as a view of Saint Gregory during a mass (E. Mâle, *L'art religieux de la fin du Moyen Age en France*, Paris, 1969, pp. 99–102). Representations of Christ alone, similar to Byzantine images, became widespread because of the enormous indulgences granted to Christians who prayed in front of them. From the fourteenth century in Italy, the Virgin, Saint John and sometimes Mary Magdalen surrounded Christ (Giovanni da Milano; Florence, Galleria dell'Accademia). As Emile Mâle wrote: "The poor image of pity then became a wonder of feeling" (ibid., p. 102).
In the fifteenth century, it was Venetian artists who were the most interested in these images, since Venice had close ties to the Byzantine world. Giovanni Bellini and Carlo Crivelli (circa 1430 – circa 1493) handled this subject several times. Their paintings, whose movement and pathos make them quite different from Vittore's, already presaged the works of the following generations which, following Lotto's and Sebastiano del Piombo's examples, never grew tired of this theme. The organization of the Rau collection *Pietà* recalls Bellini's, painted in 1460 (Milan, Pinacoteca di Brera). In his various *Pietà*, Vittore Crivelli never strayed from traditional schemas. For example, the *Christ* of Saint Lucy in Fermo still has his hands crossed, as he does in folk prints (Di Provvido, 1972, pl. 41).
The Rau collection *Pietà* shows the cross and the instruments of the Passion, which is rare in late *Quattrocento* painting. This *Christ of Pity* surmounted a retable, like most of the paintings mentioned. Its composition is all the simpler and more convincing since it complies with traditional iconography. The vertical forms of the figures are squeezed in between the horizontal lines of the low wall on the bottom and the arms of the cross above. The oblique lines start out from the instruments of the Passion, continuing on the left in the folds and edging of the Virgin's drapery and on the

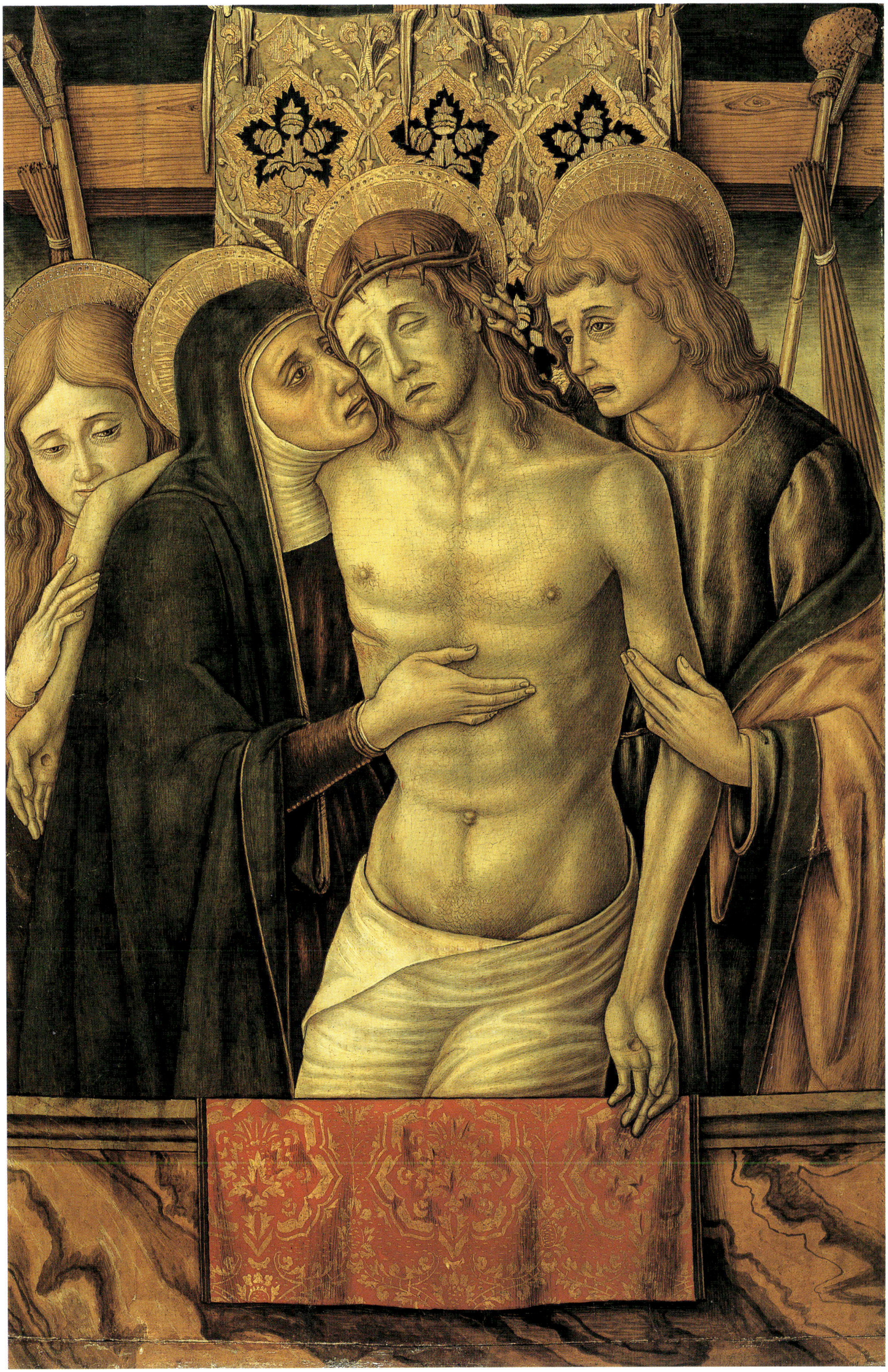

right in Christ's arm. Christ's body spreads out in this confined space. His hand stretches beyond these limits, as do the rich draperies which help give the scene its visionary character. The expressions are measured, yet the panel emanates feeling. All the gestures are delicate, especially that of the Virgin clasping Christ's head against her own. The setting and colours are rich without being excessive. Golds, oranges and browns dominate, with the blues and greens of the sky and vestments of the Virgin and Saint John slightly disrupting this harmony.
Crivelli has painted a devotional image in keeping with traditional iconography. His sound technique is devoid of all the excesses his brother was never able to resist. This work radiates a silence which compelled the believers for whom it was painted to meditate.
F. de V.

4 Bernardino Luini (circa 1485 – 1532)
Portrait of a Young Woman, 1525

Wood transposed to canvas.
H: 35 cm; W: 27.3 cm.
GR 1.869

History:
Collection of Philippe d'Orléans (1674–1723), Regent of France (1715–1723) (possibly acquired by Le Grand?); through legacy to Louis-Philippe-Joseph d'Orléans (1747–1793), known as Philippe-Egalité; sold in 1791 to a Brussels banker, then to Laborde de Méréville, with all the Italian paintings; London, sold December 26, 1798, bought by the third Duke of Bridgewater, transmitted through legacy up to the fifth Count of Ellesmere; London, Christie's, October 18, 1946, no. 113, bought by Colnaghi; London, Agnew's, 1948; Lady Malcolm Robertson; London, Christie's, December 10, 1982, no. 75.

Exhibitions:
London, Colnaghi, *Paintings of Old Masters*, 1947, no. 5; London, Agnew's, *Paintings by Old Masters*, 1948, no. 31; Manchester, City Art Gallery, *Art Treasures Centenary*, 1957, no. 55.

The first work definitely known to have been painted by Bernardino Luini (Luino, Lago Maggiore ?, circa 1485 – Milan ?, 1532) is dated 1512. It has a few hints of Leonardo's sfumato *(chiaroscuro) combined with a strong Lombard tradition inherited from Foppa and Bergognone. Details concerning the artist's training remain unknown, but it seems that Leonardo's influence overshadowed that of all others from very early on. Luini used Leonardo's motifs, facial expressions and* sfumato *for the modelling. The hypothesis of a trip to Rome, which would explain a certain Raphaelite influence, is still controversial. Luini was active throughout Lombardy and beyond, painting great, narrative fresco cycles that spread Leonardo's pictorial language far and wide.*

The Orléans family owned three paintings attributed to Leonardo da Vinci. One of them is lost, the second is the *Colombine* today attributed to Francesco Melzi and alternately identified with the paintings in Saint Petersburg (Hermitage Museum) and Richmond (Virginia Museum of Fine Arts) and the third is the one in the Rau collection. Since 1854 art historians have unanimously agreed with Waagen's attribution of it to Luini. The soft chiaroscuro's modelling of forms and the model's dreamlike air and round face are characteristic of this artist and attest to Leonardo's influence. The Rau collection painting is a fragment of a larger work, but it is not known what the original painting looked like. The young woman's complicated hair style evokes that of Leonardo's *Leda*, where the hair is painstakingly painted (Windsor Castle, inv. 12515 and 12516). This may depict the daughter of Herodias since Luini often painted *Salome Receiving John the Baptist's Head* (Paris, Musée du Louvre; Madrid, Museo del Prado; Vienna, Kunsthistorisches Museum; Boston, Museum of Fine Arts; Isola Bella, Borromeo collection). The face is similar to that found in *Susanna and the Old Men* (Isola Bella, Borromeo collection), but it may also be a fragment of a mythological scene. Angela Ottino Della Chiesa has dated this work to around 1525, during the artist's mature years, when he painted his masterpiece, the frescoes of the sanctuary of the Madonna in Saronno. These works mark the height of his career, when he harmoniously balanced Raphael's and Leonardo's influences, whose grace is reflected in this delicate face.
J.-Ch. B.

Bibliography:
P. Dubois de Saint-Gelais, *Description des tableaux de la Galerie du Palais Royal*, 1727, p. 292; J. Couché, *La Galerie du Palais Royal*, 1793–1808, vol. I, no. 1 (engraved by Massard father); W. Buchanan, *Mémoirs of Painting*, 1824, vol. I, p. 29; J. Young, *Catalogue of Pictures of the Marquess of Stafford at Cleveland House*, 1825, vol. I, no. 44; Dr Waagen, *Treasures of Art in Great Britain*, 1854, vol. II, pp. 30, 499 (presented as Luini); B. Berenson, *Italian Pictures of the Renaissance*, 1932, p. 325; A. Ottino Della Chiesa, *Luini*, 1956, pp. 46, 185, fig. 159, no. 90; B. Berenson, *Italian Pictures of the Renaissance: Central and North Italian Schools*, 1968, vol. I, p. 229; A. Chastel and A. Ottino Della Chiesa, *Tout l'œuvre peint de Léonard de Vinci*, 1968, p. 112, no. 75.

5

Antonio Solario
(Antonio Solario, known as Lo Zingaro, active in the Marches and Naples during the first quarter of the sixteenth century)
Virgin and Child

Oil on wood.
H: 59.5 cm; W: 50 cm.
Inscription on back: *IEAN BELLINO N° 174.*
GR 1.82

History:
Venice, collection of Count Johann-Matthias Schulenburg (1661–1747); Munich, Galerie Böhler, 1972.

Exhibitions:
Ancona, *Lorenzo Lotto nelle Marche. Il suo tempo, il suo influsso*, 1981, nos. 8, 9; Geneva, Palexpo, *La Fondation pour l'écrit. Salon international du livre et de la presse. Le livre et la presse dans la peinture*, 1996.

Bibliography:
Inventaire de la galerie de Feu S. E. Mgr le Feldmarechal, comte de Schulenburg, undated [printed before 1774], no. 174, published by Alice Binion; *La galleria scomparsa del maresciallo von der Schulenburg, un mecenate nella Venezia del Settecento*, Milan, 1990, p. 279, no. 174 ("from Jean Bellino, a painting representing Our Lady with a child and beautiful landscape").

Little is known about Antonio Solario's career. The sources, mainly de Dominici (1742), are unreliable except for accounts of his training in Venice. The artist's name appears for the first time in a document in the archives of Fermo (the Marches) dated April 2, 1502 as a Venice-born painter living in Fermo. Two large retables, one for Santa Maria del Carmine church in Fermo, the other for San Francesco (today San Giuseppe da Copertino) church in Osimo, were the subject of a study during the exhibition Lorenzo Lotto nelle Marche. Il suo tempo, il suo influsso *(1981, pp. 94–99). De Dominici indicated that Solario probably painted frescoes in Naples, but nothing is known about the rest of his career or the date of his death.*

In 1987, in an oral statement, E. Fahy rejected R. Pallucchini's assertion that Bartolommeo Veneto painted this *Virgin and Child*. Three years later, A. Tempestini made the more convincing argument that the work was due to Antonio Solario. His comparison with other paintings on the same theme – *Virgin and Child with the Young Saint John the Baptist* (signed; London, National Gallery), *Virgin Adoring the Child* (Copenhagen, Statens Museum for Kunst), *Virgin and Child with a Donor* (Naples, Museo di Capodimonte), and *Virgin and Child with an Angel, Saint Joseph and a Donor* (Bristol, City Art Museum) – is thoroughly persuasive.
The artist adopts the same construction on two planes. The background always features a landscape whose precision and delicate execution recall the northern European art Solario may have seen in Venice. The landscape's painstakingly rendered details and elegance, and the gold highlights on the tree trunks and foliage, are two of the artist's trademarks. So are the thin eyebrows, the eyelids curving over almond-shaped eyes, the chubby faces of the Virgin and Child and the thin gold halos. The presentation of the group, wrapped in the Virgin's heavy mantle, recalls the compositions of Giovanni Bellini and Cima da Conegliano, whose influence is evident here. This observation makes it possible to date the painting to early in the artist's career.
V. D.

6 Guido Reni (1575–1642)
David Decapitating Goliath, 1606–1607

Oil on canvas.
H: 174.5 cm; W: 133 cm.
GR 1.261

History:
Lodi collection.

Exhibition:
Bologna, Pinacoteca Nazionale, *Guido Reni*, September 5 – November 10, 1988, pp. 48–49, no. 16.

Bibliography:
S. Pepper, *Guido Reni. A Complete Catalogue of His Works with an Introductory Text*, Oxford, 1984, pp. 221–222, no. 25A, fig. 25, pl. 1; E. Schleier, "Una proposta per Guido Reni giovane", in *Arte Cristiana*, no. 713, 1986, p. 109.

Guido Reni (Bologna, 1575 – Bologna, 1642) started his training in the academy founded by the Dutch painter Denys Calvaert (1540–1614) around 1575 before frequenting the Carracci Academy. However, the artist departed from the teachings of Annibale and Ludovico Carracci, who advocated a return to the "natural", to rediscover the beauty and grace of Raphael that fascinated him so much. He was able to admire Raphael's Saint Cecilia *in the San Giovanni in Monte church at Bologna (now in the Pinacoteca Nazionale).*
Invited to Rome in 1601 by the Cardinal Paolo Emilio Sfondrato, he stayed in the Eternal City until 1614 – with frequent breaks – and went back there from 1621 to 1627. During his first stay, Reni was struck by the art of Caravaggio: Reni's Crucifixion of Saint Peter *(Vatican Museum) and the first version of* David *(Musée du Louvre) show that he adopted certain characteristics from him. Several masterpieces date from the end of the first period in Rome: the* Samson Victorious *and the* Massacre of the Innocents *(Bologna, Pinacoteca Nazionale) as well as the fresco of* Dawn *for the ceiling of the Casino Rospigliosi in Rome (1614). An independent artist, Reni came back, at the peak of his fame, to Bologna where he died several years later, carried off by a malign fever. There, his pictorial language evolved towards a greater balance and a poetry marked by a more intense spirituality and sentimentalism and an increasingly bright, refined palette.*

The book of Samuel relates the extraordinary combat between David and Goliath the Philistine (1 S 17, 49–54). David comes to the aid of the Israelite army, already ranged in a line against the Philistines led by the giant Goliath. The picture follows the unfurling narrative of the text very closely. The young David advances towards Goliath with a sling as his only weapon. A stone strikes Goliath's forehead and "he fell on his face to the ground [...]. David ran and stood over the Philistine, and took his sword and drew it out of his sheath, and killed him, and cut off his head with it. When the Philistines saw that their champion was dead, they fled away". A deeply devout painter, Guido Reni faithfully transposes this moment in religious history with clarity and a certainty which had been slightly lost since the Renaissance.
This picture has come to be recently added to the *corpus* of Reni: Mina Gregori was the first to suggest the right attribution. With our current knowledge it is impossible to establish the provenance of this painting. S. Pepper (1984) cites the mention by Oretti of a *David Decapitating Goliath* in the collection of Count Giusti del Giardino in Verona.
For stylistic reasons S. Pepper is inclined to date this painting, which is close to the *Martyrdom of Saint Catherine* (Albenga, Museo Diocesano), to Reni's Caravaggist period of 1606–1607. David has the same physical type as in Caravaggio's composition which today is in the Museo del Prado, and there is the same usage of light, in clear-cut chiaroscuro. Here the uneven light, filtering through the clouds in the tormented sky to be reflected from the armour, accentuates the composition's dramatic effect. The painting is structured along horizontal lines and a central vertical axis. It depicts the two main figures in the foreground. Later, the *Samson Victorious* (Bologna, Pinacoteca Nazionale) would be organized the same way.
Reni's Caravaggist period lasted from the spring of 1605, when Pope Clement VII's death led to an interruption of commissions from Rome, to 1608, when he began working alongside Cavaliere d'Arpino for the Cardinal Borghese.
V. D.

7 Giovanni Battista Caracciolo (1578–1635)
Joseph and the Wife of Potiphar, 1618

Oil on canvas.
H: 118.5 cm; W: 151.5 cm.
GR 1.970

History:
Brussels, Bierny collection (label on back); London, Sotheby's, July 6, 1988, no. 18.

Exhibitions:
Brussels, La Vieille Galerie d'Art (presented as Caravage, according to label on back); Naples, Castello Sant'Elmo, *Battistello Caracciolo e il primo naturalismo a Napoli*, November 9, 1991 – January 19, 1992.

Bibliography:
G. Romano, *Catalogo della pittura italiana del '600 e del '700*, Milan, 1990, p. 90.

Although it provides the earliest documentation of the artist's life, the biography written by de Dominici in 1743 – more than a century after the death of Caracciolo (Naples, 1578 – Naples, 1635) – is also the most fanciful. Archives have made it possible to identify and to date several instances in his private life which contradict the solitary character presented by de Dominici: born in 1578, married at the age of twenty, Caracciolo was the father of ten children.
His earliest recorded artistic activity dates from 1601 when, alongside Belisario Corenzio, he painted six putti in fresco for the facade of the Monte di Pietà; from this joint effort it has been deduced that he had trained beside this master. In 1607, the year Caravaggio spent in Naples, Caracciolo signed the Immaculate Conception with Saint Dominic and Saint Francis of Paul *(church of Santa Maria della Scala) which reveals indisputable links with the* Works of the Misericorde *carried out the same year by Caravaggio. Caracciolo immediately adopted Caravaggio's innovative pictorial language as well as his use of light in violent chiaroscuro. A trip to Rome in 1614 and another to Florence in 1618 brought him into contact with other artists, notably Artemisia Gentileschi. From 1622 he worked for the Carthusian monks of San Martino: the* Washing of the Feet *(1622), and later the* Adoration of the Magi, Saint John the Baptist and Saint Martin, Saint Martin with the Angel *(all circa 1626).*
A fresco painter of wide scope, Caracciolo painted, among others, Stories from the Life of San Gennaro *for the chapel of San Gennaro at the Certosa; from 1630 he showed himself open to Bolognese classicism, an indication of the diminution of Caravaggio's influence.*

This painting, which recently appeared on the art market, is one of the latest additions to the artist's œuvre, which comprises about eighty works. Above all a religious painter, Caracciolo adopts a profane manner in order to deal with this subject drawn from Genesis (Gn 39, 6–20). Potiphar, Pharaoh's eunuch, had bought Joseph, who became his majordomo. Desired by Potiphar's wife because he "was handsome and good-looking" Joseph did not give in to her entreaties but left behind a garment as he fled. In order to extract revenge Potiphar's wife, pretending that Joseph had wanted to lie with her as, according to her the cloak in her possession proved, complained to her husband, who had Joseph imprisoned.
This theme and this masterly composition have a famous precedent in Florence, in a work by Ludovico Cardi known as Il Cigoli, signed and dated 1610 (Rome, Galleria Borghese). Caracciolo's trip to Florence in 1618 suggests that he could have known this work. Nevertheless, Caracciolo opted for a more compact composition – figures at half length – but retained the same movement of flight towards the left and the subtle superimposition of four hands. He used the same typically Florentine fullness in the handling of the decoration and clothes. This technique was later taken up by other Tuscan artists, such as Giovanni Biliverti (1619; Florence, Galleria Palatina), who reproduces Il Cigoli's figures full length in his composition.
The richness and refinement of Joseph's costume, his hat decorated with big feathers – which can also be seen in *Salome with the Head of Saint John the Baptist* (Florence, Vasari Corridor) dated from the time Caracciolo visited Florence – as well as the decorative precision of the fabric of the pillow and mattress, make *Joseph and the Wife of Potiphar* a very distinct moment in Caracciolo's œuvre, to be closely linked with his 1618 stay in Florence.
The brash red notes, into which orange motif filter, contrast with the greys and blacks. Black indeed is Joseph's cloak, foreshadowing his dark fate as evidence for Potiphar's wife. An intelligent play of hands, opposed two by two and skimmed by delicate light, stands out against these three colours, echoed by an intense play of looks. The light, strong in the foreground, leaves a hand and foot of the young woman in the shadow of the background.
This picture has a dramatic yet intimate atmosphere because the two characters, who have their mouths half-opened, seem to be speaking; it was certainly a private commission.
V. D.

8

Carlo Dolci (1616–1686)
Saint John the Evangelist

Oil on canvas.
H: 102.2 cm; W: 82.5 cm.
GR 1.1020

History:
Probably painted for the artist's confessor, Domenico Carpanti; Giovanni Battista Galli; Florence, Riccardi collection, before the end of the seventeenth century; Lucien Bonaparte's collection; Oakhill, Hertfordshire, Sir Simon H. Clarke's collection; London, Christie's, May 8–9, 1840, no. 91; Thirlestane House, Cheltenham, Lord Norwick's collection; sale Philipps, July 26 – August 22, 1859, no. 1695; Bart., Sir Samuel Scott's collection; Bart., Sir Edward Scott's collection; London, Christie's, July 4, 1924, no. 140 with *Saint Matthew*; New York and Puerto Rico, Leon Medina's collection; Los Angeles, Newman Galleries, February 27, 1964 as "School of Carlo Dolci"; San Marino, California, Laurence Weitzer's collection; New York, Christie's, January 11, 1995, no. 99.

Exhibitions:
Florence, cloister of Santissima Annunziata, 1729; Florence, cloister of Santissima Annunziata, 1767?; London, British Institution, 1822, no. 95; London, British Institution, 1860, no. 25.

Carlo Dolci (Florence, 1616 – Florence, 1686), who was very young when he joined Giacopo Vignali's studio, began his career and established his reputation with religious compositions steeped in pathos. He soon received commissions from Florence's high society, which remained loyal to him throughout his career. The artist worked for members of the Medici family. Today known especially for his paintings of saints in ecstasy, Dolci also did still lives and portraits that display keen psychological insight. He had a moody temperament, painted slowly and seems to have been rather rankled by the Napolitan painter Luca Giordano's arrival in Florence in 1682. Dolci became increasingly withdrawn and died in 1686.

Saint John the Evangelist belongs to a series of the four Evangelists that were probably painted for the artist's confessor, Fra Domenico Carpanti. Subsequently purchased by Giovanni Battista Galli, a patron of artists in Florence, the four paintings were described by G. Cinelli as being in his palace on the Via Pandolfini in 1677. Later they turned up in the Riccardi collections in the Palazzo Medici-Riccardi, but there is no information on how they got there. In 1815, the *Four Evangelists* belonged to Lucien Bonaparte, a major collector who moved to Italy in 1804 and lived there several years. Bonaparte probably acquired the paintings after that date, but it is unknown whether he purchased them from the Riccardi family or obtained them after they were confiscated by the occupying French forces. In 1816, the paintings were separated. *Saint Mark* and *Saint Luke* appeared in the Lucien Bonaparte sale at Stanley's in London (May 14–16, 1816), whereas *Saint John the Evangelist* and *Saint Matthew* were purchased by Sir Simon H. Clarke, who found their quality better than that of the other two.
The nineteenth century was probably the period when Italian paintings of the *Seicento* were most highly prized by British collectors, and at that time Dolci's *Four Evangelists* were the artist's most important works on English soil. This type of work's appeal may seem surprising, considering the conspicuous display of Catholic fervor. Buchanan does not mention who purchased *Saint Mark* (wrongly believed to be Saint Luke) at the Bonaparte sale, but in 1843 the painting appeared in the collections of William II of Orange, king of the Netherlands. Sold in 1850, it entered the Fürstliche zu Wied collections, where it remained until 1968. That year it was sold (Sotheby's, July 5, 1968, no. 18). Since then it has remained in private hands.
The fate of the actual *Saint Luke* is unknown. Purchased by Edward Gray at the Bonaparte sale, according to Buchanan, it may have subsequently joined the collection of James Morrison, who provided Buchanan with funds to buy the entire Gray collection in 1838. *Saint Matthew* and *Saint John the Evangelist* were separated during the Clarke sale in 1840, where *Saint John the Evangelist* was purchased by Lord Norwick. In 1859, it was acquired at a sale of Lord Norwick's paintings by Sir Samuel Scott, who had already bought *Saint Matthew*. He exhibited both paintings at the British Institution the following year. Reunited, the works remained in the Scott collection until 1924, when they were sold together at Christie's. As time went by, the paintings' importance and their illustrious provenance gradually fell into oblivion. They appeared at the Newman sale in Los Angeles in 1964 as "School of Carlo Dolci", without any indication of their origin. At that time, *Saint John the Evangelist* was purchased by a collector and previous owner, and *Saint Matthew* was acquired by Henry Drake, who sold it to the J. Paul Getty Museum in 1969. Both paintings are still in identical Empire frames.
The existence of many known copies attests to the renown of *Saint John the Evangelist* in France. Two have been attributed to Matteo Rosselli (Nancy, Musée des Beaux-Arts; Douai, Musée de la Chartreuse; A. Brejon de Lavergnée and N. Volle, *Musées de France. Répertoire des peintures italiennes du XVIIe siècle*, Paris, 1988, pp. 299, 300). Two other, weaker versions are in the Grenoble and Nîmes museums. A copy was recently sold in Paris (Ader Tajan, Hôtel Drouot, June 26, 1992, no. 55).

Bibliography:
G. Cinelli, in F. Bocchi and G. Cinelli, *Le bellezze della città di Firenze*, 1677, p. 370; C. N. Cochin, *Voyage en Italie*, 1758, vol. II, p. 76; M. Lastri, *L'Etruria pittrice, ovvero storia della pittura toscana, dedotta dai suoi monumenti che si esibiscono in stampa dal secolo X, sino al presente*, 1791, vol. II, pl. CX; L. Lanzi, *Storia pittorica dell'Italia dal risorgimento delle Belle Arti fin presso al fine del XVIII secolo*, 1795–1796 (ed. 1809), vol. I, p. 178; W. Buchanan, *Catalogue of the Collections of Pictures of Lucien Buonaparte, Prince of Canino*, 1815, no. 18; W. Buchanan, *Memoirs of Painting*, 1824, vol. II, pp. 272, 275 and 285; F. Baldinucci, *Notizie de' professori del disegno da Cimabue in qua*, Florence, 1681–1728 (ed. 1845–1847), vol. V, 1846, p. 341; G. F. Waagen, *Treasures of Art in Great Britain*, 1854, vol. III, p. 197; A. Graves, *A Century of Loan Exhibitions*, 1913–1915, vol. I, 1913, pp. 290, 291; F. Borroni Salvadori, "Le esposizioni d'arte dal 1674 al 1767", in *Mitteilungen des kunsthistorischen Institutes in Florenz*, 1974, t. XVIII, vol. 1, pp. 29, 80; B. B. Fredericksen, *Catalogue of Paintings in the Paul Getty Museum*, 1942, no. 53; P. Tomory, *Catalogue of Italian Paintings before 1800 in the John and Mable Ringlin Museum of Art*, 1976, p. 16, no. 10; B. B. Fredericksen, "The Four Evangelists by Carlo Dolci", in *J. Paul Getty Museum Journal*, 1976, vol. II, pp. 67–73, fig. 2; G. de Juliis, "Ricerche d'archivio. Appunti su una quadreria fiorentina: la collezione dei marchesi Riccardi", in *Paragone d'arte*, no. 375, May 1981, pp. 88, 89 note 64, 91 note 81; C. Mc Corquodale, *Il Seicento fiorentino. Arte a Firenze da Ferdinando I a Cosimo III*, 1986, vol. III, p. 82; M. J. Minicucci, "Appunti per la collezione Riccardi", in *Rivista d'arte*, 1987, p. 381; F. Baldassari, in *La pittura in Italia. Il Seicento*, 1989, vol. II, p. 276; M. B. Guerrieri Borsoi, *Dizionario biografico degli italiani*, 1991, p. 421; B. B. Fredericksen, *Index of Paintings Sold in the British Isles during the Nineteenth Century*, 1993, vol. III, part 1, p. 337; F. Baldassari, *Carlo Dolci*, 1995, pp. 63–65, no. 31, fig. 31, pl. X.

A preparatory drawing for Saint John's hands is in the British Museum. He holds the book he is writing, the Gospel or the Apocalypse, on his lap with his left hand and a quill in his right hand. His attribute, the eagle, looks at him from behind in the shadow. Saint John is looking up towards heaven, his mouth half-open in an expression of divine inspiration, perhaps even ecstasy, which can often be found in works by Dolci, such as the *Mary Magdalen* in the Galleria degli Uffizi in Florence and the *Allegory of Charity* in the Cassa di Risparmi e Depositi in Prato (*Il Seicento fiorentino. Arte a Firenze da Ferdinando I a Cosimo III*, Florence, Palazzo Strozzi, December 21, 1986 – May 4, 1987, pp. 444, 448, nos. 1.250, 1.252, repr.). Space is tight around the figure, whose presence is strengthened by a scarlet drapery. This red mantle, which Christ's favorite disciple is always seen wearing, is evenly distributed in the composition and is a burst of bright colour amid the brown tones. The light that sets off the drapery's folds vividly brightens up the hands and face crowned by a halo.
Saint John the Evangelist is characteristic of Dolci's because of the interiorized but intense religious feeling and the pictorial technique: dense, precise strokes with the look of china even for the complexions, which contributed to the painter's reputation.
I. M.

9

Elisabetta Sirani (1638–1665)
Allegory of Music, 1659

Oil on canvas.
H: 99 cm; W: 73 cm.
On the back of the canvas: *BH* and the stencilled letter and numbers *L.1950*.
GR 1.657

History:
Lowther Castle, Earl of Lonsdale's collection; London, sale Appleby Brothers Ltd, June 11 – July 6, 1963, no. 14; London, Sotheby's, July 6, 1972, no. 56.

Elisabetta Sirani (Bologna, 1638 – Bologna, 1665) was the daughter and student of the painter Giovanni Andrea Sirani (1610–1670), who himself studied under and worked with the great Bolognese master Guido Reni (1575–1642). She died at the age of twenty-seven, apparently the victim of a poisoning. The Nota *she kept year after year between 1655 and 1665 and retranscribed in 1678 by Malvasia in his* Felsina pittrice *demonstrates that her brief career was intense (1841 ed., vol. II, pp. 393–400). The* tavoline *and* mezzo figure *prove that her work was highly appreciated by private collectors and important visitors passing through Bologna. They were attracted to this great artist, who had begun her career at the age of seventeen by painting a picture for the Trasasso parish in Bologna.*
Her career included two great periods. The first, somewhat academic one, followed her father's precepts and resembled Reni's "bright" period. The second, mature one, was influenced by Pasinelli and Cignani, and characterized by greater interest in light and a desire to paint more ambitious works. It began in 1663, when the Child Jesus Visiting Saint Anthony *(Bologna, Pinacoteca Nazionale) and* Mary Magdalen *(Besançon, Musée des Beaux-Arts) were painted.*

In 1659, "una mezza figura fatta per la Musica da regalare al mio maestro da suonare" appeared in the *Nota* that Elisabetta wrote on all her paintings and which was carefully retranscribed by Malvasia (1841 ed., vol. II, p. 394). This allegorical half-length figure given to her music teacher may be the one in the Rau collection, where a young, graceful and charming woman personifies Music. She is holding a score and seems to be singing while leaning her left arm on a lyre, the symbol of poetry, at the base of which lie a pair of cymbals and a hammer.
It seems that Elisabetta took music lessons for at least three years. The preceding year she had already given her teacher "una mezza figura d'un salvatore" and the following one, 1660, she offered him a half-figure representing Poetry. Music training seems to have been part of every young painter's instruction during the seventeenth century, especially in Bologna where the *Accademia degli Incamminati* offered artists the broadest possible cultural and scientific education. Guido Reni went to this academy, and he transmitted its precepts to his students, including Elisabetta's father.
The *Allegory of Music*, an outdoor scene, is extremely refined both in its study of *affetti* and carefully rendered colours. The superimposition of white, blue and violet heightened by gold attests to the artist's adoption of Reni's "bright method". A subtle play of shadow and light brushes against the two fine, delicate hands as well as the rest of the figure. They herald Sirani's growing interest in light, which at the time was influenced by Annibale Carracci, Lanfranco, Domenichino and Guido Reni's late period. Aside from the fact that this work may correspond to the 1659 note, it belongs to Elisabetta's "classic" period, when she also painted the *Sibyl* (Bologna, Pinacoteca Nazionale). After 1663, she moved more clearly away from Reni's influence, adopting rich colours and a more marked chiaroscuro.
V. D.

10

Anonymous painter, Italy / Lombardy-Piedmont (end of seventeenth – beginning of eighteenth century)
Portrait of Maddalena del Grande (1634–1713)

Oil on canvas.
H: 88 cm; W: 73 cm.
Inscription: *1711 / Maddalena del Grande Franciulla Nata il di 12 / Dicembre nel 1634 popolo della Pie vechia, Fede: /: Lissima cameriera, e cuoca dal di primo genn° 1670 / a tutto il di 26 agosto 1713 che passo a miglior vita d' / anni settantanova mesi otto, giorni 14. / Di fedel servitu anni quarantatre.*
GR 1.86

History:
Munich, Galerie Julius Böhler, 1968.

The artist who painted this splendid portrait of an old servant woman and the circumstances surrounding the commission remain unknown. The long inscription identifies the model as "Maddalena del Grande, born on December 12, 1634, died at the age of seventy-nine years, eight months, fourteen days on August 26, 1713, after forty-three years of loyal service as a cook and chambermaid". These lines suggest that the portrait was painted for Maddalena's employer, for it would have been impossible for her to pay for the commission. But when? Is the inscription alone posthumous, or the entire painting? These considerations have an influence on the attribution.
The work was certainly done by one of the "reality painters" who emerged from Caravaggism. This trend was especially strong in Lombardy and Veneto at the end of the seventeenth and beginning of the eighteenth centuries. However, Eberhard Keil (1624–1687) not being considered a portraitist, "real portraits" of the common people were rare before Ceruti or Ghislandi. If the entire painting is posthumous, a date from around 1730–1740 can be put forward, and several attributions are possible, including Giovanni Antonio Pianca (1703–1757), Vittore Ghislandi (1655–1745), Giacomo Ceruti (1691 – after 1760), Giovan Antonio Borroni (1684–1772), Antonio Cifrondi (1656–1730) or Paolo Maria Boromino (1703 – after 1779). If the inscription alone is posthumous, the possibilities are fewer and the painting can only be compared to certain works by Pietro Bellotti (1625–1700), such as the *Old Woman* in Warsaw's Muzeum Narodwe or the one in the Nîmes Musée des Beaux-Arts.
The influence of Eberhard Keil can be seen in both of these paintings as well as the one in the Rau collection, in the limited colour range as well the composition showing the figure in the foreground against a solid, dark background. Keil, who studied with Rembrandt in Amsterdam, introduced this type of "Rembrandtesque" portrait to Venice when he lived there from 1651 to 1654. According to his biographer Zanetti, Bellotti was famous for his skill as a caricaturist. If he painted this beautiful portrait of Maddalena del Grande, so full of humanity, it is a fortunate exception in his work.
J.-Ch. B.

MADDALENA DEL GRANDE FANCIVLLA NATA IL DI 12
DICEMBRE NEL 1634 POPOLO DELLA PIE VECHIA, FEDE=
LISSIMA CAMERIERA, E CVOCA DAL DI PRIMO GENN.° 1670 -
À TVTTO IL DI 26 AGOSTO 1713 CHE PASSÒ A MIGLIOR VITA D'
ANNI SETTANTANOVE MESI OTTO, GIORNI 14 ·
DI FEDEL SERVITV ANNI QVARANTATRE

11

Canaletto (Giovanni Antonio Canal, known as Canaletto, 1697–1768)
Saint Mark's Square, 1740–1750

Oil on canvas.
H: 58.5 cm; W: 103 cm.
GR 1.1017

History:
Bought by Edward Gordon Douglas Pennat, first Lord Penrhyn (1800–1886) and hung in his London residence; collection of his grandson, Edward, third Lord Penrhyn; Sotheby's, December 3, 1924, no. 60; [Ellis and Smith]; [London, Arthur Tooth and Sons, 1925]; [Knoedler]; New York, John Levy's collection, 1925; Bloomfield Hills, Michigan, George C. Booth's collection; New York, Sotheby's, May 18, 1972, no. 71; private collection; London, Christie's, December 9, 1994, no. 59.

Exhibitions:
Toronto, Art Gallery of Toronto – Ottawa, National Gallery of Canada – Montreal, Museum of Fine Arts, *Canaletto*, 1964–1965, p. 60, no. 21, repr.; London, O. and P. Johnson, *Quintessence of Civilisation*, 1971, p. 15, no. 5, repr.

Bibliography:
K. T. Parker, *The Drawings of Antonio Canaletto in the Collection of His Majesty the King at Windsor Castle*, Oxford-London, 1948, p. 34, no. 26; W. G. Constable, *Canaletto*, Oxford, 1962, vol. I, pl. 14, vol. II, p. 190, no. 17; L. Puppi, *L'opera completa del Canaletto*, Milan, 1968, no. 183, repr.; W. G. Constable, *Canaletto*, 2nd ed. revised by J. G. Links, Oxford, 1976, vol. I, pl. 14, vol. II, p. 193, no. 17; J. G. Links, *Canaletto. The Complete Paintings*, Saint-Albans, 1981, p. 16, no. 23; A. Corboz, *Canaletto. Una Venezia immaginaria*, Milan, 1985, vol. II, p. 649, no. P300, repr.

The son of the theatrical painter Bernardo Canal, Canaletto (Venice, 1697 – Venice, 1768) began as a scene painter, but soon moved away from this purely decorative genre. During a stay in Rome in 1719–1720, where he painted scenes for Scarlatti's operas, he discovered Vanvitelli. On his return to Venice, his Roman experience was enriched through acquaintance with Carlevaris and Marco Ricci. He then painted a stream of views of Venice, the vedute.
Very soon appreciated by art lovers, in particular the British, he produced for them a number of large series of views of Venice. In 1744 Canaletto dedicated to John Smith, later British consul, who had become his "patron-dealer", the series of etched views which today are counted among the masterpieces of Venetian painting. Between 1746 and 1753 he made several trips to England where he painted views of London and English manor houses. He returned to Venice, where he finished his career. The Academy, which had for a long time held him at arm's length, finally admitted him in 1763.
Canaletto's work marks an important step in the development of landscape painting. Aside from the direct influence he exercised over Venetian painters such as Bellotto, Guardi or Marieschi, he opened a path which, passing through the English landscape painters of the eighteenth century and Constable, led to the nineteenth century and Corot's landscapes.

In this painting, Canaletto shows the eastern side of Saint Mark's square, with the basilica's main facade and, slightly set back, the western facade of the Doges' Palace. On the right, the Loggetta is plunged in the Campanile's shadow, which stands out against the bright background, while part of the bell tower takes up the far right of the composition almost to the top of the canvas. On the left, the northern side of the square, between shade and sun, recedes towards the houses and the less official part of the city. The composition centers on a long horizontal line formed by a series of different facades. The three poles and the Campanile create four vertical lines that give the painting rhythm and are gently echoed by smaller vertical lines in the slightest architectural features: pinnacles, pilasters and columns.
Bathed in late-afternoon sunlight, this *Saint Mark's Square* features Canaletto's usual palette of grey, beige, blue and pink. A luminous effect heightens these soft colours and causes them to vibrate. The square bustles with numerous figures going about their business, walking and greeting each other. Children play with dogs; small tents formed by parasols and cloth stretched over market-stalls shelter merchants. Constable dated this painting to the 1740s.
Another, probably earlier version seen from a slightly higher angle is in the National Gallery of Art in Washington (F. Shapley, *Catalogue of the Italian Paintings*, Washington, 1979, vol. I, pp. 101–103, vol. II, pl. 69, fig. 1). In that work, the outlet to the lagoon between the Doges' Palace and the Loggetta can be seen. A pen-and-ink drawing over pencil showing variations of the same figures, but which is very similar to the Rau collection painting, is in the Royal Collections at Windsor. The point of view is similar, but the composition is somewhat tighter: the houses on the left do not appear (Parker, 1948, pl. 14).
I. M.

12

Bernardo Bellotto (1721–1780)
The Tower of Marghera, 1735–1742

Oil on canvas.
H: 43 cm; W: 56.5 cm.
GR 1.861

History:
Sir Hugh Lane's collection; London (?), Christie's, July 9, 1917, no. 157; Cox collection; London, art market, 1956; London, Christie's, July 29, 1973, no. 65; London, Christie's, July 10, 1981, no. 73.

Bibliography:
W. G. Constable, *Canaletto* [1st ed. 1962], 2nd ed. revised by J. G. Links, Oxford, 1976, vol. II, p. 379; S. Kozakiewicz, *Bernardo Bellotto*, London, 1972, vol. II, p. 457, no. Z 289; E. Camesasca, *L'opera completa del Bellotto*, Milan, 1974, p. 122, no. 306 A.

Canaletto's nephew, Bernardo Bellotto, also known as Canaletto the Younger (Venice, 1721 – Warsaw, 1780) trained in his uncle's studio from 1735. In 1742 he started to travel around Italy, stopping first in Rome and probably Florence and Lucca as well. He spent 1744 in Lombardy before working in Turin for Charles-Emmanuel III of Savoy in 1745.
As Canaletto's influence on him gradually diminished, he found his own style, giving his urban scenes a naturalistic aspect which is unmistakably his. He developed this style in the great European capitals, where he worked under the patronage of princes. For example, he settled in Dresden in 1747, where Frederic-Augustus II of Saxony appointed him court painter. It was there that he painted some of his most beautiful works, including the many Views of Dresden *and* Views of Pirna *(Dresden, Gemäldegalerie). He worked in Vienna from 1758 to 1761 at the court of Maria-Theresa before moving on to Munich and back to Dresden in 1762. In 1767 he decided to go to Saint Petersburg but stopped in Warsaw where Stanislaw August Poniatowski appointed him court painter. Once settled in Poland, Bellotto lived there until he died.*

The tower of Marghera, the painting's subject, was built in the fifteenth century on one of the many small islands in the southwest of the Venice lagoon. It was demolished during the first half of the nineteenth century. The tower occupies the right-hand side of the painting, with two low houses whose chimneys, typical of Venetian architecture, stand out against a mountainous background. A small landing stage is shown on the left. The Euganean hills are outlined against the sky, forming a shallow diagonal which rises gently up to the tower.
In this early work, which was surely painted during the artist's Venetian period when he worked with his uncle, Bellotto used one of Canaletto's compositions, known today through one of his etchings. The original painting, once in the Dimitri Tziracopoulo collection in Berlin, has been missing since 1939. Besides the etching, two other versions are known. According to Constable, one is partly a studio painting (once in the collection of Count S. Vitale), the other the work of a follower (Venice, Ca' Rezzonico; Constable, ed. 1976, vol. II, p. 379, no. 369). E. Camesasca and S. Kozakiewicz, who had not seen the picture in the Rau collection when they published their work, agree with Constable's opinion in attributing the work to Bellotto. Bernardo Bellotto's composition differs from the original by its closer viewpoint and changes in the figures, who add life to the scene. In the lower right-hand corner, Bellotto replaced the two workers on the water's edge by part of a pier on which a man is seated. The artist removed the small boats in the foreground, keeping only those moored to the landing stage. He also brought the shore closer to the bell tower and the hills. The rose-tinted, grey-beige tower is delineated against a muted blue sky. Clear lines divide the sun-lit areas from the shadows, but the contrasts are softened by the humid atmosphere in which the shimmering light bathes the scene, a light characteristic of Venetian painting since the Renaissance. A certain abrasion of the paint surface, particularly in the sky, allows the red ochre underpainting of the canvas to show through in places, perhaps accentuating this impression of the colours' softness.
I. M.

13 Giandomenico Tiepolo (1727–1804)

Allegorical Portrait of a Young Woman with Flowers, 1780–1790

Oil on canvas.
H: 60.5 cm; W: 51 cm.
GR 1.525

History:
Paris, Marquis de Biron's collection; London, Knoedler Gallery, 1922; New York, A. F. Mondschein; New York, Louis and Mildred Kaplan's collection; London, Christie's, March 23, 1973, no. 79.

Exhibition:
New York, Finch College, *Venetian Paintings of the 18th Century*, 1961, no. 42.

Bibliography:
A. Mariuz, *Giandomenico Tiepolo*, Milan, 1971, p. 129, fig. 224.

At a very early age, Giandomenico Tiepolo (Venice, 1727 – Venice, 1804) was an apprentice in his father's bottega. *They often worked side by side, including on monumental frescoes. Giambattista's work overshadowed his son's, but Giandomenico's own style clearly emerges in the frescoes, beginning with the ones for the Villa Valmarana in Vicenza, which they painted together in 1757. His personal sensibility simply and intelligently conveys his contemporaries' mores. Works such as the* Charlatan, *the* Peasants' Meal *and the* Declaration of Love *are forerunners of the famous Punchinello scenes (1759–1797, paternal villa in Zianigo, today deposited in Venice, Ca' Rezzonico) and the many drawings on Commedia dell'Arte themes, the great human comedy where everyone can recognize him or herself in Punchinello.*
He followed his father to Würzburg (1750–1753) and Spain (1761–1770). They painted the Glorification of Spain *at the Madrid royal palace between 1764 and 1766, and Giandomenico composed* Christ in the Olive Orchard *(Madrid, Museo del Prado) and seven stations of the cross for Saint Filippo Neri church in Madrid (today in the Prado). Shortly after the demise of the Republic of Venice in 1797, Giandomenico executed his last major official decoration, the ceiling of the Palazzo Contarini in Venice. The exhaustion of his style shows through this work.*

Spontaneity and a brisk, pertinent and refined touch are the main factors that make this fanciful portrait so appealing. Giandomenico painted colour in its pure state. He used it in the same way the Impressionists would later. The flowers look natural and are alive with light. Red, yellow, blue and white contrast without clashing. As a colourist, Giandomenico knew how to make the most of luminous Prussian blue, which was invented at the beginning of the eighteenth century, by integrating it into his palette. Strands of blue run through the young sitter's auburn hair, the colour for which Venetian women are famous. Giandomenico portrayed a beautiful, feminine, expressive and energetic face modelled by a strong light that comes from the left, leaving the entire right side in shadow. The plain clothing is painted with the same spirited, incisive touch as the rest of the composition. The colours – white, yellow, ochre, brown and pink – are aimed at achieving a harmonious effect. The artist's use of them is especially intelligent in the gradual shading of yellow to brown. The thick yellow varnish that once covered the paint has been partially removed, making it possible to admire this portrait's liveliness in all its original splendor.
A. Mariuz dates this work from the 1780s, a period when the artist was in full maturity. This is reflected by the extreme ease with which Giandomenico captured the model, who seems to have posed several times for him. The technique and style of the Rau collection portrait make it similar to the paintings in the Nat Leeb collection in Paris and the van Horne collection in Montreal. Here Giandomenico has moved well away from the pompous portrait so popular during the eighteenth century. He enjoyed painting free interpretations of this kind, where he could give free rein to his sensibility and the expression of his inner feelings.
V. D.

The Flemish and Dutch School

While Italy had, as early as the fifteenth century, a genuine artistic revival, art in northern countries reveals a greater degree of continuity; this slower evolution did, however, lead to fundamental discoveries. The real founder of the Flemish School was the painter Jan van Eyck who, from 1425, was in the service of Philip the Good, a great art patron; van Eyck's fundamental contribution was, if not the discovery of oil painting, at least the manner in which the new technique could be employed to provide effects of luminousness and transparency hitherto unknown. These stylistic characteristics point up the difference with Italy: Flemish artists attempted to provide depth of space by means of colour, whereas the Italians, in order to achieve this, used the mathematical principles of monofocal perspective according to which all lines meet in a single vanishing line. One should also mention the mysterious Master of Flemalle – or Robert Campin – whose art still imbued with International Gothic shows a great interest in detail and a pronounced taste for religious symbolism. There were many artists who were profoundly influenced by these two great masters' teachings to achieve a typically Flemish style; among them we could note Colyn de Coter, Rogier van der Weyden, Petrus Christus, Dirk Bouts.
In the sixteenth century, Flemish painting was deeply marked by the figure of Hieronymus Bosch. He created a totally personal style which produced fantastical figures with caricatural faces and who often illustrate human folly.
His work provided an exceptional impact on the art of his own time, by its sense of mystery, as well as by the richness of its inventive iconography. Simultaneously, Italian influence is increasingly obvious, like in the works by Hendrick Ter Brugghen. In the seventeenth century, with the inheritance of Pieter Brueghel the Elder and the Matthieu brothers, profane themes (landscapes, genre or story scenes, portraits and still lives) took over from religious iconography.
The most important figures from that time are without doubt Rubens, Rembrandt and Frans Hals. The first, informed by his many travels in Italy, was the greatest representative of the Baroque movement in Flanders. His iconographic repertoire happily mingled mythology and history and his palette showed a brilliant chromatic scale. In a style far removed from that, Rembrandt basically concentrated on historic painting and on portraits through which he developed an exacerbated naturalism. His palette shows violent contrasts between browns and ochres and thus provides some amazing chiaroscuros. His influence on Frans Hals' work is obvious.
In the eighteenth century Flemish painting underwent a definite waning and found it hard to compete with the French taste which at that time swept throughout Europe.

14

Colyn de Coter (active in Brussels between 1480 and 1525)
Saint Veronica, circa 1510

Oil on wood.
H: 29.5 cm; W: 20 cm.
GR 1.688

History:
Oxon, Cornbury-Park, C. Vernon Watney's collection; Munich, Galerie Julius Böhler (*Gemälde alter Meister Plastiken Zeichnungen Kunstgewerbe*, fall 1973, no. 6).

Bibliography:
V. J. Watney, *A Catalogue of Pictures [...] at Cornbury*, Oxford, 1915, no. 66.

Colyn de Coter seems to have come under the influence of the Master of the Legend of Saint Catherine (generally identified with Pieter van der Weyden) during his formative years. Active in Brussels between 1480 and 1525, in 1493 he was sufficiently well-known to receive a commission for decorating the Saint Luke's guild chapel in Antwerp. Nurtured on the models of Robert Campin and Rogier van der Weyden, his vocabulary began displaying the influence of Bernard van Orley in 1515.

In the early twentieth century, this panel belonged to the Vernon Watney family in Oxon, England, which probably acquired it from a French collection. The pictorial surface is in good condition, and the network of craquelures reveals a noticeable difference between the treatment of the figure and that of the landscape, which was probably repainted in the mid-eighteenth century.
The right-hand side and the upper section have been cut. The trace of a hinge on the left-hand side approximately two centimetres from the upper edge, and the direction in which Saint Veronica is facing, demonstrate that the panel is obviously the right wing of a triptych. Veronica is directly inspired by the famous Vienna triptych painted by Rogier van der Weyden around 1440. Dressed in a flowing mantle, she is wearing an opaque veil and delicately holding the sudarium, on which Christ's face appears. A few tears flow down her downcast face, which is intended to arouse compassion in the believing viewer.
A label in French glued to the back indicates that in the late nineteenth century the work was attributed to Lucas Cranach the Elder. Considered a Flemish work by V. J. Watney in 1915, at the Böhler sales the painting was correctly attributed to the Brussels artist Colyn de Coter, a late interpreter of van der Weyden's style.
Characterized by sharp lines and powerful chiaroscuro effects, the work displays many similarities to the Saint Alban retable and, even more so, the Trinity altarpiece in the Louvre (M. J. Friedländer, *Early Netherlandish Painting. IV. Hugo van der Goes*, Leiden-Brussels, 1969, nos. 90, 94; C. Périer-D'Ieteren, *Colyn de Coter et la technique picturale des peintres flamands du XVe siècle*, Brussels, 1985, pp. 60–65, 101–106). Therefore *Saint Veronica* must date to circa 1510 and provides invaluable information about Rogier van der Weyden's triptych which, mentioned for the first time in 1659 in Leopold-Wilhelm's Vienna collection, may have been in sixteenth-century Brussels.
F. E.

* 15

Jan Mandyn (1502–1560)
Temptation of Saint Anthony, 1540–1550

Oil on wood.
H: 40 cm; W: 59 cm.
On the sword embedded in the tree: *ECTOZ*.
GR 1.175

History:
London, Sotheby's, March 26, 1969, no. 77; London, Hallsborough Gallery, 1972.

Exhibitions:
Amsterdam, Kunsthandel en Verzamelaar, *Collection Rex Nan Kivell*, 1970, no. 39, fig. 85 (presented as Jan Mostaert); Amsterdam, Historisch Museum, *CINOA*, 1970 (presented as Jan Mostaert); Zurich, Landesmuseum – Cologne, Wallraf-Richartz-Museum, *Himmel, Hölle, Fegefeuer. Das Jenseits im Mittelalter*, 1994, no. 145; Cologne, Wallraf-Richartz-Museum – Zurich, Kunsthaus – Vienna, Kunsthistorisches Museum, *Das Capriccio als Kunstprinzip*, 1996–1997.

Bibliography:
The Connoisseur, April 1970, p. 258, repr.

Jan Mandyn (Haarlem, 1502 – Antwerp, 1560) settled in Antwerp by 1530, training several students there, including Spranger and Gillis Mostaert the Elder. Like Pieter Huys he followed Hieronymous Bosch in painting "Devilries" and "Droleries". Huys and Mandyn are difficult to differentiate, although Mandyn is more imaginative. His only signed work, a Temptation of Saint Anthony, *is in the Frans Halsmuseum in Haarlem.*

The narrative of the temptations of Anthony, the hermit saint, compiled by Jacopo da Varagine (French ed.: Jacques de Voragine, *Légende Dorée*, Paris, 1967, vol. I, pp. 130–134) were used in art from the twelfth century and, in the fifteenth, more individually by Bosch. Here the saint seems to dream the scenes in very unclear symbols which are shown to his left. However, some are comprehensible. For example, the vine which climbs round the tree against which Saint Anthony leans recalls the holy vine of the Antonites, a religious order whose duty was to cure the *mal des ardents*, an illness evoked by the fire which glows in the distance, a frequent motif with Bosch. The female corpse at the same time evokes allegories of Death, Time, Pride and Love in a threatening image reminiscent of Baldung. It replaces the young and beautiful women who are normally shown as envoys of the devil to tempt Anthony. The other symbols are more esoteric, such as the sword bearing the letters "ECTOZ", whose meaning is still obscure, or the decapitated head placed on a plate, possibly that of Saint John the Baptist. The hermit, who may be sleeping, is holding a rosary with the open Bible and crucifix nearby. He appears besieged by armed demons and creatures ready to torment him. The temptation is not as direct as it is with Bosch, for example, and this painting could also be called *Visions of Saint Anthony*.
Through its fantasy and poetic imagination, this world, worthy of Bosch, is distinguished from the average works by the followers of the master, such as Pieter Huys', who, in spite of his quality, does not avoid an excess of realism. This lack of invention may be evident in his two signed paintings of *Temptation of Saint Anthony* (Paris, Musée du Louvre; Antwerp, Museum Mayer van den Bergh).
The painting in the Frans Halsmuseum in Haarlem, Mandyn's only signed work, possesses the same verve as the Rau picture and the same composition open on the left, with wings and a lower horizon than in the panoramic landscapes of Patinir, but with similar, rather strange rocks. This similarity of spirit certainly suggests an attribution to Mandyn.
The handling of the Rau panel mixes the fifteenth-century tradition with the more innovative experiments of Bosch and Brueghel: fine, porcelain-like, but enlivened with several grisailles and frottis. The figure of Anthony is reminiscent of those of old men by Pieter Coecke, a painter who spread Italian discoveries in Flanders. This opening beyond tradition is confirmed by the correct way the composition goes beyond Patinir's methods.
It is therefore correct to locate Mandyn's work not far from more modern versions, such as those of Matthys Cock or of Met de Bles, to whom, at an unknown date, this *Temptation of Saint Anthony* was once attributed (Heim-Gairac Documentation).
O. Z.

16

Frans Pourbus the Younger (1569–1622)
Portrait of Guillaume Duvair, 1616–1621

Oil on canvas.
H: 62 cm; W: 53.5 cm.
GR 1.843

History:
Paris, Baron E. de Beurnonville's collection; Paris, sale of Baron E. de Beurnonville's collection, March 21–22, 1883, no. 423 (wrongly presented as "on wood"); Geneva, Pereire's collection; London, Sotheby's, March 9, 1983, no. 8; Cologne, sale at Abels, July 1972.

Exhibition:
Geneva, Musée Rath, *Trésors des collections romandes*, 1954, no. 26.

Frans Pourbus the Younger (Antwerp, 1569 – Paris, 1622) was the son of Frans Pourbus the Elder and grandson of Pieter Pourbus, who were sixteenth-century painters in Antwerp. In 1591 he became free-master in this Flemish city before being named painter to Archduke Albert and Duchess Isabelle of Austria in Brussels. From 1600 to 1609 he worked for the court of Mantua, travelling often to paint portraits in Innsbruck (1603), Turin (1605), Paris (1606) and Naples (1607). In 1610 Maria de' Medici named him court painter and had him come to Paris, where he was naturalized French in 1618 and spent the rest of his life.

Guillaume Duvair (Paris, 1556 – Tonneins, 1621), Louis XIII's Minister of Justice, was the son of Jean Duvair, a gentleman from Auvergne who was a member of the king's court. Since his father left him nothing but a prebend at the church of Meaux, he became an ecclesiastic and lawyer. In 1584, he became a member of the Parliament of Paris. He remained faithful to Henry IV during the League, quelled the revolt in Marseille and brought the city back under the King's rule. Afterwards he became ambassador to England, and upon his return was named first president of the Parliament of Provence, where he worked for the freedom of the Gallican church, quarrelling with the Archbishop of Aix. In 1616 Louis XIII appointed him Minister of Justice to replace Sillery. Six months later he had to resign because of court intrigues, and he withdrew to the Bernardin monastery. The king recalled him to the same position after the death of the Marshal of Ancre. In 1617 he was consecrated Bishop of Lisieux. He was close to Louis XIII, accompanying him to Normandy in 1620 and the siege of Clerac in 1621. On one of his voyages with the king he was struck by fever and had to stop in Tonneins, where he died. His body was brought back to Paris and buried in the church of the Bernardins, where Molinier gave the eulogy.
Duvair was a friend of the scientist Peiresc and had a passion for medals and antiques. He wrote treatises on piety and philosophy as well as legal writs. His portrait by Pourbus was certainly painted between 1616 and 1621, a period when he was in Louis XIII's favour and at the height of his political career. Pourbus was an heir to sixteenth-century Flemish artists, adapting their models to the circles he frequented. He painted full-length portraits of King Henry IV and Queen Maria de' Medici, but preferred a less solemn quarter-length format for Guillaume Duvair. Pourbus' style, which is similar to Pulzone's, blended the Flemish and Italian traditions. He gradually loosened up his technique while remaining highly reserved towards the Baroque. The *Portrait of Guillaume Duvair* conveys this quality in the subtle rendering of the soft flesh and especially in the sumptuous colours of the garments, which signify the sitter's position. The facing and plush red vestment stand out powerfully against the black velvet doublet. The Louvre has a very similar portrait (inv. 1712) by the same artist, wrongly considered a studio work until a recent cleaning.
Ph. L.

17

Hendrick Ter Brugghen (circa 1588 – 1629)
Backgammon Players, 1627

Oil on canvas.
H: 119.5 cm; W: 156.5 cm.
Signed and dated lower left on the side of the table:
H Brugghen fecit 1627.
GR 1.641

History:
Possibly Amsterdam, Willem Schrijver's collection (mentioned in an inventory dated October 26, 1661 as "Van Terbrugge, sijnde Van Verkeerders", published by A. Bredius, *Künstler-Inventare*, 1915–1922, p. 216); certainly Stockholm, private collection, 1941; Geneva, A. Savanini's collection, 1961; Stockholm, Mrs. Streletsky's collection; London, Christie's, December 8, 1972, no. 60, repr.

Exhibition:
Geneva, Musée d'Art et d'Histoire, 1961.

Bibliography:
G. Isarlo, *Caravage et le caravagisme européen*, 1941, pp. 234–236 (presented as *Soldats*; private collection, Stockholm); B. Nicolson, "The Rijksmuseum 'Incredulity' and Terbrugghen's Chronology", in *The Burlington Magazine*, April 1956, vol. XCVIII, p. 108; B. Nicolson, *Hendrick Terbrugghen*, The Hague, 1958, no. A67, pl. 84; *Panorama du monde*, February 1958, p. 57, repr. ("Le tableau du mois" – The painting of the month); *Apollo*, March 1973, fig. 10; *The Burlington Magazine*, January 1974, p. 35.

Hendrick Ter Brugghen (Deventer ?, circa 1588 – Utrecht, 1629) was Abraham Blœmaert's student in Utrecht, where his family moved in 1591, a few years after his birth. He left for Italy in 1604, visited Naples and, during his ten-year stay in Rome, certainly met Caravaggio, who died in 1610. He spent the summer of 1614 in Milan before returning to Utrecht, where he joined the painters' guild in 1616. Ter Brugghen is believed to have made a second voyage to Italy at the end of the 1620s because his later works are more similar to those of the Italian Caravaggists.

The subject of backgammon players is related to the Northern Europeans' moralizing depictions of the gambling scene at the foot of the cross. Dutch and Flemish artists such as Lucas of Leiden isolated the card players motif, featured by Caravaggio during the early seventeenth century in a painting now lost. Among the seventeenth-century Dutch artists, Baburen and Ter Brugghen illustrated this subject by drawing on Caravaggio's harsh realism.
Ter Brugghen painted his *Backgammon Players* in 1627, during his mature period. The tightly framed scene shows half-length figures playing around a table that is seen obliquely, which allowed the artist to skilfully arrange them. The young soldier shown from the back in the foreground is wearing armour that reflects the light, which is painted in several nuances of grey. This magnificent detail is found in *Mars Sleeping* in Utrecht's Museum Centraal, dated from the early 1620s (Nicolson, 1958, no. A71). The figure in the background on the right also served as a model for the *Violon Player* of 1626 (New York, David Koester Gallery, 1955; Nicolson, 1958, no. A51). His smiling face demonstrates the influence of Frans Hals. Although the relationship between the two artists cannot be dated with certainty, the link between them is obvious. Finally, the turbaned figure in the centre is counting points by writing lines on a slate with a piece of chalk. The working-class theme and realistic figures were the main aspects this painting drew from Caravaggio. Ter Brugghen used a softened chiaroscuro to attain a "decorative realism". He made light play on the truth-filled faces and colourful clothes, which take on a special brilliance. For example, the bright nuances of the helmeted soldier's black-striped red shirt on the left is echoed by the short pants of the figure on the right and the turban of the one in the centre. This genre scene is impressive for a painting dated 1627 because of its ambitious, generous composition with several figures.
Ter Brugghen, who also handled the game players theme in a work dated 1623 (The Minneapolis Institute of Arts, Dunwoody Fund Purchase), painted mostly single figures, such as the *Drinking Man* of 1627 (Augsburg, Staatliche Gemäldegalerie; Nicolson, 1958, no. A5). The same year he also painted grandiose works such as *Jacob, Laban and Leah* (London, National Gallery; Nicolson, 1958, no. A40), using a horizontal format and, as in the *Backgammon Players*, arranging the figures around a table bathed in a soft light.
Ph. L.

18

Jan van Goyen (1596–1656)
Storm, 1637

Oil on wood.
H: 23.5 cm; W: 36.5 cm.
Signed and dated lower left:
V.G. 1637.
GR 1.212

History:
Lochem's Gravenhage, Nystad Antiquairs; Wassenaar, C. H. Muntz's collection, 1963; London, Sotheby's, March 16, 1966, no. 108, repr.

Exhibition:
Dordrecht, Municipal Museum, *Nederlandse Landschappen uit de zeventiende euw*, 1963, no. 33, fig. 63.

Before entering the studio of Eseias van de Velde in Haarlem for a year in about 1617, which was a decisive and particularly formative stay, van Goyen (Leyden, 1596 – The Hague, 1656) was the student of C. A. Schilderpoort, I. van Swanenburg and J. A. de Man. This painter was very successful, as the number of his imitators demonstrates. He was also a speculator who died ruined by several bad business deals.
From 1620 to 1626 he painted landscapes in the manner of those of Eseias van de Velde, although in many respects they were more Flemish. Towards 1625, on the initiative of Pieter de Molijn and jointly with his master and Salomon van Ruisdael, he developed the Dutch monochrome landscape type: a palette reduced to green, yellow and brown in a composition centered on a light-coloured diagonal which leads back from a dark foreground under a forbidding and heavy sky. As the years proceed his works tend towards a greater monochrome and their rhythm to greater monumentality. In Leyden from 1619 to 1631, he finally settled in The Hague in 1634.

The only person in this painting, a peasant poorly sheltered by a timber lean-to, several sheaves of straw and a bare tree, contemplates a storm in a landscape of dunes. The overall black and yellow tone, undisturbed by any other colour, is typical of van Goyen in the years after 1630. Such restraint in the use of colour is fairly specifically his, as is the grand simplicity of the composition centered on the single figure and his frail shelter, placed on a little rise and violently illuminated by a slightly oblique sheet of lightning. A band of dark ground opens onto the middle area, which stands out from the dim, sketchy background. Movement towards the background is created by the varied strength of contrast and by lively and suggestive brushwork. It is the principle of the diagonal landscape which the artist practised from about 1625. The firmly modelled shapes and the vigorous branches of the tree pushing against the background of sky, which takes up more than three quarters of the panel, finally convince us of its authenticity, even if Beck did not include it in his well thought-out catalogue.
The composition of the *Wooden Fence* (1631; Brunswick, Herzog Anton Ulrich Museum) is similar to the Rau panel, but the strong contrasts of light and overall dark tone recall the stormy atmospheres of some of Frans de Hulst's paintings such as the *Haarlem Castle* in the Riom museum.
Van Goyen did not often treat the theme of a storm on land, though he painted many tempests at sea such as that in the Národni Galeri in Prague. In the first half of the seventeenth century seascapes were for him and for the Porcellis the best field for presenting a more realistic view of these picturesque manifestations of nature. Rembrandt, with the *Bridge*, 1637 (Amsterdam, Rijksmuseum) and the *Storm*, 1638–1639 (Brunswick Museum), and Rubens, with the *Shipwreck of Aeneas*, around 1620 (Berlin, Staatliche Museen), gave versions of the storm on land that were more tragic and of almost cosmic scope. Van Goyen is part of a more contemplative, intimist poetic vein.
O. Z.

19

Salomon van Ruisdael (after 1600 – 1670)
River Landscape, 1634

Oil on wood.
H: 26.5 cm. W: 39.5 cm.
Signed and dated lower right:
SvR. 1634.
GR 1.933

History:
Frankfurt, sale "Mittelrheinische Standesherren", May 3, 1932, no. 99; Almelo, Tj. Bendien's collection; London, Christie's, May 4, 1979, no. 116; London, Sotheby's, December 19, 1985, no. 67, repr.

Bibliography:
W. Stechow, *Salomon van Ruysdael*, Berlin, 1975, pls. 136, 137, no. 442.

Salomon van Ruisdael (Naardem, after 1600 – Haarlem, 1670) was the brother of Isaack van Ruisdael and the uncle of Jacob van Ruisdael, both great landscape painters. It is not known where he was trained, but in 1623 he registered in the guild in Haarlem, and painted his first landscape in 1626, when Pieter de Molijn, van Goyen and Esaias van de Velde were inventing the naturalist monochrome landscape. After 1640, he moved towards a more decorative style. His few still lives are similar to van Aelst's.

In 1631 Salomon van Ruisdael began painting river banks, perhaps following the example of Jan van Goyen, who was a little ahead of him in this way. A signed picture, the *River Landscape*, dates from this period, and only the relative lack of imagination and undifferentiated brush strokes allow it to be distinguished from other contemporary works and the same subject painted by van Goyen.
The banks of a calm stream on a fine day are a constant motif for van Ruisdael. A dark area of the river acts as a foreground and emphasises the diagonal which gives the picture depth. This is also suggested on the next plane by the clear streak of water and the dark screen of the bank and its trees, while the sky occupies two thirds of the picture. This composition is similar to the style developed by van Goyen and de Molijn in the years 1625–1630 and adopted by van Ruisdael in 1627. No less characteristic is the almost monochromatic grey-green, olive green colour scheme simply brought to life by a blue nuance in a sky that is lighter and more serene than in most of van Goyen's works.
The date and style of the Rau work make it comparable with the *Boat Ride on the River* (1632; Hamburg, Kunsthalle), the *River Bank* (1633; The Hague, Mauritshuis). The Rau picture is a forerunner of the works of the 1640s, taking greater liberty with the principle of the diagonal. The painting's dominant line, marked by the bank, is balanced by the central tree, whose arabesque clearly stands out from the foliage, and by the boat's vertical mast, slowing down the eye's movement to the bottom of the horizon. Here van Ruisdael manages to express the omnipresence of water in the atmosphere. The ray of sunlight crossing the clouds lights the big tree in the centre and, further away, the side of one of the nude fishermen on the riverbank. The subtlety of the luminous touches as well as their scarceness are worthy of the master.
O. Z.

20

Judith Leyster (1609–1660)
Young Girl with a Straw Hat, 1630–1640

Oil on wood.
H: 36.2 cm; W: 31 cm.
GR 1.285

History:
Bulwero Quebec House, East Dereham (presented as Frans Hals on a label on the back of the painting); presented by the Galerie Meissner at the 14th Swiss Fair of Antiques and Art in 1973; Zurich, Galerie Meissner, 1974.

Exhibitions:
Haarlem, Frans Halsmuseum – Worcester, Mass., Worcester Art Museum, *Judith Leyster: A Dutch Master of the Golden Age*, 1993; Washington, The National Museum of Women in the Arts, *Judith Leyster: Leading Star*, 1993–1994.

Bibliography:
Pantheon, 1973, no. 22, p. 220, repr.

Judith Leyster (Haarlem, 1609 – Amsterdam, 1660) was born with the family name Willemsz. She acquired the nickname Leyster because that is what her father's bar, "The Lodestar", was called. Ampzing's work on Haarlem mentions Judith Leyster as a painter as early as 1626–1627. In 1628 the artist and her family left for Vreeland, near Utrecht, before settling in Zaandam, near Haarlem, in September 1629. In 1631 she was present at the baptism of one of the children of Frans Hals (1580/1585–1666). Their friendship went back to at least 1629, if we are to judge by the artist's influence on her work. In 1633 she became a member of the Haarlem painters' guild. On January 1, 1636, she married the painter Jan Miense Molenaer (around 1609 – 1668) and in 1637 they left for Amsterdam, where they lived for eleven years. In 1648 the couple settled in Heemstede, near Haarlem, where Judith Leyster spent the rest of her life.

The painting illustrates Frans Hals' influence on Judith Leyster. Sometimes the student did as well as her teacher, and it is difficult to tell their work apart. This is the case of the Rau collection painting, as the label on the back indicates. The model can be found in another, similar painting by Leyster (oil on wood, diameter 31 cm; Rouen, sold on June 2, 1970, no. 34, repr.). In the circular painting, the little girl's hair is unkempt and she is looking to the right. The technique is even sketchier than in the Rau collection work, which gives it a more spontaneous character.
This yellow and brown-toned painting perfectly renders the scene's sunniness with an astonishing, refreshing naturalness. Leyster contrasted textures. She painted the shirt and light brown jacket with broad, visible brushstrokes, giving the former a lacy effect with a few intertwining white lines. The face is handled differently, with reflections of light provided by the white impasto on the chin, edge of the lips and nose. The expression is no less lively, as the firmly drawn corners of the lips as well as the vitality in the child's eyes demonstrate. The most beautiful, most delicate part of the painting is the golden curls, where some yellow impasto accents stand out against strokes that are first blurred, then dark, providing the hair with a sense of volume. The composition fills the frame because of the hat, which combines elegance and rusticity. This painting surely dates from the 1630s, the period when Leyster and Hals were the closest to each other. Dr Bisboer, director of the Frans Halsmuseum in Haarlem, has pointed out that the handling of the hair and face is characteristic of Leyster. The artist found inspiration for her early works in the genre scenes of the Utrecht Caravaggists. By 1629 she was under Hals' influence, although she never attained the master's smooth, expressive technique.
Nevertheless, this *Young Girl with a Straw Hat* proves that Leyster could equal her contemporary in a small work with an individualized subject. Her style remained more conventional in more elaborate paintings. After 1630 she and Frans Hals lost touch with each other, and her work became more similar to that of Dirck Hals and Jan Molenaer.
Ph. L.

21

Frans Post (1612–1680)
The Episcopal Church of Olinda, 1662

Oil on wood.
H: 34.5 cm; W: 47 cm.
Signed and dated lower right:
F. Post 1662.
GR 1.634

History:
Cologne, Moll's collection; Paris, Jacques Kugel's collection; Amsterdam, sale at Sotheby's of the Max van Waay collection, November 7, 1978, no. 82, pl. 47.

Exhibitions:
Paris, Hôtel de Rohan, *France et Brésil*, 1955, no. 98; Basel, Kunstmuseum, *Im Lichte Hollands*, 1987, no. 74, repr.; Basel, Kunsthalle, *Im Lichte Hollands*, 1987, no. 68; Basel, Kunsthalle – Tübingen, Kunsthalle, *Frans Post 1612–1680*, 1990, p. 68, repr.

Bibliography:
E. Larsen, *Frans Post interprète du Brésil*, Amsterdam – Rio de Janeiro, 1962, p. 202, no. 121; J. de Sousa-Leao, *Frans Post*, Amsterdam, 1973, pp. 84–85, no. 37; P. Ten Doesschate Chu and P. H. Boerlin in *Im Lichte Hollands*, Basel, Kunstmuseum, 1987, no. 74, repr.

The landscape artist Frans Post (Leiden, 1612 – Haarlem, 1680) came from a family of artists. His father Jan Jansz (died 1614), a stained glass painter, and his brother Pieter (1608–1669), a painter and architect, who left with him for Brazil in 1637 in the expedition of Prince Jean Maurice of Nassau-Siegen. From that year until his return to Holland in 1644, Frans Post executed numerous drawings and paintings of which few survive. At Haarlem in 1644 he registered in the guild of Saint Luke and continued to paint landscapes in a style close to that which he had worked out in Brazil, with the same themes.

A possibly Portuguese nun, a Dutch settler, a native woman, and a black woman, probably a slave, stand surrounded by tropical vegetation amidst a few traces of Olinda, a coastal town to the north of Recife (Brazil). Frans Post depicted this city thirteen times and its church five times (Sousa-Leao, 1973, nos. 36, 78, 79, 80, 81).
Olinda, which was founded in 1537, was the seat of the Portuguese colonial government, a bishopric and a centre for sugar production. It was captured and laid waste by the Dutch in 1630 and then abandoned. Post, in Brazil from 1637 to 1644, did not paint the site until fifteen to twenty years after visiting it. The Rau picture is the one that shows the Baroque cathedral's ruins the least; the portico can be seen on the left. Further to the right, the planters' residences are flanked by the slave cabins, in front of some crumbling walls. It has been suggested that this picture contains moralistic overtones linked to the image of the decline of Catholic and Portuguese power, or more generally that all things decay (Boerlin, 1987, no. 74). Nevertheless it could be that Post was simply inspired by the picturesque site. This picture, dated 1662, shows the trademarks of Post's work during the period of his return. The intense colour, which is distributed in an almost compound way (brown, green and blue), does not have the clarity and strange iridescence which give their originality to the *São-Francisco River and Fort Maurice* (1638) and the *Countryside around Port-Calvo* (1639), both in the Louvre, painted in Brazil when he was so fascinated with its foreignness.
A viewpoint from the small knoll on the right opens out onto a composition whose depth is organized by increasingly lighter strips parallel to the panel's plane and by the wing formed by the church portico, the background rising in tiers below on the right. From his training at Haarlem – Larsen suggests Pieter de Molijn as his master before 1637 (1962, p. 134) – Post kept a penchant for the horizontal and the preponderance of the sky. This influence was stronger when he was painting in Brazil and applied the principles of landscape with deep diagonals. By contrast, the high point of view here is a reminiscence of Cornelis Vroom, or it has a Flemish source, whose origin should be sought in Joos de Momper and his school. Like the *Engenho* in the Copenhagen Statens Museum for Kunst, the *Episcopal Churches of Olinda* in the Museu do Instituto Historico e Geografico of Rio de Janeiro, and the Bareto and De Caldas collections (Larsen, 1962, no. 48, fig. 50; Sousa-Leao, 1973, nos. 78, 80, 81) have the same high, informative and analytical viewpoint, giving an almost documentary image to Post's Dutch clients interested in paintings of Brazil. However, this landscape of Brazilian ruins seems to be an exotic echo of Breenberg's and Nieulandt's paintings of Roman ones. The same human life reigns over the theatrically presented debris of the past.
O. Z.

22

Gerard Dou (1613–1675)
The Cook, 1660–1665

Oil on wood, polished.
H: 29 cm; W: 23.2 cm.
GR 1.207

History:
Paris, sale of Baron Delessert's collection, March 15, 1869, no. 19; Paris, sale of Baron Narischkine's collection, April 5, 1883, no. 12 (engraved by Daniel Mordant); Paris, Baron Erlanger's collection; Vienna, Galerie Sankt-Lukas, 1931; Stuttgart, at Bühler's, 1958.

Bibliography:

J. Smith, *Catalogue raisonné*, supplement, London, 1842, p. 22, no. 72; C. Hofstede de Groot, *Beschreibendes und kritisches Verzeichnis der Werke der hervoragendsten holländischen Maler des XVII. Jahrhunderts*, Esslingen-Paris, 1907, vol. I, p. 399, no. 175; W. Martin, *Gerard Dou: des Meisters Gemälde in 247 Abbildungen*, "Klassiker der Kunst", vol. XXIV, Stuttgart-Berlin, 1913, p. 102, repr.

Gerard Dou (Leiden, 1613 – Leiden, 1675) trained with the engraver Dolendo and the glass painter Pieter Couwenhorn before working with his father, who was also a glass painter. In February 1628 he joined Rembrandt's workshop, which was very close to his home, where he rubbed shoulders with Jan Lievens and Joris van der Vliet until the Master left for Amsterdam in 1631–1632. Dou joined the Saint Luke's guild, which had just been founded in Leiden, in 1648. From 1641 the Swedish diplomat Spiering gave him a generous annual allowance which gave him first refusal of the painter's works. In 1660 the Dutch states bought three paintings from the artist, including the Young Mother *in The Hague's Mauritshuis as a gift to Charles II of England, who was visiting the Dutch capital. Gerard Dou's became so renowned that a permanent exhibition of twenty-nine of his paintings belonging to the collector Jan de Bye was held in the house of the painter Hannot from 1665. Dou, who founded the School of Fine Arts in Leiden, had many pupils, including Gabriel Metsu, Frans van Mieris the Elder, Pieter van Slingelandt, Godfried Schalken, Dominicus van Tol, Carel de Moor and Naiveu.*

The monogramme *Dou* mentioned by Walther Bernt in his appraisal, and which shows up clearly in old photographs at the base of the window frame below the pot, is a falsification which was removed when the work was restored. Today only a circle remains, painted as if it had been carved into the stone. The two letters *o* and *u* had been added to them in order to lend the work greater authenticity. However, this painting is so typical of Gerard Dou's work of the years 1660–1665 that it did not need such treatment.
The model of an old woman was inherited from the studies Rembrandt made during his Leiden period of the heads of old people, who were usually the artist's parents. They were reworked by the young Dou and can also be seen in the *Spinning Woman*, which is in the Hermitage in Saint Petersburg. In this work the woman is wearing glasses and working on a skein of wool. The same model can be found once again in the *Old Woman at the Window* in Vienna's Kunsthistorisches Museum (inv. 624), a painting dating from between 1660 and 1665. Here the old lady, facing left, is holding a pitcher. Lastly, she appears in the *Woman Watering Plants* in the English Royal Collection.
Dou was admired for small pictures of this kind, painted with a finesse that remained famous because it lent its name to the School of Leiden. He reworked elements borrowed from Rembrandt, such as the window painted in *trompe-l'œil*, which frames the painting and makes it more realistic, and the old woman's picturesqueness. He updated them for working-class scenes showing simple people going about their daily occupations. The *Cook* is a mature work that is still similar to Rembrandt's style. It does not have the coldness and excessive precision of later works. Dou made the old woman more lifelike by depicting her against a dark background brightly lit in the embrasure of the false window. The details of the wrinkled, toothless face with its flaccid flesh are astoundingly realistic. Similarly, the play of light on the varnished, three-legged clay pot, achieved by using white impasto on its charred brown surface, is worthy of one of Rembrandt's students.
Ph. L.

23

Emmanuel de Witte (1615/1617–1691/1692)
Interior of the Oude Kerk, Amsterdam, circa 1655

Oil on wood.
H: 47 cm; W: 58 cm.
GR 1.526

History:
Tsarkoje Selo, princely collection; Berlin, sale at Lepke's of the Saint Petersburg museums, June 4, 1929, no. 100, repr., pl. 35; Aerdenhout (Netherlands), sale at Moser's; New York, 1952; Silvano Lodi's collection, 1973.

Exhibition:
Rotterdam, Boymans-van Beuningen Museum, *Vermeer Oorsprender Invloed Fabritius, de Hooch, De Witte*, *Rotterdam*, 1935, no. 53.

Bibliography:
H. Jantzen, *Das Niederländische Architekturbild*, Leipzig, 1910 (new ed. Würtzbourg, 1979), no. 689; E. Trautscholdt, in *Thieme-Becker*, 1947, vol. XXXVI, p. 124; I. Manke, *Emmanuel de Witte, 1617–1692*, Amsterdam, 1963, no. 76.

Emmanuel De Witte (Alkmaar, 1615/1617 – Amsterdam, 1691/1692) was trained by Evert van Aelst, brother of the celebrated still life painter also represented in the Rau collection. He registered with the Alkmaar guild of Saint Luke in 1636 before working in Rotterdam (1639–1640), Delft and, after 1656, Amsterdam. He painted portraits and historical pictures until 1650, afterwards specializing in church interiors.
He was influenced by Gerard Houckgeest's works of 1650–1651, abandoning Pieter Saenredam's axial, monochrome view for a more colourful and diagonal alternative showing only a corner of the building. De Witte would paint an increasing number of real or imaginary churches. He focused especially on expressing the softness of the light, which looks like it comes from outdoors. His depiction of light is similar to Carel Fabritius' and Pieter de Hooch's.
The same soft, peaceful atmosphere can also be found in his few genre scenes.

The *Interior of the Oude Kerk, Amsterdam* was one of de Witte's favourite themes. Here a view from the early fourteenth-century Gothic church's choir aisle and north transept is shown. Jantzen, Manke and Walther Bernt (certificate dated 1973) attribute this painting to de Witte. Liedtke implicitly agrees by not mentioning it in his corrections of Manke's lists. This work, which harks back to Houckgeest and van der Vliet, is characterized by a greater concentration on the refined treatment of the light, which firmly models the bodies, and a refusal to provide the painting with depth by giving the same tones to the choir screen and transept. The golden chiaroscuro and straightforward bursts of light surrounding the dark patches, making them vibrate like those near the foreground figures, are worthy of Fabritius. Manke dates this picture to around 1655 and notes that the little organ on the left is a model from before 1659. The awkwardness of the perspective's construction, both in the transept and ambulatory, is evidence for such a dating. The *Oude Kerk in Amsterdam* in the Musée des Beaux-Arts in Strasbourg, also dated to around 1655 by I. Manke (1963, no. 66), is very similar to the Rau picture, although the contrasts between light and dark are more accentuated. In both cases the central column of the north wall of the nave has been omitted, and the column supporting the pulpit has a diaphragm arch in the Strasbourg example that is missing here. This is proof that de Witte interpreted his motifs, probably both for aesthetic and plastic reasons. Another panel of the same subject, also attributed to this artist (55 × 49 cm, signed; Cologne, Lempertz sale, November 14, 1974, no. 208, fig. 45), is less symmetrically organized, but still depicts the choir and transept from a fairly similar angle and includes similar figures.
O. Z.

24 Gerard Ter Borch (1617–1681)
Portrait of a Gentleman, 1670

Oil on wood.
H: 40 cm; W: 34.5 cm.
GR 1.895

History:
Geneva, François Tronchin's collection, circa 1750; Geneva, Bessinge cabinet, Tronchin family; Haras de la Flocellière (Vendée), Marquis de Hillerin (born Tronchin), until 1953; Paris, Dr Benedict's collection; London, Julius Löwenstein's collection; private collection; London, Christie's, December 2, 1983, no. 118, repr.

Exhibition:
Rome, Palazzo delle esposizioni – Milan, Palazzo Reale, *Mostra di pittura olandese*, 1954, no. 32.

Bibliography:
C. Hofstede de Groot, *Beschreibendes und kritisches Verzeichnis der Werke der hervoragendsten holländischen Maler des XVII. Jahrhunderts*, Esslingen- Paris, 1913, vol. V, no. 293; S. J. Gudlaugsson, *Gerard Ter Borch*, The Hague, 1951, vol. I, pl. 229; 1960, vol. II, no. 229.

Like his brother and sister Moses and Gesina, Gerard Ter Borch (Zwolle, 1617 – Deventer, 1681) was pushed into an artistic career by his father, himself an artist. He apprenticed with Pieter de Moijn in 1633 before becoming master in the painters' corporation in Haarlem two years later. From 1637 to 1640 he travelled from England to Italy, then to Spain, before going to France. On his return to Holland he did not settle at Deventer until 1654. He painted mostly portraits, especially full lengths, and, from the 1650s, genre scenes illustrating middle class life. Isolated from painters in Leiden or Delft, such as Dou, Mieris, Metsu, de Hooch or Vermeer, Ter Borch brought himself up to their level by practising an intimate and intense kind of painting, in which each object shown becomes essential.

This portrait, which has long been attributed to Gerard Ter Borch (Hofstede de Groot, 1913) has an exceptional history. It comes from the first picture gallery of the Geneva collector François Tronchin (1704–1798), in which the Northern European schools were already predominant. It was neither part of the sale to Catherine II of Russia in 1770, nor of the 1801 auction in Paris, as it belonged to the Tronchin heirs' Bessinge cabinet. François Tronchin, a great lover of Dutch art, had chosen a highly characteristic portrait by Ter Borch from the years 1660–1670, when the painter attained great virtuosity in the use of grey, blue and violet nuances.
S. J. Gudlaugsson dates this work to about 1670 because of the shape of the sitter's hat and points out that it is one of the first examples of a half-length figure in which a table appears nearby. *Nicholas Pancras* in the Kunstalle in Hamburg (oil on canvas, 38 × 31 cm, signed, dated 1670) and *Adriaen de Graeff* (oil on canvas, 40,5 × 30 cm, signed, dated 1674; private collection) are highly comparable works, also painted at this time, when the artist above all painted portraits. Like the genre scenes which Ter Borch gave up at this time, they feature smooth brushwork, a play of tone on tone and a strong concentration on the sitter, who mysteriously emerges from the dark, neutral background, where only the table can be discerned. The model, who is still unknown, is psychologically well characterized and seen with Ter Borch's customary distancing, which does not stress the features.
O. Z.

25

Willem van Aelst (circa 1626 – after 1683)
Still Life with Herring's Head, 1650–1660

Oil on canvas.
H: 43.5 cm; W: 35.5 cm.
Signed upper right.
GR 1.543

History:
Lady Abel Smith's collection, CVO; London, Sotheby's, July 7, 1976, no. 26, repr

Willem van Aelst (Delft, circa 1626 – Amsterdam, after 1683) was trained in the studio of his uncle Evert in Delft before being admitted to the same town's guild of Saint Luke in 1643. From 1645 to 1649 he lived in France, and in 1656 went to Italy, where he met Otto Marseus van Schrieck, becoming his student and co-worker. The following year he settled in Amsterdam, where he lived until his death, the exact date of which is unknown but which was probably after 1683.

Willem van Aelst was his generation's most gifted still life painter. He surpassed the simple technical exercise of trompe-l'œil, striving to put together variously-textured objects in a world bathed by a gentle light and inventing compositions whose originality equals their simplicity.
His early works, painted in Italy around 1650, took after the Northern European tradition of food-laden tables combined with the more decorative one of the Italian Baroque. The opulence of the colours in these paintings, inherited from Italy, is striking. This contrasts with the sobriety of early seventeenth-century Flemish painting, a moderation that nevertheless persisted in van Aelst's grouping of objects. The pictures he painted upon returning to the Netherlands in 1657 continued to feature these Baroque characteristics, but their draughtmanship and colours were different, with van Aelst experimenting with rich tonal harmonies while constantly refining his touch. The artist, who was more than a straightforward illusionist, unified his *Still Life with Herring's Head* with a soft, uniform light that bathes the table cloth, is reflected in the glasses and models the herring's head and half lemon. Serenity emanates from this cleverly composed group of objects which invites contemplation. The left-hand glass clearly marks the vertical plane, while the horizontal one is solidly established by the table covered in a red cloth. The knife on the right-hand side, sketching a diagonal, suggests depth. The glasses, lemon and remains of the herring clearly stand out against the dark background. They take on a special relief imbued with mystery. This painting can be dated to the 1650s. Its sobriety and extreme elegance make it similar to works such as the still life in the Glasgow Museum, composed of a herring's head on a dish, some glasses and bread, as well as the one in the Pitti Palace in Firenze, dated 1652. The herring's head can be seen again in a picture in the Göteborgs Konstmuseum , dated 1659 (oil on canvas, 49 × 40 cm; inv. 905), in another now in the Akademie der bildenden Künste in Vienna, and even in much later and more decorative works such as the one in the Gemäldegalerie in Dresden, dated 1679 (oil on canvas, 56 × 45 cm; inv. 1331).
Ph. L.

26

Jan Siberechts (1627–1703)
The Art Lover's Cabinet, 1661–1672

Oil on canvas.
H: 57 cm; W: 64 cm.
GR 1.502

History:
Vienna, A. Kleinschmidt's collection (presented as David II Teniers); Vienna, Clerck's collection, 1845 (presented as David II Teniers); Budapest, Georg Rath's collection, 1870; Vienna, Max Strauss collection, 1872; Vienna, sale at Wawras of the Strauss collection, March 22–23, 1926, no. 37, repr., bought by Vienna's Schnitzler; London, sale at Sotheby's of the van Pölnitz collection, December 12, 1973, no. 106, repr.

Exhibition:
Vienna, Königliches Österreichisches Museum, *Ausstellung von Gemälden alter Meister aus dem Privatbesitz*, 1873, no. 140 (Strauss collection).

Bibliography:
O. Eisenmann, *Zeitschrift für Bildende Kunst*, IX, 1874, p. 60 (presented as Gonzales Coques); Th. Frimmel, *Gemalte Galerien*, p. 36; Th. Frimmel, "Das Sittenbild des Siberechts in der königlische Galerie zu Copenhagen", in *Blatter für Gemäldekunde*, III, p. 20; W. Suida, *Kunstschätze der Galerie Max Strauss in Vienne*, 1921, p. 61; R. Eigenberger, *Catalogue de la vente Strauss*, Vienna, 1926, no. 37, repr.; G. Von Terey, *Trésor de l'art belge au XVIIe siècle. Mémoire de l'exposition d'art ancien à Bruxelles*, Brussels, 1911–1912, p. 258; T. H. Fokker, *Jean Siberechts*, Brussels-Paris, 1931, p. 119; *The Burlington Magazine*, November 1973, no. 848, repr.

The landscape painter Jan Siberechts (Antwerp, 1627 – London, 1703) was master in his native city in 1648 or 1649. He certainly travelled to Italy before working in Antwerp again until 1673, when he was invited to London by the Duke of Buckingham. His early style was influenced by the Italianate Dutch landscape artists Both and Berchem. From 1661 to 1672 he created an original style showing countryside, farmers and animals in a cold, glittering light.

For a long time art historians believed this painting to be the work of Teniers or Coques. The attribution to Siberechts was based on obvious stylistic similarities with a signed interior scene painted in 1671 (oil on canvas, 60 × 57 cm; Copenhagen, Statens Museum for Kunst; Fokker, 1931, p. 91, pl. 20), which makes it possible to date the Rau collection picture to the years between 1661 and 1672. Until 1864 the Boymans-van Beuningen Museum in Rotterdam had a similar *Young Girl at Her Toilet*. The similarity of styles is unmistakable. All three have a low viewpoint of a side-lit room designed like a cube.
The *Art Lover's Cabinet* demonstrates an especially keen interest in depicting light. Here it is warm and not cold, as in the landscapes from the years 1661–1672. It also reflects the painter's desire to render the bodies' round volumes, which is so striking in the landscapes and genre paintings mentioned above.
This type of interior scene was highly popular in seventeenth-century Antwerp, but it is rare for an artist like Siberechts. There are only four known examples in his body of work. The *Art Lover's Cabinet* shows a couple surrounded by their collection of paintings and sculptures which Fokker and Eigenberger have identified as works by actual artists. The Dutch-style *Seascape* may be by the Flemish painter Bonaventura Peeters. The picture of a *Woman Milking a Cow* is typical of Siberechts' own "landscape-genre scenes" from the years 1661–1672. Similarly, Siberechts showed two of his own paintings hanging on the walls in the works in Copenhagen and Rotterdam. The still life with fish may be by Alexander Adriaenssen. The portrait held by the young woman recalls Thomas Key and Pourbus and the chiaroscuro beauty of the very decorative, busy still life of fruit, game, a monkey and a cat evokes Jan Fyt. Finally, Eigenberger has identified the grisaille above the cabinet with van Dyck's *Samson Being Arrested* in Vienna's Kunsthistorisches Museum. The sculptures are patterned after ancient models. The painting is dominated by Flemish art before 1660, reflecting the content of collections in Flanders.
Eigenberger argues that in this picture Siberechts portrayed himself with his family before his departure for London. Beyond its anecdotal interest, this wonderful, rare, gold-toned painting unifies the colours of the paintings and walls covered in embossed Cordova leather. It demonstrates Siberechts' concern for observing light, so typical of Dutch painting but so original in Flanders. It is a superb example of his rare interior scenes, upon which he conferred the monumentality found in his depictions of rural life.
O. Z.

The German School

In the fifteenth century, two great outside events brought the German painters to seek out a new way: the use of oil painting in Flanders and the outbreak of the first Renaissance in Italy. The influences which followed are clear in the works of the Master of the Life of Mary, and in those of Stefan Lochner, both active in Cologne. During the years 1470–1490, a wave of anguish and anxiety swept through people's minds due to the climate of religious intensity. This phenomenon is fully realized in Martin Schongauer and Matthias Grünewald's works. The latter became a master of the fantastical, capable of representing pain to an extraordinary degree (the *Isenheim Altarpiece*, Colmar, Musée d'Unterlinden).
In the sixteenth century, Dürer's art in itself embodies the synthesis between the German tradition and Italian innovations. His contemporary, Lucas Cranach the Elder, was noteworthy for having introduced, in spite of his fervent Protestantism, female nudes with extreme grace and sensuality. It should be noted that among those painters there was a great taste for the strange and the dreamlike. Furthermore, a pagan sensuality is curiously mixed in with a profound religious fervour. Holbein the Younger was mainly a portrait painter. His quest for truth, and his sharp sense of observation led him to an almost scientific rigour, which made him one of the best in his field at that time.
In the seventeenth century, Germany's contribution to the Baroque movement is mainly in the field of architecture, whereas painting showed a taste for genre scenes, still lives and allegories, such as Vanities.
In the eighteenth century, German painting came under a double influence: that of French painting as well as the taste for, and rediscovery of, antiquity, which led some years later to the appearance of Romanticism.

27

Master of the Life of Mary (active from 1460 to 1490)
Last Judgement

Oil on wood.
H: 57 cm; W: 40.5 cm.
GR 1.127

History:
Vienna, E. Engländer's collection; Vienna, Baron Ferstel's collection; Berlin, sale at Ball and Graupe's, May 12, 1930, no. 29; London, sale at Sotheby's of the Ingram's collection, March 11, 1964, no. 125, repr.; London, Hallsborough Gallery, May 1965.

Exhibitions:
Cologne, Wallraf-Richartz-Museum, Melster zu Köln, Herkuntt-Werke, *Stefan Lochner*, Wirkung, 1993, p. 380, no. 70; Zurich, Schweizerisches Landesmuseum – Cologne, Wallraf-Richartz-Museum, *Himmel, Hölle, Fegefeuer. Das Jenseits im Mittelalter*, 1994, no. 131.

Bibliography:
G. Troescher, "Weltgerichtsbilder in Ratshäusern und Gerichtsstätten", in *Wallraf-Richartz-Jahrbuch*, 1939, vol. XI, pp. 139–214, fig. 170; A. Stange, *Deutsche Malerei der Gotik*, Munich-Berlin, 1952, p. 47, fig. 75; "The Hallsborough Gallery Exhibition", in *Apollo*, May 1965; *Connoisseur*, May 1965, no. 3, repr. (detail); *Die Weltkunst*, June 1, 1965, repr.; H. M. Schimdt, *Der Meister des Marienlebens und sein Kreis*, Dusseldorf, 1978, fig. 41; A. Stange, *Kritisches Verzeichnis der deutschen Tafelbilder vor Dürer*, 1978, vol. I, no. 187.

Around 1460–1465 this painter and draughtsman from Cologne created a series of eight panels depicting the Life of Mary *in his native city's Saint Ursula's church. Seven of them are in Munich's Alte Pinakothek (inv. WAF 618–624), and one in London's National Gallery. Other paintings that are now in Augsburg, Berlin, Cologne, Nuremberg etc. have been linked to this body of work, making it possible to recontruct the master's artistic personality. The strong Dutch influence on his work suggests that he travelled to the Low Countries. His style is very similar to that of the Master of the Lyversberger Passion. These two artists, often confused, were the most talented representatives of the Cologne school during the second half of the fifteenth century.*

The composition of this *Last Judgement* is divided into two scenes. In the upper section is a crowned, open-armed Christ enthroned in His Glory dressed in red robes and surrounded by a halo of golden light. On either side, angels announce His victory by blowing trumpets. The saints surrounding him, bearing the symbols of their martyrdoms, are divided into two groups. On the left, Mary the Mother of Christ can be recognised among the women in the first row. Around her is Saint Barbara, holding a tower, and Saint Catherine of Alexandria, with a sword and a book, together with Saint Agnes and the lamb in the second row. Seated on the right-hand side are Saint Peter with his key, Saint John the Baptist dressed in an animal skin and with a lamb on his book, Saint John the Evangelist holding the poison cup and Saint Matthew holding a sword. Behind them are Saint Augustine in bishop's dress holding a flaming heart and Saint Lawrence holding a grille. In the lower section Saint Peter, shown a second time, and two angels welcome the Chosen, who are going to heaven on the left. On the right, two devils are pushing the Damned to Hell. In the centre of the composition a landscape stretches into the distance, with a view of a town and some living figures accompanied by either angels or demons. The meaning of the scene is clear: eternal life depends upon life on Earth; those who are led by angels will go to Paradise, the others, guided by demons, will suffer in the fires of Hell.
This painting, formerly attributed to the fifteenth-century French School, was linked by Max J. Friedlander to the work of the Master of the Life of Mary. Stange clarified this attribution by seeing in this piece the hand of a studio assistant influenced by the paintings of Stefan Lochner, who was active in Cologne from 1442 to 1451. The composition was inherited from this artist's, but the figures, particularly that of Christ, and landscape are very similar to the works of the Master of the Life of Mary. A studio copy of this painter's *Last Judgement* is in the Wallraf-Richartz-Museum in Cologne.
Ph. L.

*28

Lucas Cranach the Elder (1472–1553)
Triptych, circa 1510–1515

Oil on wood.
Central panel: H: 148 cm; W: 99.5 cm.
Wings: H: 148 cm; W: 43.5 cm.
GR 1.259

History:
Tilburg, private collection; Cologne, Lempertz, November 29, 1968, no. 31.

Bibliography:
Jubiläums-Austellung Tilburg 1898–1948. Alte Kunst in Brabanter Besitz, Tilburg, 1948, no. 82; C. Grimm, J. Erichsen and E. Brockhoff, *Lucas Cranach. Ein Maler-Unternehmer aus Franken*, Augsbourg-Regensburg, 1994, pp. 156–157.

Lucas Cranach the Elder was active in Vienna in 1501. Three years later, he became court painter for the Saxon elector-prince Frederick the Wise in Wittenberg, where he directed a productive studio. In 1508, Cranach travelled to the Low Countries. Seven years later, he was famous and working on Emperor Maximilian's Book of Hours. In the 1520s, the artist executed commissions from Cardinal Albert of Brandenburg and Luther, his personal friend. Later, he left an increasing share of his work to the studio, where his sons Hans worked from 1525 to 1537 and Lucas the Younger from 1537. In that period, his vocabulary tended to become simpler and more standardized.

Inscribed in a modern frame, the triptych was exhibited in Tilburg in 1948.
The work poses numerous iconographic and stylistic problems. Open, it has an arched profile with spandrels that have been entirely regilded. The triptych depicts *Christ among the Doctors*, flanked by the *Multiplication of the Loaves* and the *Marriage at Cana*. The extremely rare plan, which may have been dictated by a humanist, appears to draw a connection between the bread, the wine and the Word. Closed, the work depicts *Saint Elizabeth of Thuringia Giving Alms*, uncustomarily and rather clumsily accompanied by the *Nativity*. The only likely explanation for this juxtaposition is the desire to emphasize the eucharistic character of the whole.
The very uneven surface has many repainted sections on the wings, especially the architectural parts, which seem to have been reconstituted during a relatively recent period. On the other hand, the central panel is in a satisfactory state of preservation. It consists of seven lindenwood planks approximately five millimetres thick that are horizontally glued and consolidated with strips of canvas. With the exception of a few touch-ups in the architecture, which can be glimpsed through the door, and in the group of five Jews in the foreground, the painting surface is of high quality, as can be observed in the four figures grouped around the lectern and the repainted white hound.
Attributed at the Lempertz sale to the circle around Hans Süss von Kulmbach, the triptych must have been painted by Lucas Cranach the Elder, probably with help from his studio for the wings. Characterized by a broken perspective and a well-punctuated composition, it is halfway between the works influenced by the painter's stay in the Low Countries, such as *Christ Driving the Merchants from the Temple* by Mölbis and the *Holy Family* in Vienna, and those displaying a more expressive style, such as the *Massacre of the Innocents* in Dresden (M. J. Friedländer and J. Rosenberg, *Lucas Cranach*, Paris, 1978, nos. 25, 34 and 70).
The bride and groom in the scene from the *Marriage at Cana* are dressed in the style of Emperor Maximilian's court, indicating that the painting must date to circa 1510–1515.
F. E.

29

Lucas Cranach the Elder (1472–1553)
Judith, circa 1525

Oil on wood.
D: 14.6 cm.
Signed with the dragon with outstretched wings and dated: *1525*.
GR 1.691

History:
England, Hawkins collection; Calmann collection; London, Baron Hatvany's collection since 1943; London, Christie's, December 1, 1978, no. 82.

Bibliography:
D. Koepplin and T. Falk, *Lukas Cranach. Gemälde, Zeichnungen, Druckgraphik*, Basel-Stuttgart, 1974, fig. 143.

This tondo passed through different British collections before entering the Rau collection. Inscribed in an old frame, it is relatively well preserved. The pictorial surface, covered by a regular network of craquelures, reveals that parts of the work were repainted, especially the upper section of the dark background and the costumes worn by the three symmetrical half-figures. In the centre, Judith is wearing a lavish, low-cut dress and a large, red velvet barrette in her hair. She is holding Holofernes's head in one hand and the sword with which she has just cut it off in the other. She is, uncustomarily, flanked by two attendants. The one on the left has a youthful face, whose profile seems partially touched up. The woman on the right looks older. On the far right-hand side, her flowing hair merges with the date 1525 and Lucas Cranach the Elder's emblematic signature: a dragon with outstretched wings. Cranach and his studio frequently featured Judith in their paintings, especially after around 1530, as the Vienna and Berlin versions illustrate (M. J. Friedländer and J. Rosenberg, *Lucas Cranach*, Paris, 1978, nos. 230 and 234). By combining eroticism and tyrannicide, the artist justifies the Lutheran princes' uprising against the Emperor and offers a Biblical legitimization of the nobility's anti-puritan morals (J. Wirth, "La Réforme luthérienne et l'art", in *Problèmes d'histoire du christianisme*, 14, 1984, p. 42). In this context, the panel takes on a certain importance, considering its early date. The tondo's inventiveness and modelling make it comparable to a series of roundels that, like the *Young Woman* in Stuttgart and the *Virgin with Child* in a private collection (Koepplin and Falk, 1974, p. 277), can be attributed to the master's hand and dated to circa 1525.
F. E.

30

Jakob Strüb (active in Veringenstadt in the early sixteenth century)
Saint Acacius and the Ten Thousand Martyrs, around 1505–1510

Oil on wood.
H: 44.8 cm; W: 62.5 cm.
GR 1.630

History:
London, Sotheby's, March 19, 1975, no. 15.

Probably born in the 1470s, Jakob Strüb was trained in his father Peter's studio in Veringenstadt, near the Swabian town of Sigmaringen. In 1505, he worked with his younger brother Hans on a large retable in the Augustinian monastery of Inzigkofen. His vocabulary – halfway between that of Bartholomäus Zeitblom and Bernhard Strigel – is more archaistic than his brother's.

Cleaned by Pierre Boissonnas in Zurich in 1989, the panel is in a satisfactory state of preservation. It consists of two horizontally-assembled pine planks and has come down to us completely intact. However, it does not appear to have been conceived as an independent work. The direction in which Saint Acacius is facing strongly suggests that the painting belonged, with another panel of the same dimensions, to the wing of a triptych. According to a twelfth-century legend based on the story of Saint Maurice and the Theban Legion, Acacius inspired ten thousand Roman legionnaires who, refusing to sacrifice to pagan gods, were martyred in the name of the Christian faith. Traditionally depicted as a soldier, in this painting the saint holds the attributes of an archbishop. Seated on a wooden throne, he is flanked by the ten thousand martyrs impaled on the trees of Mount Ararat. His cult was highly popular in the Germanic countries between the late fifteenth and early sixteenth centuries (A. Desvaux, *Les dix mille martyrs*, Bellême, 1890).
Attributed to a southern German painter at the 1975 Sotheby's sale, the work is related to Swabian culture and recalls the incisive lines of Bartholomäus Zeitblom, a painter from Ulm, and the plastic softness of Bernhard Strigel, an artist from Memmingen. It seems to have been painted by the same hand as the wings Jakob Strüb made in 1505 for the Inzigkofen retable (H. D. Ingenhoff, *Der Meister von Sigmaringen. Die Malerfamilie Strüb aus Veringenstadt*, Stuttgart, 1962). Similarities with the grassy parterre of Strüb's *Visitation* Thyssen (I. Lübbeke, *The Thyssen-Bornemisza Collection. Early German Painting 1350–1550*, London, 1990, pp. 378–383) and the volumetric definition of the *Presentation of the Virgin* in the Donaueschingen museum (C. Grimm and B. Konrad, *Die Fürstenberg Sammlungen Donaueschingen. Altdeutsche und schweizerische Malerei des 15. und 16. Jahrhunderts*, Munich, 1990, p. 13) also indicate that *Saint Acacius and the Ten Thousand Martyrs* was painted by the same hand. A few details of the costumes, such as the shoes and the headpiece worn by a martyr in the lower right-hand corner, strongly suggest that it was painted shortly afterwards, in other words around 1505–1510.
F. E.

*31 Jeremias van Winghe (1578–1645)
Servant in a Kitchen, 1635

Oil on wood.
H: 115 cm; W: 85 cm.
Monogrammed and dated, lower centre: *I. F. 1635.*
Marked with the stamp of the Kaunitz's collection, Vienna, lower right.
GR 1.957

History:
Vienna, Kaunitz's sale, March 13, 1820, no. 197; Paris, sale at Palais Galliéra, December 10, 1962, no. 115, repr.; Monaco, Sotheby's, June 20, 1987, no. 351, repr. (presented as *Monogrammiste I. F.* with the date 1635).

Bibliography:
E. Greindl, *Les peintres flamands de nature morte au XVIIe siècle*, Brussels, 1983, pp. 89, 370, no. 1, fig. 161 (presented as *Monogrammiste I. F.* with the date 1655; private collection, Paris); S. Segal, *A Prosperous Past: The Somptuous Still Life in the Netherlands 1600–1700*, The Hague, 1988, p. 57, fig. 4.1 (attributed to Jeremias van Winghen with the date 1615); C. Grimm, *Stilleben: Die niederlandischen und deutschen Meister*, Stuttgart-Zurich, 1988, fig. 129, p. 201 (attributed to Jeremias van Winghen with the date 1615).

Jeremias van Winghe (Brussels, 1578 – Frankfurt, 1645) specialized in still lives, portraits and genre and market scenes. He was active in Frankfurt, where his father, the painter Joducus van Winghe, brought him in 1584 to flee anti-Protestant persecutions. He studied under his father before training with Frans Badens in Amsterdam. Van Winghe was clearly influenced by Beuckelaer and Aertsen, and recalls the decorative innovations of Rubens' Flemish followers. He may have known Snyders, among others. Sam Segal has recently attributed high quality works to this almost forgotten master.

There is a weak copy of this painting (oil on wood, 115.5×86.5 cm; Paris, sale at the Théâtre des Champs-Elysées, November 22, 1987, no. 24, repr.; attributed to the studio of the *Monogrammiste I. F.*). It and the Delff of the Rau collection belonged to the famous Kaunitz collection in Vienna. For a long time the inscriptions were attributed to the *Monogrammiste I. F.* The date was read as *1635* for the 1987 sale and *1655* by Edith Greindl, who considered this anonymous painter a follower of Frans Snyders and the earlier painters Aertsen and Beucklaer (Greindl, 1983, p. 89) and attributes two other still lives to him (ibid., nos. 2, 3). In 1988 Sam Segal read the date as *1615* and convincingly established a link between this work and the *Kitchen* in Frankfurt's Historisches Museum, signed and dated *Jeremia. Van. Winghe. Fecit. 1613* (oil on canvas, 115.5×146 cm; inv. 1972).
The similarities are obvious. The Beuckelaer-style composition features background scenes in the same spirit as the drinking men in the Rau collection painting. The identical motifs of the fish in a plate and cutting board on the tub appear in both works. Finally, the handling of the objects, especially the pewter plate, is the same. Sam Segal has shown that the *I* in the monogram stands for *Jeremias* and the *F* for *fecit*. Claus Grimm also argues that the *I* is the initial for Jeremias, but that the *F* is for *Francoforte*, van Winghe's nickname. The clothing of the figures in the background differ in the two works. The garments in the Frankfurt painting correspond to those of the early seventeenth century, while those in the Rau collection picture are later, from the 1630s. The date should therefore be read as *1635* rather than *1615*; the upper downstroke of the *3* has been effaced. The year 1655 would have been too late. This hypothesis is confirmed by the style of the Rau collection panel, which is more modern than that of the Frankfurt painting. The still life's monumental forms and dynamic organization, with the cat reaching for the slab of meat, go beyond Aertsen's and Beuckelaer's styles, which recall Snyders', who in 1635 had been active for a long time and whom, furthermore, van Winghe probably knew. The background scene is similar to those found in paintings by the Flemish artists Simon de Vos and Christophe van der Lamen. This current was practised by van Winghe's early German teachers Binoit, Flegel as well as the Strasbourg painter Stosskopff. In the end this sombre, warmly coloured and splendidly executed *Servant in a Kitchen* brings to mind Samuel Hoffmann, the German artist who worked with Rubens in 1622.
O. Z.

32

Anton Graff (1736–1813)
Portrait of a Gentleman, 1790–1800

Oil on canvas.
H: 61.5 cm; W: 51.8 cm.
GR 1.166

History:
Munich, sale at Böhler's, January 1970.

Bibliography:
E. Berckenhagen, *Anton Graff. Leben und Werk*, Berlin, 1967, p. 391, no. 1562A, repr. p. 392.

Anton Graff (Winterthur, Switzerland, 1736 – Munich, 1813) entered the school of drawing and painting in his native town in 1753, which at that time was directed by Johann Ulrich Schellenberg. Leaving for Augsburg in 1756, he worked with the engraver Johann Jacob Haid. Ten years of trips to Ansbach, where he met Johannes Kupetzki, Augsburg, Regensburg, Winterthur and Zürich enabled him to acquire mastery of the portrait. After sending one of his self-portraits to Dresden in 1766, Graff was made painter of the court of Saxony and a member of the Academy. In 1771 he painted Lessing's portrait and in 1778 met Goethe in Berlin. A member of the Berlin Academy in 1783, he painted portraits and a few landscapes until 1802. Because of an eye disease his output declined until of his death, which was soon after his admission to the Munich Academy in 1812.

This *Portrait of a Gentleman* is not, as was previously supposed, a self-portrait. In fact, comparisons with those that are definitely by the painter prove that it is not his face. Moreover, confirming this view, he looks towards the right, and not at the viewer as when a painter was looking at himself in a mirror. If the identity of this man about forty years old remains unknown, certain stylistic traits nevertheless make it possible to date the painting to the 1790s.
This portrait is distinguished by the desire to depict the sitter's character with an economy of means that is contrary to the Baroque style, which consisted of giving the character numerous attributes referring to his social status and military, economic, literary or artistic activities. Here, sobriety reigns. The accent is on truth in the rendering of the face. The head is tightly framed, the clothes reduced to a dark jacket with a white shirt and a chestnut coloured scarf. The fully lit face is brought to life by the corners of partly-opened lips and the strongly outlined eyes. The expression is resolute, the sitter seeming to have been caught in full action. Two oblique lines, those of the nose and the scarf, enliven the composition. In the development of his style Anton Graff owes much to Johannes Kupetzki (1667–1740), whom he met in 1757 at the court of the Margrave of Ansbach. The sobriety of Kupetzki, whose intense depiction of reality and personality were so different from the Baroque, had an impact on him.
It is above all from the 1770s that Graff definitively opted for the realistic and psychological portrait, rejecting the Baroque pomp or Rococo charm which he had previously tried to capture. The colours became darker, as in the portraits of Rembrandt and of Kupetzki. After 1775 the palette changed again under the influence of French and English painting. Here the tones, chosen in a range of browns, light for the face, darker for the jacket, give the portrait an atmosphere of gentleness.
At this time Graff discovered the line as a means of expression. It can be seen especially in the look and the corner of the lips, the two major points of every realistic portrait, but also in the drawing of the shirt collar and scarf. These simple details give the expression strong firmness.
Ph. L.

The French School

During the fifteenth and sixteenth centuries, French painting, while remaining faithful to the Gothic tradition, did not manage completely to avoid Flemish and Italian influences. While, under John the Good, Paris held the rank of artistic capital, in the fifteenth century, the city of Tours took over with the artist Jean Fouquet. This artist, who had at length studied the discoveries of the renewal in Italy, can be seen as the first French artist of modern times.

The transition between the Middle Ages and the Renaissance took place under the impulse of François I who, in 1528, decided to settle in Fontainebleau. To restore the castle he called upon Michelangelo, Il Rosso and Primaticcio. And so Tuscan Mannerism found itself embedded in France, and engendered the Fontainebleau School.

Therefore the French School as such did not, in fact, put in an appearance until the seventeenth century. Henceforth, the French artists went to Italy to complete their training. The chief representatives of the start of the century were Valentin de Boulogne, Nicolas Tournier, Claude Vignon and, above all, Simon Vouet. The latter, named first painter of the king by Louis XIII, had a style very clearly influenced by Caravaggio. On the contrary, Philippe de Champaigne, who had started with Flemish culture, developed a more "classical" style. The austere rigourousness obvious in his portraits became even more pronounced when he got to know the Jansenists in Port-Royal.

Strangely enough, it was in Rome, where Baroque reigned supreme, that Poussin and Le Lorrain, the two great masters of Classicism, expressed their genius. The former admired Titian and Raphael and borrowed from the mythological repertory as well as from history, his favourite themes. His painting, like that of Jean-François Millet, is an example of a profound intellectual meditation on the harmony existing between man and nature. Like Poussin, Le Lorrain lived in Rome and very early on carried out a minute observation of nature; the major representative of classical landscapes, his art provides an idealized vision of nature.

Under Louis XIV's reign, painting expressed the grandeur of the State's power. Thus, Le Brun carried out frescoes integrated into large architectural programmes, whereas Largillière made portraits of the main figures in high society. During the Regency, the Duke of Orleans favoured an art which was more deliberately focused on life's pleasures; hence we have the *fêtes galantes* painted by Watteau and Pater. This tendency reached its paroxysm under the reign of Louis XV, with Boucher, whose style saw the apotheosis of Rococo. Animal paintings, still lives, genre scenes and landscapes also found many adepts at the end of the eighteenth century (Chardin, Oudry), as well as sentimental portraits (Greuze, Vigée-Le Brun). This sentimentality reached its culmination in Vernet and the Chevalier Volaire's landscapes, and in the paintings of "ruins" by Hubert Robert. But, without a doubt, the painter best able to express the quintessence of these different approaches was Fragonard.

33

Jacques Linard (circa 1600 – 1645)
Vanitas with Candle, 1644

Oil on canvas.
H: 39.8 cm; W: 48.6 cm.
Signed lower right:
I'. LINARD.
Dated on the paper:
ce XX janvier 1644
GR 1.131

History:
Paris, private collection; Geneva, J.-P. Durand, June 1971.

Exhibitions:
Paris, Orangerie des Tuileries, *La nature morte de l'Antiquité à nos jours*, 1952, catalogue by Ch. Sterling, pp. 77–78, pl. XXII; Geneva, Palexpo, *La Fondation pour l'écrit. Salon international du livre et de la presse. Le livre et la presse dans la peinture*, 1996.

Bibliography:
A. Hulftegger, *Bulletin des musées de France*, July 1946, p. 4; K. Benedict, *Maandblad voor Beeldende Kunsten*, February 1948, p. 30, repr. p. 34; K. Benedict, "Notes sur Jacques Linard", in *Etudes d'art publiées par le musée national des Beaux-Arts d'Alger*, no. 13, 1957, p. 31, repr.; J.-F. Revel, "Linard", in *Connaissance des Arts*, September 1958, no. 79, p. 63, repr.; M. Faré, *Le grand siècle de la nature morte en France, le XVIIe siècle*, Fribourg, 1974, p. 40, repr.; *Les Vanités dans la peinture au XVIIe siècle*, notice by J. Foucart, Caen, Musée des Beaux-Arts, July 27 – October 15, 1990, p. 58, fig. 3.

Jacques Linard (Paris ?, circa 1600 – Paris, 1645) was probably born at the turn of the century because his death certificate, in 1645, stated that he was "about forty-five" (Dreyfus-Bruhl, 1948, pp. 1, 3). Nothing is known of his training nor his beginnings, but he is mentioned as being in Paris in 1626, and his first certain picture is dated 1627. The office of valet de chambre *to the King which he held in 1631 attests to his presence at court and a certain affluence. Linard's surviving works show him to be an exclusively still life painter. Indeed he participated with Moillon, Stosskopf and Baugin in the development of this genre, new to France in the early seventeenth century.*

The *Vanitas with Candle* is the last known dated painting by Jacques Linard. It was executed a year before his death. Should one read a particular significance into this moving testimony by an artist who feels his end is approaching ? This reflection on death, on the ephemeral and transitory nature of earthly life, developed in the seventeenth century, particularly under influence from Northern European artists. It became fairly popular in France.
Linard was one of the first French artists to handle the theme of the Vanitas. Nevertheless, they were rare in his œuvre, which was essentially dedicated to still lives with flowers or fruits, sometimes populated by birds or butterflies. Only three examples remain. The most complete composition, the *Vanitas with Moth* (Faré, 1974, pp. 38–39), dated 1634, presents various elements of the rebus which illustrates the vanities of the world. The shell, flute, open book, vase of flowers, fruit and hourglass, a symbol of the passage of time, show that it should be interpreted as an allegory of the senses. The *Vanitas with Carnation* (Madrid, Museo del Prado; Faré, 1974, p. 40), which is very similar to the Rau collection painting, seems to predate by several years this *Vanitas with Candle*, a true *memento mori* where the artist limited the composition to the theme's essentials. On the stone table a skull rests on a book bound in brown leather. Beside it, a fragile bouquet of carnations, tulips that are just beginning to fade, and a button rose are in a glass vase reflecting a window. The candle on the wall has just gone out. An inscription on the crumpled paper which is slipping out of the closed book clearly gives the painting's meaning: *Voilla comment tous noz beaux jours deviennent. ce XX janvier 1644* (This is how all our beautiful days end, January 20, 1644). But despite the subject, Linard refused pathetic depiction which, for example, with a comparable economy of means, Philippe de Champaigne expressed in his only known *Vanitas* (Le Mans, Musée Tessé). The *Vanitas with Candle* puts forward a sobriety and melancholic poetry proper to early seventeenth-century French still life painting.
I. M.

voilla comment tous noz beaux iours deuiennent.
ce xx janvier 1644
I. LINARD

34 Philippe de Champaigne (1602–1674)
Portrait of Doctor Boüin, 1625

Oil on canvas.
H: 60 cm; W: 47 cm.
Ancient inscription upper left: *n (?) Boüin docteur / ppal de poitier / an 1625.*
GR 1.896

History:
Great Britain, private collection, 1976; Paris, sale at Palais d'Orsay, June 16, 1977, no. 60, repr.; London, Gallery Colnaghi and Co Ltd, 1978; London, Christie's, December 2, 1983, no. 36, repr.

Exhibition:
London, P. and D. Colnaghi and Co Ltd, 1978, *Paintings by Old Masters*, no. 24, repr.

Bibliography:
B. Dorival, *Philippe de Champaigne 1602–1674*, Paris, 1976, vol. II, p. 388, no. 2051, repr. p. 518, fig. 2051A.

Philippe de Champaigne (Brussels, 1602 – Paris, 1674) received his earliest training in Brussels and in 1621 settled in Paris. In the French capital he met the young Poussin on the eve of his departure for Italy, where he would never go. He worked for Lallement and Nicholas Duchesne, whom he succeeded and whose daughter he married in 1628. Champaigne was granted French nationality in 1629 and became one of the favourite painters of Louis XIII and Richelieu, of whom he painted several portraits. He was a founding member of the Royal Academy in 1648 and painter of the Paris aldermen. He was also a church painter and formed a special bond with Port Royal and the Jansenists. He painted many altarpieces imbued with a grave and sober religious sentiment, but was also a fashionable portraitist, sought after by his contemporaries.

Nothing is known about Dr Boüin's life except that he belonged to a well-known family in Poitou. Bernard Dorival notes a portrait of a *Madame Boüin*, drawn by Daniel Dumonstier, dated 1641, in the Cabinet des Estampes in the Bibliothèque Nationale (J. Adhémar, "Les Dessins de Daniel Dumonstier du Cabinet des Estampes", in *Gazette des Beaux-Arts*, March 1970, p. 149, no. 94, ill.).
The clumsy inscription in the painting's upper left corner makes it difficult to date the work. It provides a piece of information about the life of the model, who was undoubtedly appointed chief doctor of Poitiers in 1625, but has led the London exhibition catalogue's author to consider this portrait one of the artist's early works. Bernard Dorival argues that it is a late work painted around 1645. It is closely related to the *Portrait of Philippe de la Trémoïlle* (Amsterdam, Rijksmuseum; Dorival, 1976, vol. II, no. 172) which dates from around 1643. Furthermore, the sitter's moustache and goatee as well as his costume are characteristic of the fashion in the years 1640–1645: slashed sleeves, sombre doublet decorated with lace, buttoned up high below the collar and opening lower over the shirt, the collar fastened with a tasselled cord.
Philippe de Champaigne used a limited colour range. The three-quarter figure stands out against a light grey and beige background. The golden white of the sleeves and shirt and the colder, almost transparent white of the collar set off the black doublet. The artist concentrated his attention on the model's face and psychology. He painted the pink complexion, the greyer zones where the beard appears below the skin, the half-opened ruby lips, and the lively, sparkling look which directly addresses the spectator with precision and delicacy.
I. M.

n. Boüin docteur
ppal de poitier
an 1625.

35

Jean-François Millet
(Jean-François Millet, known as Francisque Millet, 1642–1679)
Heroic Landscape

Oil on canvas.
H: 112.8; W: 145.3 cm.
CR 1.262

History:
Vienna, Czernin's collection; Silvano Lodi's collection, 1972.

Bibliography:
P. Rosenberg and Fr. Bergot, *French Masters Drawings from the Rouen Museum, from Caron to Delacroix*, Washington-New York-Minneapolis-Malibu, 1981–1982, pp. 63–64, repr.

Jean-François Millet (Antwerp, 1642 – Paris, 1679) was born in Antwerp where his French father was a sculptor in Ivory. In 1659 he came to Paris, where in 1662 he married the daughter of his Antwerp master Laureys Franck. Accepted into the Academy in 1673, he showed two landscapes in the Salon of that same year. He travelled in Flanders, Holland and England, but died prematurely in 1679. His deep compositions which open out onto vast horizons, as well as the subjects depicted, make Millet one of the best representatives, in France, of the heroic landscape as defined by Nicolas Poussin.

Only a few of Francisque Millet's pictures exist today. Not one is signed or dated. The twenty-eight engravings by his student Théodore however, have made it easier to know his œuvre (Davies, 1948). Although Théodore did not make an engraving of it, the attribution of this heroic landscape to Millet is not in doubt. The composition, with a view of a distant blue-tinted horizon seen from above, the handling of the brown-green foliage and the quality of the colouring are characteristic of the artist.
The painting is very similar to the *Landscape with Christ and the Woman from Canaan* (Toledo, the Toledo Museum of Art; *La peinture française du XVIIe siècle dans les collections américaines*, Paris, Grand Palais, January 29 – April 26, 1982, pp. 290–291, no. 71). A succession of mountain ranges in the background and the *fabriques*, whimsical little structures that ornamented gardens, can be found there, as well as the two figures of the man starting to cross the bridge and the one behind him, who is turned toward his companions. Engraved by Victor Pillement (Rosenberg and Bergot, 1981–1982), the composition is entitled *Regulus Returning to Carthage*. This title is not critically accepted. Is it not rather a Biblical scene, as in the Toledo picture? Probably not. The person in the foreground is holding a book. The leaves of a laurel crown protrude from under the cloth covering his head, portraying him as a poet. The bust of a man and a false inscription can be found on the facade of the first building, perhaps a mausoleum. In the distance, on the upper right, two men are carrying an idol, preceded by torch-bearers even though it is a daytime scene. It is possible that this is a funerary scene taken from an episode in Antiquity.
Another version of this picture exists with several differences, particularly in the trees. It was in the collection of Lord Wilton at Ditchley (sold Sotheby's, June 9, 1955, lot 180) and is now in the museum at Southampton (*Pictures from Southampton*, London, 1970, no. 14, repr.). The Rouen Musée des Beaux-Arts also has a red chalk drawing, a preparatory work for this composition (Rosenberg and Bergot, 1981–1982, pp. 63–64, no. 78).
I. M.

36

Nicolas de Largillière (1656–1746)
Portrait of a Woman with Carnation, 1740

Oil on canvas.
H: 92 cm; W: 73 cm.
Once signed and dated on back of the original canvas: *peint par N. de Larguillière / 1740* today masked by the recanvassing of 1842 (according to the sales catalogue of December 9, 1959).
GR 1.608

History:
Mrs. Beryl Leslie Urquhart's collection, 1930; Sotheby's, December 9, 1959, no. 55, repr.; London, Old Masters Galleries, 1966; London, Sotheby's, March 27, 1968, no. 57, repr. (under the title *Portrait dit de Catherine Dujardin*); London, Christie's, July 17, 1970, no. 214, repr. (under the title *Portrait de la comtesse Wachtmeister*); Christie's, January 29, 1971, no. 122; Broad Gallery; Clifford Duits collection; London, Sotheby's, December 8, 1971, no. 114, repr.

Exhibition:
London, Old Masters Galleries, 1966, no. 20, repr.

Bibliography:
M. N. Rosenfeld, *Largillière, portraitiste du dix-huitième siècle*, Montreal, 1982, pp. 254–255, repr. fig. 50d.

Nicolas de Largillière (Paris, 1656 – Paris, 1746), the son of a Paris hatter, was trained by Antoine Goubau in Antwerp in 1672 before being sent to the studio of the portraitist Peter Lely in London. In 1682 he returned to Paris, where he devoted himself mainly to portraits, although he worked in other genres as well. Four years later the Royal Academy received him with a Portrait of Le Brun, *today in the Louvre. Largillière was gifted with a sound constitution – he lived to the age of eighty-nine – and an aptitude for work. According to his contemporaries he painted more than 1,500 works. His portraits of women, which are always a bit idealised, put more emphasis on the models' social rank and accessories than their personalities.*

It is often difficult to positively identify Largillière's portraits of women. Like many others, this one, has gone under many names – Catherine Dujardin, Countess of Wachtmeister – during the twentieth century. The artist simplified and embellished the faces of his vain clients in order to live up to their expectations better. This approach was in keeping with the spirit of the eighteenth century. Roger de Piles recounted that women did not tolerate as much realism in their portraits as men did. The work's composition and technique confirm that it was painted between 1720 and 1740.
The artist's style changed significantly and at the end of his career was defined by a smooth, delicate finish, intense colours, minute details in the clothing and background decor and a great amount of cohesion between the various elements. The static pose is enlivened by the dynamism of the beautiful, brittle-looking blue velvet drapery, the profusion of lace and the stormy landscape that creates a sense of depth. The flesh tones and shining eyes have life-like colours but despite this brightness, the features of the face, somewhat thickened by age, are a bit blurred and idealized to make them more attractive. Largillière always composed his portraits sumptuously to the detriment of any psychological intensity. The technically brilliant blue, white and ivory tones of the model's clothes, which overall are fairly cold although enlivened with red here and there, are characteristic of the artist's mature works. He painted several layers of varnish, giving the texture a clear, limpid look that further heightens the sheen of the colours. The carnation, whose bright tints stand out against the dark drapery, recalls the still lives painted by the artist when he was young. His Flemish training shows through in the play of light on the fabrics and subtle, meticulous rendering of each detail.
Largillière used this type of composition countless times throughout his career, for example in the *Portrait of a Woman* in Milan (oil on canvas, 82 × 65 cm; Milan, Pinacoteca di Brera). Among many other examples, the same gold-embroidered dress with a matching dark blue velvet mantle can be found in the *Presumed Portrait of the Duchess of Beaufort* (oil on canvas, 80 × 64 cm; signed, dated 1714; Paris, Musée Cognacq-Jay). M. N. Rosenfeld argues that it is a studio costume because it appears often in the artist's portraits of women (1982, p. 254).
Largillière's method explains these similarities. He worked directly on the canvas, often painting his heads with the model sitting in from of him, but used detailed oil sketches for the draperies, hands and background landscapes. His training in Antwerp undoubtedly explains this process (see, for example, the *Study of Hands* in the Louvre, inv. DL 1970–7).
C. B.

37

Jean-Baptiste Pater (1695–1736)
Stopping at an Inn, after 1728

Oil on canvas.
H: 53 cm; W: 64 cm.
Signed lower left: *Pater*.
GR 1.624

History:
Lord Shrewsbury of Alton Tower's collection; van Cuyk's collection, 1860; Isaac Péreire's collection, 1866; Paris, sale of the Isaac Péreire collection, March 6–9, 1872, no. 72, repr. engraved; Paris, sale of the Oppenheim's collection, April 23–28, 1877, no. 80; Paris, sale of Mrs. Oppenheim's collection, June 17, 1890, no. 23; London, sale at Sotheby's of the Greffuhle collection, July 22, 1937, no. 75, repr.; Duke of Gramont's collection; Paris, Galerie Cailleux, 1954; Netherlands, private collection; J. H. Loudon's collection; Silvano Lodi's collection, 1973.

Exhibitions:
Paris, Galerie Martinet, *Exposition des tableaux et dessins de l'Ecole française, tirés de collections d'amateurs*, 1860, no. 221; Paris, Palais des Champs-Elysées, *Tableaux anciens empruntés aux galeries particulières*, 1866, no. 130; London, Royal Academy of Arts, *Winter Exhibition*, 1954–1955, no. 233A.

Bibliography:
H. Mireur, *Dictionnaire des ventes d'art*, 1911, vol. V, p. 509; F. Ingersoll-Smouse, *Pater*, 1928, p. 72, no. 448; J. Cailleux, *Cailleux 1912–1962*, 1962, unnumbered page, repr.

Jean-Baptiste Pater (Valenciennes, 1695 – Paris, 1736) was the son of the sculptor Antoine. In 1704 he was apprenticed to a painter in Valenciennes, Jean-Baptiste Guidé. His real master, however, was Watteau, with whom he studied twice. The first time was around 1710–1713, the second in 1721 in Nogent, shortly before Watteau's death. In 1728 he was admitted to the Royal Academy as a painter of gallant fêtes. He was strongly inspired, through Watteau's style, by Italian theatre. According to Gersaint, he was a tireless, prolific worker who wielded an easy brush. Despite his premature death he left a considerable body of work whose seductive, lively spirit marked the beginning of the eighteenth century.

A procession of women, children and soldiers is taking place in a rustic landscape with a bluish, somewhat Flemish background. The figures, who are following close behind each other, have varied poses. They are reminiscent of Rubens' joyous *Fair* (Paris, Musée du Louvre). Pater was above all a colourist. Gersaint recalled that he did not like to draw. In this painting he livened up his composition with brisk strokes of green, red and yellow. *Stopping at an Inn* cannot help evoking Watteau and his *Relaxations* and *Fatigues of the War* (oil on copper, 21.5 × 33.5 cm, around 1712; Saint Petersburg, Hermitage Museum).
Like his teacher, Pater saw the ravages of the wars of Louis XIV's late reign in Valenciennes, a border town. However, in contrast with Watteau, he did not focus on the misery of the soldier's life and demonstrated neither compassion nor realism. On the contrary, the painting reflects a cheerful, enchanting spirit, full of life and movement. It is genteel and good-natured, making it more similar to the gallant fête rather than the sad depiction of a military camp. This painting has been catalogued under different names during its various sales and exhibitions, including the *Camp* and *Stopping at an Inn*. In his monograph devoted to Pater, F. Ingersoll-Smouse put this painting into the *Marching Troops* category. Pater painted this subject, one of his favourites, many times. A number of versions still exist, explaining how the artist worked. He inherited his methods from Watteau. Pater chose the figures most suited to his composition from his collections of sketches and put them together by groups in a given setting. This is why a few details vary from one scene of marching troops to another. Pater was concerned with rapidity and efficiency. In fact, throughout his short career he was haunted by the fear of poverty (*Catalogue raisonné des diverses curiosités du cabinet de feu de M. Quentin de Lorangère*, Paris, 1744, pp. 193–197).
The work was probably painted after 1728, when Pater was admitted to the Academy with a painting of *Soldiers Rejoicing*. A version of this painting is the pendant to another *Soldiers Marching* (Ingersoll-Smouse, 1928, no. 447), which is very similar to the Rau collection work. All of these paintings may have been done during the same years.
C. B.

38

François Boucher (1703–1770)
The Flute Lesson, 1751

Oil on canvas.
H: 63.2 cm; W: 101 cm.
GR 1.607

History:
Anonymous sale, February 1, 1839, no. 76; anonymous sale, April 19, 1843, no. 2A; anonymous sale, March 23, 1872, no. 7; Paris, Baronne de Rothschild's collection; Wildenstein's collection, until 1968; London, Sotheby's, March 24, 1971, no. 103.

Exhibitions:
Cincinnati, Art Museum, *French Paintings of the 18th and Early 19th Centuries*, 1937, no. 1; New Orleans, Louisiana State Museum, *The Great Tradition of French Painting*, 1940, no. 9; Toronto, Art Gallery, *Exhibition of Great Paintings in Aid of the Canadian Red Cross*, 1940, no. 48; New York, Wildenstein, *The Woman in French Painting 15th to 20th Century*, 1950, no. 16; Caracas, Museo de Bellas Artes, *Obras clásicas de la pintura europea*, 1956, no. 15; New York, East Hampton, Guild Hall, *Pleasures of Summer*, 1958, no. 6.

Bibliography:
A. Ananoff, *François Boucher*, Lausanne-Paris, 1976, vol. II, p. 74, no. 374.

The son of an ornamentalist and dealer in engravings, François Boucher (Paris, 1703 – Paris, 1770) was a student of his father's before joining François Lemoyne's studio. He worked as an illustrator before winning the Royal Academy's first prize in 1723 with Evilmerodach Delivering Jehoiachin, Prisoner of Nebuchadnezzar. *Boucher did not leave for Rome, but lived in Italy for a short time later. He devoted the years 1726–1728 to drawing and engraving, copying drawings by Watteau for the collector Julienne. In so doing, Boucher acquired an ease that enabled him to demonstrate his skill with his earliest commissions.*
His reception by the Academy in 1734 with Renaud and Armide *(Paris, Musée du Louvre) marked the start of a long career during which the artist worked for the king and Madame de Pompadour. For thirty years, he displayed a tremendous capacity for work in several areas of activity: he became a professor at the Academy in 1737, its director and the king's first painter in 1765, supplied models for the Gobelins and Sèvres factories, where he held official positions, and designed many sets for the theater and opera. A painter, decorator and ornamentalist, Boucher revitalized history painting with his repertory of* mythologie galante.

The *Flute Lesson* is a charming, bucolic scene in which Boucher features children: a young shepherd takes advantage of a timely opportunity to show a little shepherdess how to play the flute. The artist uses a palette of very soft colours. The characters stand out against a grey-green background encircled by red foliage. A dark mass of trees fills up the painting's right-hand side, while the distant, open blue-grey sky appears on the left. The little girl is dressed in white, pink and blue pastel tones. The shepherd is wearing the same colours, heightened by a yellow sleeve and red drapery, the composition's only bright notes. Blue unites all the group's components, from the ribbon on the straw hat to the boy's trousers, the cuff of the sleeve, the girl's dress and the cord with which she holds her sheep. The scene was painted with brisk brushstrokes and various kinds of paint to achieve different effects. The child's left leg, coat and red drapery beneath the hat are surrounded by brown lines drawn with quick strokes that give the figure a sense of motion. Boucher used thick layers of a richer paint for the sheep and foreground with the dog.
A. Ananoff gives 1751 as the date of the *Flute Lesson*. In this work, Boucher returned to a subject he had already painted in 1748 (Ananoff, 1976, vol. II, p. 7, no. 311) using an oval format with older figures. The composition is exactly the same. That painting was exhibited at the Salon in 1748 and 1750 and engraved by R. Gaillard under the title the *Pleasant Lesson*, which served as the model for a china group, the *Flutist*, that many factories in France and other countries reproduced until the late 1770s (terra cotta; Sèvres, Musée National de Céramique; *François Boucher 1703–1770*, 1987, pp. 359–360, no. 98). The three sheep are a direct quotation from a painting that had been shown at the 1747 Salon, *Are They Thinking of the Grape?* (Ananoff, 1976, vol. II, pp. 4–5, no. 310). That work shows a group of four sheep on the right. Three of them appear here in the same positions, and they can be found again in an engraving by Gilles Demarteau based on a drawing by Boucher (ibid., p. 5, fig. 891).
The *Flute Lesson* served as a model for tapestries; the composition appears on the back of a sofa in the National Gallery of Art in Washington. In 1751, Boucher also supplied the models for a series of backrests that Madame de Pompadour commissioned from the Gobelins, which probably depicted nude Cupids (*François Boucher 1703–1770*, 1987, p. 34).
I. M.

39

Maurice-Quentin de La Tour (1704–1788)
Portrait of Charles-Jacques Colin, 1750–1760

Pastel on paper.
H: 59 cm; W: 49 cm (upper part enlarged with a strip of paper between 2 and 4 cm wide).
GR 1.974

History:
Stayed in the Colin family until the beginning of the twentieth century; Rouen, Président Couvet's collection; Henri Marion's collection; Paris, sale at Drouot's, December 12, 1988, no. 15, repr.

Exhibition:
Rouen, Musée des Beaux-Arts, *Art du XVIIIe siècle*, 1929, no. 141.

Bibliography:
P. Vitry, "Un pastel de La Tour au Musée de Rouen", in *Bulletin de la Société d'Histoire de l'Art Français*, 1929, 1st fascicule, pp. 73–74; *Figaro*'s art supplement, April 1929, no. 229, repr. on cover; C. Debrie, *Maurice-Quentin de La Tour*, 1991, pp. 100–101.

*In 1723 Maurice-Quentin de La Tour (Saint Quentin, 1704 – Saint Quentin, 1788) went to Paris for training. Tardieu recommended that he join Jean-Jacques Spoëde's studio, but La Tour above all benefitted from advice from Louis de Boullogne and Jean Restout. Vivien and Rosalba Carriera had updated the pastel, which attracted La Tour to the point where he specialized in it. In 1746 he was accepted into the Academy as a painter of portraits in pastel. He actively took part in the Salons and became painter to the king in 1750. From then on a crush of clients crowded his studio and Mariette said that he did portraits of "all the people most distinguished by their birth or by their talents" (*Abecedario*, published by P. de Chennevières, A. de Montaiglon, 1853, vol. III, p. 71).*

There is no reason to challenge the identification of the model, whose portrait was owned by his descendants until the beginning of the twentieth century. Charles-Jacques Colin (or Collin) was in Madame de Pompadour's service for many years. In 1748 the king's favourite asked the man who had been her family's attorney to sell his position at Châtelet and become intendant of her house. He moved to Versailles, where his house on Saint Louis street, La Collette, still stands.
He is wearing a gold Maltese cross fastened to his chest by a red ribbon. The white enamelled decoration with *fleurs de lys* is the decoration of the Order of the Knights of Saint Louis. The *Almanach Royal* (1753, p. 113; 1765, p. 130) indicated that from 1750 to at least 1765 Colin held the position of the order's comptroller general. In 1693 Louis XIV created the Order of Saint Louis, which was reserved for army and navy officers regardless of birth. The model is shown frontally, his body imperceptibly turned three-quarters to the left to give the composition movement. He is looking at the viewer. The sober theatricality emphasises his physiognomy. The pleasant expression, full of life and vigour, and the moving eyes and smiling mouth are firmly and supply modelled. The painter wonderfully captured his model's personality and life. Mariette rightly said that La Tour "had the precious talent of making true-to-life portraits" (*Abecedario*, vol. III, p. 71).
La Tour, who was above all a draughtsman, enclosed colour within form. The colour range is limited, intelligent and does not detract from the balance of the composition. The figure stands out against a neutral green background. He is wearing a velvet jacket whose softness and reflections are still highlighted by the pastel's powdery look. A few red notes are the only touches that brighten up the austere palette. The composition, which is very similar to that of the *Portrait of Montalembert* exhibited at the Salon of 1753 (pastel, 65 × 55 cm; Paris, Doeuillet sale, Galerie Georges Petit, April 27, 1932, no. 34, repr.; Bernard and Wildenstein, 1928, no. 81). It can be dated to the 1750s or 1760s, when the artist, who had reached the height of his career, painted many official portraits. The dating is borne out by the model's position, which he held from 1750 to 1765.
C. B.

40

Jean-Baptiste Greuze (1725–1805)
Portrait of a Young Woman, 1760

Oil on canvas.
H: 47 cm; W: 38.9 cm.
Signed and dated upper right: *J. B. Greuze. 1760.*
GR 1.542

History:
Mr. C. J. West's collection, 1835; London, Christie and Manson's, 1835; Louis Paraf's collection, 1909; London, C. J. Galloway's collection; Paris, Baron d'Erlanger's collection; Paris, sale at Drouot's, May 21, 1941, no. 12, repr.; Paris, Baronne Lopez-Tarragoya's collection; London, Christie's, June 29, 1973, no. 89, repr.

Exhibitions:
London, Guild Hall, 1898, no. 79; Paris, Palais de Bagatelle, *Exposition rétrospective de portraits de femmes sous les trois Républiques*, 1909, no. 90, repr.

Bibliography:
J. Smith, *Catalogue Raisonné of the Works of the Most Eminent Dutch, Flemish and French Painters*, London, 1837, vol. VIII, and *Supplement*, London, 1942, no. 114; J. Martin, Ch. Masson and C. Mauclair, *Jean-Baptiste Greuze*, Paris, 1906, p. 37, no. 532; G. Mourey, "Exposition rétrospective de portraits de femmes", in *Les Arts*, July 1909, no. 91, p. 30, repr. p. 22; "Le mariage malheureux de Jean-Baptiste Greuze", in *Connaissance des Arts*, July 1955, pp. 14–17, repr. p. 15.

Jean-Baptiste Greuze (Tournus, 1725 – Paris, 1805), who was born in Burgundy, did not arrive in Paris until around 1750. In 1755 he was admitted to the Academy. The same year he exhibited at the Salon for the first time and was acclaimed by the critics. His moralising genre scenes made an impression on the public and ushered in the beginnings of a new aesthetic. His portraits, which were at every exhibition, were no less popular and his renown earned him official commissions. Greuze was a good businessman who understood all the advantages that dissemination of his works through printing could bring, and he encouraged engravers to make copies of his works.

The many surviving portraits of Madame Greuze suggest that she is the artist's young model in the Rau collection painting. Edgar Mulhall confirmed this traditional identification in a written statement dated February 25, 1992. On February 3, 1759 Greuze married Anne-Gabrielle Babuti (1732 – around 1812), the daughter of a Paris bookseller, in Saint-Médard's church in the French capital. In August 1793 Greuze and Gabrielle divorced after a stormy twenty-six years together.
In a letter to the sculptor Falconet dated August 1767, Diderot, who nevertheless found the young woman charming, described the couple's relationship in these terms: "I enjoy hearing him speak to his wife. It is a spectacle where Punch beats back the blows, which makes the fellow meaner" (*Correspondance*, annotated by G. Roth, 1955–1970, vol. VIII, p. 104).
The catalogue of the June 29, 1973 sale affirms that the painting was exhibited at the 1761 Salon under number 99, entitled *Portrait of Madame Greuze as a Vestal*. Its size (64.8 × 48.6 cm) as well as Diderot's description (p. 134) make it a distinctive work. The catalogue of the May 21, 1941 sale compared the painting to one of those appearing under number 104 and of which Gabriel de Saint-Aubin did a sketch (E. Dacier, *Catalogues de ventes et livrets de Salons illustrés par Gabriel de Saint Aubin*, 1907, vol. VI, p. 64, repr. p. 25). However, this small drawing does not seem to exactly match the Rau collection painting. The young woman's body is turned in another direction and she is wearing a bonnet tied under her chin. It may be possible that the painting, dated 1760, was exhibited at the 1761 Salon under the number 104, *Several Heads Painted under the Same Number*. However, neither descriptions nor the size specified makes it possible to confirm this hypothesis. These small portraits did not attract the attention of the critics, who were overwhelmed by number 100, *Village Harmony*. A laconic Diderot was the only critic who mentioned it, saying: "There are several very life-like heads by Greuze" (p. 135). Nevertheless, this charming figure is eye-catching. The young, round, child-like face is caught in a natural pose. The light impasto of the cheeks provide it with life and substance, while the subtle glaze of the veil covering the shoulders underscores the young woman's fragile grace. A few touches of colour add a fresh, delicate note. Diderot, recalling the past, described Gabrielle flatteringly: "A white doll straight as a lily, red as a rose" (*Œuvres complètes*, édition critique et annotée, H. Dieckman, J. Proust and J. Varloot, 1979, "Salon de 1765", p. 152), G. Mourey quoted the Enlightenment philosopher as describing "a child's face, a round, unified forehead, eyebrows high above the eyes that lend her physiognomy a naive expression, a straight, alert little nose of a young girl, a moist, well-outlined, coquettish, oval, still full mouth, soft, delicate flesh, an amiable roundness, a little air of feeling heightening and enlivening what was a little too sheepish about the face" (quoted by Mourey, 1909).
C. B.

41 Chevalier Volaire (Pierre-Jacques Volaire, known as Chevalier Volaire, 1729 – before 1802 or 1790)
Still Waters, Fishermen, 1766

Oil on canvas.
H: 55 cm; W: 72 cm.
Signed and dated lower right, partly effaced: *le [c]he[valier] Volair[e] / Roma 176...*
GR 1.115

History:
Vienna, Czernin's collection, 1926; Vienna, Sankt Lucas Gallery, 1963.

Bibliography:
Catalogue of the Czernin collection, pp. 94–95, no. 157; F. Ingersoll-Smouse, *Joseph Vernet, peintre de marine*, Paris, 1926, vol. II, p. 47, no. 1235A (presented as Joseph Vernet).

Pierre-Jacques Volaire (Toulon, 1729 – Naples, before 1802 or Lerici, 1790?) came from a family of artists. His early training was probably dispensed by his father, Jacques, official painter of the city of Toulon. In 1754 Joseph Vernet, whom the King had commissioned to paint a series of the Ports of France, *arrived in Toulon and took the young Volaire under his wing. Volaire followed his teacher from port to port, leaving him in 1763 to return to his home town for a while before going to Rome, where he lived until 1769 and painted works that were very similar to Vernet's. Afterwards he left for Naples where he seems to have lived until his death, the date of which has not been clearly established.*

Volaire remained with Joseph Vernet for eight years, helping him with his commissions, especially the *Ports of France*. This experience marked his style for the rest of his life. These two pendants, for example, were considered to have been painted by Vernet, as Ingersoll-Smouse's catalogue demonstrates, until a restoration in 1989 revealed Volaire's partially effaced signature. The works are extremely similar to Vernet's. The same composition, with one side filled with land and architecture and the other opening out on to the sea and ships, the same big, cloudy sky taking up two-thirds of the canvas, the same soft, orange-tinted morning light contrasting with the violent midday storm and even the same small, gesticulating figures in the foreground, so characteristic of Vernet, can be found in Volaire's Rau collection paintings.
The figures, especially in paintings of shipwrecks, were very popular during the eighteenth century because of their dramatic aspect. The poses of the barely escaped women weeping or squeezing their children, the lifeless figures and tired, desperate faces not only won viewers' hearts, but liven up the foreground of this quasi-theatrical scene as well. Everything in the two scenes is contrasted. *Still Waters* is characterized by a static composition of horizontals and verticals and the stiff poses of the figures, who are unveiled by the light of a warm, pink morning sun. The *Storm at Sea* furiously rocks to the rhythm of curves and obliques which seem to embody the wind of the tempest. A harsh light models the landscape and bitterly illuminates the little group of unfortunate shipwreck victims and their saviours. Lively colours and a marked chiaroscuro round off the painting, which is imbued with a tragic flavour. Many compositions that could have inspired Volaire can be found in Vernet's work. For example, *Still Waters* and *Storm at Sea* are very similar to two famous works, *Morning, Calm Weather* and *Midday, Shipwreck*, part of a series of decorative works entitled the *Four Parts of the Day*, commissioned by the Marquis de Marigny for the Dauphin's library at Versailles. They were painted in 1762 and are still in their original location (oil on canvas, 83 × 135 cm; Ingersoll-Smouse, 1926, nos. 763, 764, repr.).
Volaire, who probably helped paint these scenes, may have remembered them four years later when he did these two pendants in Rome. The choice of the times of day, the organization into contrasting light and dark scenes and the location of the paintings' various elements are similar. The same spirit can be found in the *Storm* by Vernet, which was certainly painted after the Rau collection works and exhibited at the 1769 Salon (private collection; *Diderot et l'art de Boucher à David*, Paris, Hôtel de la Monnaie, 1984–1985, p. 395, repr.).
This comparison demonstrates the close relationship between the master's work, which changed little over time, and his student's. The influence remained powerful until at least 1769, when Volaire settled in Naples and the landscapes of Campania and eruptions of Mount Vesuvius breathed new life into his style. These new subjects became his specialty and perpetuated his fame.
C. B.

42

Jean-Honoré Fragonard (1732–1806)
Portrait of François-Henri, Duke of Harcourt, circa 1769

Oil on canvas.
H: 81.5 cm; W: 65 cm.
GR 1.560

History:
Duke of Harcourt's collection; London, Sotheby's, December 8, 1971, no. 21, repr.

Exhibitions:
Paris, Musée des Arts Décoratifs, *Exposition d'œuvres de J.-H. Fragonard*, 1921, no. 90 (catalogue by G. Wildenstein); Paris, Musée Carnavalet, *Le Théâtre à Paris*, 1929, no. 31; Paris, Gazette des Beaux-Arts, *Le siècle de Louis XV vu par les artistes*, 1934, no. 133; Bern, Musée des Beaux-Arts, *Fragonard*, 1954, no. 22; Paris, Galerie Charpentier, *Cent chefs-d'œuvre de l'art français, 1750–1950*, 1957, no. 33; Paris, Galeries Nationales du Grand Palais – New York, Metropolitan Museum of Art, *Fragonard*, 1987–1988, no. 140, repr. (catalogue by P. Rosenberg).

Born in Provence, Jean-Honoré Fragonard (Grasse, 1732 – Paris, 1806) was ten years old when his parents settled in Paris, where he briefly studied under Chardin and, more successfully, Boucher. Winner of the Prix de Rome in 1752, he left for Italy in 1756. Contact with Antiquity and works by the great masters of painting rounded out his training. He was influenced by Hubert Robert with whom he worked a great deal, and befriended the abbot of Saint-Non, his first patron.
On his return to France, as a recognised painter, he hesitated between an official career (Corésus and Callirhoé, *1765; Paris, Musée du Louvre) and lighter works, likable or gallant genre scenes which carried on the tradition of Boucher and fanciful figures where the freedom of the brush reached its heights. Forgotten in the first half of the nineteenth century, Fragonard has since regained an undying celebrity.*

The *Portrait of François-Henri, Duke of Harcourt* is one of the fifteen fanciful figures by Fragonard known today. Painted around 1769, these identically sized paintings have not yet yielded all their secrets. The patrons and most of the figure's costumed models are unknown, but the Rau collection portrait is still one of the least mysterious.
Mentioned for the first time in 1921, the *Portrait of François-Henri, Duke of Harcourt* and its pendant, the *Portrait of the Duke of Beuvron* (Paris, Musée du Louvre), were not separated until 1971. The Fragonard exhibition in Paris and New York in 1987–1988 reunited them, with P. Rosenberg offering a full study. The models were identified from 1921. They include François-Henri, Duke of Harcourt, Governor of Normandy (1726–1802) and his younger brother, Anne-François d'Harcourt, Duke of Beuvron (1727–1797). Exhibited and published, they have often been mixed up, with the one taken for the other. Recent studies, and notably the comparison between Fragonard's work and a portrait of François-Henri d'Harcourt drawn by Anicet-Charles-Gabriel Lemoinier (Rouen, Musée des Beaux-Arts), have confirmed the identification of the model (Rosenberg and Compin, 1974; Rosenberg, 1989). The suggestion of this is given by an old inscription stuck to the back of the picture: "[..] Duc d'Harcourt né le 11 janvier 1726 / lieutenant général de Normandie en 1764 / Gouverneur du Dauphin sous Louis XVI, Ambassadeur du Roi Louis XVIII en Angleterre / pendant la Revolution Française / mort a Selaine canton de [...] juin 1802 / Il avait épousé Catherine Scholastique / d'Aubusson de la Feuillade morte à Paris rue de Babylone / le 18 novembre 1815" (Duc d'Harcourt born January 11, 1726 / Lieutenant General of Normandy in 1764 / Governor of the Dauphin under Louis XVI, Ambassador of King Louis XVIII to England / during the French Revolution / died at Selaine, canton of [...] in June 1802 / He had married Catherine Scholastique / d'Aubusson de la Feuillade who died in Paris, rue de Babylone, / November 18, 1815.)
Dressed in a sea-green jerkin and a red and black short cape, his sword at his side, the Duke of Harcourt is holding a hat with a white plume in his right hand, proudly clamped on his hip, and is clutching a fine gold chain. The face stands out against a white ruff, a reminder of portraits by Rubens. The garment is brushed in an almost transparent manner, dominated by brown tones. The coloured accents are marked by heightenings of pure colour, a dazzling red for the folds of the cape and, for the sleeves, an almond green lightened by a single yellow note at the hollow of the left arm. The lively touch and free brush, which runs over the canvas in large, rapid strokes, gives the portrait its dynamism. Fragonard was keen to express the vitality of his model, surprised at the moment he turns round.
I. M.

Bibliography:
G. Wildenstein, "L'exposition Fragonard au Pavillon de Marsan", in *Revue de l'Art français*, July 1921, no. 7, p. 360; L. Reau, *Fragonard*, Brussels, 1956, pp. 88, 174 pls. 93, 181; *Journal de l'Amateur d'Art*, 10 May 1957, detail reproduced on cover; G. Wildenstein, *The Paintings of Fragonard*, Aylesbury, French ed., 1960, pp. 16–17, no. 240, pl. 36; J. Wilhem, *Fragonard* (unpublished monograph), 1960, p. 113; Ch. Sterling, *Portrait of a Man (The Warrior), Jean-Honoré Fragonard. An Unknown Masterpiece by Fragonard*, Williamstown, 1964, p. 86; J. Thuillier, *Fragonard*, Geneva, 1967, pp. 79, 86; Y. K. Zolotov, *Le portrait français du XVIIIe siècle*, Moscow, 1968, p. 160, repr.; D. Wildenstein and G. Mandel, *L'opera completa di Fragonard*, Milan, 1972, no. 256, repr. (presented as portrait of Anne-François); P. Rosenberg and I. Compin, "Quatre nouveaux Fragonard au Louvre", in *Revue du Louvre*, no. 3, 1974, pp. 184–186, fig. 4; *Art de Basse Normandie*, no. 78, 1979, p. 34; J.-P. Cuzin, *Fragonard, vie et œuvre*, Fribourg-Paris, 1987, pp. 113, 192, no. 176, fig. 133 p. 106; P. Rosenberg, *Tout l'œuvre peint*, Paris, 1989, no. 205, repr.; M. D. Scheriff, *Fragonard. Art and Eroticism*, Chicago-London, 1990, pp. 183–184, notes 45–46 pp. 245–246.

43

Hubert Robert (1733–1808)
Monumental Staircase, 1770–1775

Oil on canvas.
H: 55 cm; W: 46 cm.
GR 1.955

History:
New York, Christie's,
March 26, 1987, no. 148.

Bibliography:
Will be included in the *Catalogue raisonné* of Hubert Robert's paintings in preparation at the Wildenstein Institute, Paris.

Hubert Robert (Paris, 1733 – Paris, 1808) did his apprenticeship in the studio of the sculptor Michaelangelo Soldtz, who encouraged him to go to Rome, where, the French Ambassador, the future Duke of Choiseul, took him under his wing. In 1759 the aristocrat got him into the French Academy without taking part in the Prix de Rome competition. He became friends with Fragonard and the Abbot of Saint-Non, and visited Naples with the latter in 1760. During these few years, the artist produced a great number of drawings inspired by Italian ruins and landscapes.
On his return to Paris in July 1765, Hubert Robert quickly became famous. He exhibited regularly at the Salon and led a brilliant career, close to the court, for twenty years. He developed the drawings sketched in Italy into larger compositions, executed numerous views of Paris and celebrated parks and, in 1783, began a series on the monuments of southern France, now in the Louvre.
The artist did not escape the upheavals of the Revolution. He was arrested in 1792 and saved by the 9th Thermidor. In 1795 he was appointed to an official position, chairing with Fragonard the Commission for the Central Museum of the Arts, the future Louvre Museum founded on July 27, 1793.

This painting, monumental despite its small size, is fairly representative of Hubert Robert's talent and interest in architecture. During his stay in Italy he was able to closely observe, study and draw the monuments of antiquity and the palaces and churches of modern Rome. Beyond these accurate records of real buildings, the artist often chose one architectural element or another to develop it elsewhere, sometimes in combination with other features. The monumental staircase is one of his favourite motifs. Here it is used to reconstruct an imaginary site.
The scene is viewed through an arcade forming a frame for the composition. On either side there is a statue on an elevated plinth. In the foreground two men chat in the shadows, their silhouettes standing out against a lighter background. The group of women is bathed in a ray of light coming in through a large arch on the left. The great, shaded staircase guides the viewer's eye into the painting's depths, where a few figures stand out against the light. The painter used beige and grey monochromes tending towards blue in the stairwell. The stationery figures on the steps are sketched in almost tone upon tone. The ones leaning against the balustrade are more brightly lit and attract attention. A miniscule red accent lends them presence. Only the female figures entering under the vault are coloured. Their clothes are painted with light, brisk brushstrokes. The vermillion, white and blue strokes dress the figures and catch the light.
Joseph Baillio dates this small, very beautiful painting to the years 1770–1775.
I. M.

44

Elisabeth-Louise Vigée-Le Brun (1755–1842)
Portrait of Charlotte Ritt, 1797

Oil on canvas.
H: 49.5 cm; W: 35.5 cm.
Inscribed in the paste, lower right: *L E V Le Brun / a petersbourg / 1797.*
GR 1.134

History:
Danzig, collection of Mrs. F. X. Frantzius, born Ritt; with her heirs in 1925; Munich, sale by Weinmüller, November 28, 1968, no. 1245, repr.

Bibliography:
J. Baillio, "Identification de quelques portraits anonymes de Vigée-Le Brun aux Etats-Unis", in *Gazette des Beaux-Arts*, XCVI, November 1980, pp. 166, 168, fig. 15, note 28.

Elisabeth-Louise Vigée (Paris, 1755 – Paris, 1842) studied under her father, Louis Vigée, before training with Joseph Vernet and Greuze. In 1776 she married the art dealer J.-B. Le Brun. She was the appointed portraitist of Queen Marie-Antoinette and the ladies of the court, and in 1783 was received by the Academy. In 1789 she left France, staying away until after the Revolution. From 1789 to 1792 she lived in Florence, Rome and Naples, from 1792 to 1795 in Vienna and from 1795 to 1802 in Saint Petersburg and Moscow. In 1796 she became a member of the Academy of Saint Petersburg, where she was highly esteemed by the Russian aristocracy. Her Souvenirs, *published between 1835 and 1837, reveal that she painted at least forty-eight portraits in Russia, a country she considered her second homeland.*
In 1802 she returned to Paris but continued travelling, this time to England, Holland and Switzerland. Elisabeth Vigée-Le Brun is, along with Adélaide Labille-Guiard and Marie-Victoire Lemoine, one of the most famous woman painters of the late eighteenth century.

This portrait of a woman was published for the first time by Joseph Baillio in 1980. The model has been identified as Charlotte Ritt, wife of the great Russian miniaturist Augustin-Christian Ritt (1765–1799). The painting's provenance has made this identification possible. It belonged to the heirs of Mrs. F. X. Frantzsius, born Ritt, before being offered to the Louvre in 1925 (Baillio, 1980, p. 168, note 28). Moreover, a *Portrait of Charlotte Ritt* drawn in one of the artist's travel notebooks (Paris, private collection, 1980) and a miniature portrait of her daughter Julie Le Brun painted by August Ritt in 1796 attest to the relationship between Elisabeth Vigée-Le Brun and the Ritt family (Baillio, 1980, p. 166).
Joseph Baillio was aided in his identification of the model by a portrait of a woman, located in a private New York collection and considered at the time to be of Madame Razoumoffska, whom Vigée-Le Brun painted in Vienna sometime between 1792 and 1795. The discovery of a date and inscription on this work, engraved, like here, in the paste, "L. E. Vigée / Le Brun / a petersbourg / 1798", revealed that this work was from the Russian, rather than Viennese, period. A comparison with the Rau collection work, whose location was unknown at the time, shows a striking resemblance between the models.
The *Portrait of Charlotte Ritt*, which was also painted in Saint Petersburg and dated 1797, shows a young, tender-looking woman. It may be related to the second and more ambitious portrait, dated 1798, where a three-quarter length figure of a woman is seen sitting on a rock, her elbow leaning on a grassy mound. In both cases, the model is wearing fabric in her long, curly hair and fine muslin under the chin. The same ornamentation, which must have been fashionable in Russia at the time, can be found in the *Portrait of the Grand Duchess Elisabeth Alexievna* (1798; Montpellier, Musée Fabre).
A detail that had not been visible in photographs emerged when a recent study of the Rau collection portrait was again submitted to Joseph Baillio for examination in view of the present catalogue's preparation. Here the young woman's eyes are blue-grey, but those of the figure in the portrait in the American collection are brown. Therefore, although the models look strikingly alike, they cannot be the same person. According to Joseph Baillio (written statement, February 1992), the Rau collection painting is indeed a portrait of Charlotte Ritt, while the work in the United States shows the princess Maria Grigorievna Galitsine.
I. M.

The Spanish School

In Spain the Renaissance did not produce any remarkable painters. We have to wait until the second half of the sixteenth century to find geniuses such as El Greco and de Ribera.
The former had travelled to Venice, and he assimilated in a very personal way the lessons of Titian and Tintoretto. He rapidly found a really personal style, very far removed from the pictorial traditions of the Renaissance; he confirmed his tendency towards a visionary representation, steeped in spirituality, which magnified colour, luminous contrasts as well as a profound sense of drama. De Ribera also lived in Italy during his formative years; he was especially aware of Caravaggism, whose luminousness and naturalism were carried to excess.
The following century, known as the Golden Century, witnessed the birth of one of the greatest artists of that time: Velázquez. His early works, although still under the influence of Caravaggio's naturalism, soon evolved towards a style in which colour became totally free.

45

El Greco (Domenikos Theotokopoulos, known as El Greco, 1541–1614)
Saint Dominic in Prayer

Oil on canvas.
H: 75 cm; W: 58 cm.
Signed on the stone,
lower left.
GR 1.45

History:
Madrid, Marqués de Aldama's collection; London, Tomas Harris, 1931; Florence, Contini Bonacossi's collection; Munich, Galerie Julius Böhler, 1970.

Exhibition:
London, Tomas Harris, *Old Masters by Spanish Artists*, June 1931, p. 11, repr.

Bibliography:
H. E. Wethey, *El Greco and His School*, Princeton, 1962, vol. II, no. 206, fig. 250;
T. Frati, *L'opera completa del Greco*, Milan, 1969, no. 70d;
J. Gudiol, *El Greco. 1541–1614*, Barcelona, 1971, no. 197;
J. M. Pita Andrade, *El Greco*, Milan, 1981, Paris, 1983, no. 234, repr. p. 183.

The first twenty-five years of El Greco's life (Candia, Crete, 1541 – Toledo, 1614) are still quite mysterious. He spent some time in Venice and may have trained in Titian's studio, but his work is strongly derived from Bassano's and Tintoretto's. He was undoubtedly attracted to Spain by the big Escurial project, coming to Toledo in 1577 and living there until his death in 1614. His early Spanish works combine the Venetians' smooth touch with the Mannerists' tart polychromatism. From 1580 to 1583, he worked for Philip II, who did not like the Martyrdom of Saint Maurice *(Madrid, Escurial, Real Monasterio). After this failure, El Greco turned towards a clientele made up of Toledo jurists and humanists who were more likely to appreciate his eminently intellectual work. He had a brilliant career as a painter of portraits and religious history, but during the Golden Century the only artist who really understood him was Velázquez.*

Dominique de Guzmán (1170–1221), a Castillian gentleman who founded the Order of the Friar Preachers, or Black Friars, was canonized in 1234. He sparked a giant preaching and prayer campaign to fight the Cathar and Albigensian heresies, which at the time were ravaging the Church. The Dominicans were preachers and beggars who split their time between prayer and study and seemed as revolutionary as the Franciscans. Saint Dominic never became as popular as Saint Francis of Assisi, who was ten years younger than he, but was particularly venerated in Italy, southern France and, of course, Spain.
In Toledo, El Greco imagined new iconographic types that were in accordance with the very specific wishes of the Counter-Reformation's exegetes. He imported a new type of Saint Francis from Italy, a thin ascetic more in keeping with historical accuracy. He painted many examples that were exceptionally popular in Spain. *Saint Dominic in Prayer*, dialoguing with a crucifix in an austere Castillian landscape, certainly fulfilled the Black Friars' wishes to spread the grand, solitary image of their order's founder.
The composition is very similar to that of *Saint Francis in Meditation* (San Francisco, M. H. de Young Memorial Museum, studio replica in Lille, Musée des Beaux-Arts). The severe Dominican costume – the white robe and scapular and deep black cope and hood – reduce the palette to cold tones that are perfectly suited to the theme of the hermit in prayer. The artist focuses attention on the saint's folded hands and aristocratic face, imbued with mildness and interiority, and made longer by the pointed goatee.
The apparently simple composition is rigorously ordered around a central axis emphasized by the scapular's vertical fall. The fairly low viewpoint accentuates the slender pyramidal shape filling the space on a summarily sketched landscape background. The number of times El Greco painted the same scene attests to the success of this powerful image, which was one of the artist's major creations. Three signed versions with slight variations, especially in the face and folds of the robe and scapular, are considered authentic by all of the critics. El Greco painted them several years apart. The first *Saint Dominic in Prayer*, currently in the Plácido Arango collection in Madrid, dates from between 1585 and 1590. The version in the Toledo cathedral sacristy can be dated from between 1600 and 1605. The picture in the Boston Museum of Fine Arts, which is slightly smaller than its predecessors, was painted between 1605 and 1610. Harold E. Wethey, one of the greatest El Greco historians, says that the even slightly smaller Rau collection painting was probably painted by the master and his studio between 1600 and 1610. Other versions, such as the one in the Hispanic Society of New York, are undoubtedly old copies. El Greco certainly helped paint the Rau collection painting. It is very similar to the Arango version, but a few differences, especially in the shape of the wrists and scapular, rule out the possibility that this may be a copy. The freedom of technique, unrealistic shapes and very elongated figures confer an undeniably mystic accent on El Greco's paintings that was in perfect harmony with the spiritual revival taking place in Counter-Reformation Spain.
O. D.

46

José de Ribera (1591–1652)
Saint Jerome, 1636

Oil on canvas.
H: 73.5 cm; W: 59.5 cm.
Signed and dated middle left:
Jusepe de ribera español F. / 1636.
GR 1.78

History:
Bought for 150 pounds from a noble family before 1741: Verona, collection of Marshal von der Schulenburg (1661–1747), no. 112; Munich, Galerie Julius Bölher, 1970.

Bibliography:
Inventario Originale della Galleria di Sua Ecc.za Maresciallo Conte di Schulenburg colle differenti Spedizioni e Prezi del Costo..., Venice, 1741, folio 6: *Inventaire de la Gallerie* (sic) *de feu S.E. Mgr. Le Feldmaréchal comte de Schulenburg*, Berlin, [175...], p. 5, no. 112 (pen-numbered copy in Hanover, Niedersächsisches Hauptstaatsarchiv).

José de Ribera (Jativa, 1591 – Naples, 1652) was a Spanish as much as an Italian artist. He was born in Valencia province and may have worked in Ribalta's studio. At an early age he left for Italy, visiting Parma and Bologna before spending time in Rome in 1615 and settling in Naples in 1616. De Ribera was one of Caravaggio's finest and most faithful followers. Protected by the Spanish viceroys, he quickly became the city's most influential painter, receiving major commissions from the aristocracy and religious orders. His style, which was thoroughly tenebrist at first, changed around 1635. The artist's Baroque dynamism and clear, colourful range of colours reveal a familiarity with Venetian and Flemish painting. De Ribera's rich, serious personality deeply marked not only the Neapolitan school, but Spanish painters such as Zurbarán, Murillo, Pereda and Claudio Coello, who saw his works sent by the viceroys to the land of their birth.

Saint Jerome was one of the four great Doctors of the Roman Catholic Church. His cult grew at the time of the Counter-Reformation. Jerome was born in Stridon, Dalmatia, baptized in Rome at the age of nineteen and ordained a priest in Antioch. He withdrew to solitude in the Syrian desert for several years before going to Rome, where he became both Pope Damasus' secretary and a closely followed spiritual director. He founded monasteries in Palestine, where he led a life of austere penitence entirely devoted to meditation and translation of the Bible. He died in 420. He laid down the definitive Latin text of almost the entire *Vulgate* version of the Bible, which was officially adopted by the Church at the Council of Trent, 1545–1563.
The anchorite sage, along with Saint Peter and Mary Magdalen, became an emblematic figure of the sacrament of penitence, which was much debated by the Protestants. His depiction was a popular theme in seventeenth-century art, and repeatedly returns as a dramatic leitmotif throughout de Ribera's career. In his catalogue of the artist's works (Milan, 1978), Nicola Spinosa lists forty-seven paintings of this saint, nineteen of which are definitely signed. The Rau collection picture as well as a recently published painting in Genoa (M. Roethlisberger, *Archivo Español de Arte*, no. 253, 1991, pp. 87–89, fig. 1), signed and dated 1647, should be added.
De Ribera seemed fascinated by this mortified old man whom, at the beginning of his career, he depicted full-length, listening to the Last Judgment trumpet (Seville, Ossuna collegiate church; Naples, Museo di Capodimonte; Saint Petersburg, Hermitage Museum). Later works show him three-quarter length, writing or beating his *mea culpa* with a stone (*Saint Jerome*, signed and dated 1643; Lille, Musée des Beaux-Arts).
The Rau collection version is simple, yet has a powerfully expressive force. The head of an aged man with a full beard and silvery hair stands out in full light against a solid dark background. His gleaming eyes seem sunk into heavily shadowed sockets with red-lined lids. The face is modelled by fine, coloured strokes and broad, dense or transparent ones, producing an extraordinarily natural impression of life. In the foreground, the hands laid on a skull are similarly handled with long, crossed, red, grey and white brushstrokes. The red cape concealing the left shoulder is more smoothly and sketchily handled. The sun and scourging have dried out the bare, taut skin. Saint Jerome himself described "this rebellious skin that I have attempted to tame through weeks of fasting [..] burned by the

Jusepe de Ribera español F.
112

sun [..] with a film of filth that made my skin look like an Ethiopian's" (*Epistola XXII ad Eustochium*).
This version strives to accurately illustrate the subject in accordance with Counter-Reformation instructions. It is dated 1636, in the middle of de Ribera's fully mature period, shortly before he received the major commission for the San Martino charterhouse. The painting belonged to Count Johan Matthias von der Schulenburg, a German field marshall who entered the service of the Republic of Venice in 1715 and, beginning in 1724, gathered together a huge collection of more than 950 works, most of them by earlier and contemporary Italian artists. The number 112, which can be seen on the painting's lower left, was added during a gallery inventory carried out in French after the marshal's death. An original inscription reading *Giusepe di Ribera, zugenannt lo Spagnoleto. Px St. Hyeronimus. N. 112* appeared on the back of the old canvas reinforcement, which was removed during restoration in 1970.
O. D.

The British School

British painting, compared to that of France or Italy, received very little support in the way of patronage from individuals or institutions. It was only in the eighteenth century that the first English academies came about. One of the begetters of academic training was the painter Reynolds. Anxious to promote his country's art in the face of France and Italy, he developed what he called a "grand style", i.e. painting devoted to portraits, according to the classical canons of antique statuary. But Reynold's most basic innovation in British painting, was to have used as models people from different social classes. Unlike Gainsborough, who was self-taught, and who carried out, following van Dyck, fashionable portraits which he placed within the English countryside. His refined style borrowed from the Rococo a clear and luminous chromatic scale, along with a certain lyricism. If these two artists signify the apex of Classicism in England, their influence nonetheless opened the way for Romanticism.

47 John Michael Wright (1617–1694)
Portrait of Sir Hugh Wyndham, 1670–1680

Oil on canvas.
H: 125.5 cm; W: 102 cm.
GR 1.948

History:
London, Christie's, November 18, 1983, no. 34; London, Anthony Dallas, 1984; London, Sotheby's, November 19, 1986, no. 29.

Exhibition:
London, Anthony Dallas and sons Ltd, *British Paintings*, 1984, no. 4.

Bibliography:
Apollo, December 1984, p. 27 (advertising for the exhibition mentioned earlier, only existing colour reproduction of the painting).

John Michael Wright (London, 1617 – London, 1697) apprenticed with the painter Jamesone in Edinburgh before going to Italy. From 1642 to 1656 he lived in Rome. On his way back to London he became Archduke Leopold William's antiques buyer. His long stay on the continent imbued his work with a French and classical flavour unknown in England, which earned him the favors of Charles II. Between 1660 and 1670 he was a successful portraitist, but in Restoration England his sometimes austere naturalism and Catholic convictions prevented him from playing the leading role, which fell upon Sir Peter Lely.

The model for this portrait was the eighth son of Sir John Wyndham of Orchard Wyndham. Sir Hugh (1603–1684) was brought up at Wadham College, Oxford and made sergeant-at-law in May 1654. Although this promotion to the magistrature was declared illegal during the Restoration, he not only kept his position but in June 1660 was named judge and in June 1670 Exchequer. He was married three times, first to Jane, daughter of Sir Thomas Wodehouse of Kimberley, then to Elisabeth, daughter of Sir William Minn of Woodcott and, in 1675, to Katherine, widow of Sir Edward of Beveridge. This portrait, which can be dated to after 1660 because the model is wearing a judge's robes, features Wright's main trademarks: discreet sobriety and elegance as much in the figure's pose as in the setting which, reduced to the basics, enhances the absolutely truthful, psychologically realistic face. This painting is similar to Wright's more famous portraits, such as *Brian Duppa, Bishop of Winchester* (1660; Oxford, Christ Church) and *Colonel John Russell* (1659; Ham House, Victoria and Albert Museum). Between 1671 and 1675 Wright painted twenty-two full-length portraits of judges who had settled the difficult legal questions arising from the Great Fire of London in 1666. These works, which are in Lincoln's Inn, London, include the *Portrait of Sir Wadham Wyndham* (1610–1668), Sir Hugh's brother. This commission may have persuaded Sir Hugh to have Wright paint his own portrait, which would date it to between 1670 and 1680 or so. Sara Stevenson, who has suggested the same date, has confirmed the Rau collection painting's traditional attribution to Wright (oral statement, 1992).
J.-Ch. B.

48

Joshua Reynolds (1723–1792)
Portrait of Rebecca Watson, 1758

Oil on canvas.
H: 76.4 cm; W: 62.9 cm.
GR 1.942

History:
Sir W. J. Watson's collection; Christie's, May 7, 1904, no. 127, bought by Gooden & Fox; London, Christie's, April 22, 1983, no. 90 p. 151, repr.; London, Christie's, April 18, 1986, no. 113, repr.

Exhibition:
Berlin, Kaiser Friedrich-Museums-Vereins, *Ausstellung von Werken Alter Kunst*, 1906, no. 112 p. 32.

Bibliography:
A. Graves and W. Vine Cronin, *A History of the Works of Sir Joshua Reynolds, p. R.A.*, 1889, vol. III, p. 1039.

Joshua Reynolds (Plympton, 1723 – London, 1792) was the son of a Devonshire clergyman. He left London at the age of seventeen and chose as his teacher the portraitist Thomas Hudson. After a stay in Italy (1750–1752), he moved to London definitively and opened a workshop where commissions were soon flooding in. The portraits from the 1750s are characterized by their Venetian style and the influence of Rubens and Rembrandt. Around 1757 the more delicate style of his rival, Ramsey, began influencing them. Between 1755 and 1760, Reynolds' diaries (M. Cormack, "The Ledgers of Sir Joshua Reynolds", in Walpole Society, *XLII, 1970, pp. 105–169), show that the artist received up to six sitters per day, each staying about one hour. He worked every day and had up to 150 patrons in a year.*

Joshua Reynolds was always very comfortable doing childrens' portraits. In this work he painted the daughter of Rebecca Buller of Morval and Admiral Charles Watson (1714–1757). The eight-year old Rebecca (1750–1811) sat for Reynolds in April 1758, shortly after the death of her father who had distinguished himself in India many times, especially during the battle of Plassey (June 1757). His recent death may explain the serious, dreamy, almost sad expression of the child, who is solemnly standing ramrod straight. Some beautiful blue, grey and yellow harmonies complement one another, from the sky to the magnificent dress covered with embroidery and lace. The impasto technique and rich, powerful colours, so characteristic of Reynolds' work, attract the eye. As with the heavy clothing, the necklace's large pearls accentuate the young girl's fragility and gentleness.
The *Portrait of Lady Elizabeth Hamilton* (117 × 80 cm; Elkins Park, J. E. Widener collection), executed in the same year, resembles the previous painting in its technique as well as in the sitter's pose. Reynolds particularly liked painting children and knew how to make them appealing, intimate and friendly in his art. He made the long sittings more pleasant by telling amusing stories or fairy-tales to his young models. Thus Northcote, student and biographer of the artist, recalled "What a huge racket filled the studio when the children were there! He played and fought with them, speaking to them in their own language; and while he was doing this he caught their fleeting expressions which make his child portraits so captivating" (*Conversations of James Northcote R. A. with James Ward on Art and Artists*, published by E. Fletcher, London, 1901, p. 78).
C. B.

49 Thomas Gainsborough (1727–1788)
Portrait of Mrs. Gainsborough

Oil on canvas.
H: 75 cm; W: 62 cm.
GR 1.902

History:
Margaret Gainsborough until her death in 1798; Margaret Gainsborough, her daughter, until her death in 1820; by legacy to Elisabeth Green (born Gardiner), her first cousin; Rev. William Green, her husband; Miss Laetitia Green, a relative, second wife of Mr. Thorne; John Mills Thorne, his son, 1859; Rev. William Edward Green, son of William Green, 1876; bought in 1876 by John Heugh; London, Christie's, May 10, 1878, no. 236, bought by Thomas at Agnew & Sons Ltd; Sir Robert Loder, 1882; sale, May 29, 1908, no. 528, bought by Asher Wertheimer; Rio de Janeiro, E. Guinle, 1911; Paris, Galerie Charles Brunner, 1912; Toronto, bought by Georges A. Morrow, 1917 (1927); Toronto, Waddington's, Mac Lean & Co. Ldt, June 1983; Monaco, Sotheby's, June 26, 1983, no. 512, repr.; London, Sotheby's, July 5, 1984, no. 274, repr.

Exhibitions:
London, British Institution, 1859, no. 135; London, Royal Academy of Arts, *Old Masters*, 1882, no. 12; London, Grosvenor Gallery, *Gainsborough Exhibition*, 1885, no. 175; London, *Japan-British Exhibition*, 1910, no. 17; Paris, Galerie Charles Brunner, 1912, vol. III, no. 14, repr.; London, Pembroke Galleries, 1921; Toronto, Art Gallery, 1927, no. 27.

Thomas Gainsborough (Sudbury, 1727 – London, 1788) was born in Suffolk. He was always sensitive to the landscapes of his youth, which he would later work into his great portraits of English society painted in the grand manner. He apprenticed in London from 1740 to 1748, settling definitively in the capital city in 1774. Once famous, he painted numerous official portraits, both of members of the Royal family and the aristocracy. The outstandingly simple portraits he painted of his family or friends, devoid of all artifice, present an alternative facet of his work. They bear witness to his virtuosity and consummate skill in the art of portraiture and in the rendering of expression and personality.

Thomas Gainsborough married Margaret Burr in the summer of 1746. Adrienne Corri recently published an article revealing the young woman's origins ("Gainsborough's Early Career: New Documents and Two Portraits", in *The Burlington Magazine*, April 1983, pp. 212–214; *The Search for Gainsborough*, London, 1984). Born in Holland around 1728, Margaret was the illegitimate daughter of Frederick, Prince of Wales, son of George II, who gave her an annual allowance of £ 200 a year through the intermediary of Henry, Duke of Beaufort. Despite strong personality differences, the couple was inseparable and had two daughters: Mary, born in 1748, and Margaret, born in 1752. Gainsborough often executed portraits of his family. He painted his wife every year on their wedding anniversary, but few of these works have survived (*Gainsborough*, Paris, Grand Palais, 1981, p. 147).
Until the Heugh sale of 1878, the Rau collection painting had the same provenance as the portraits of *Mary* (77.5 × 65 cm; London, Tate Gallery, no. 5638), dated 1777, and *Margaret Playing the Lute* (76 × 67.3 cm; formerly in the Adolf Hirsch collection). However, it would seem that the latter is more likely a painting of Mary. It is still difficult to determine whether they were produced in the same year, but their free and easy execution nevertheless certainly makes them very close in date. All the artist's tenderness towards his sitter shows through in this work. The artist very carefully depicts her handsome face with its rather sad, tired expression which is in marked contrast with the rapid, spirited handling of her costume. The warm brown and red tones and the vibrant, confident touch make this a moving, lively and realistic portrait. The *Portrait of Mrs. Gainsborough* in the Courtauld (oil on canvas, 77 × 64 cm), painted circa 1778, is very close in spirit to the Rau collection piece, whilst the *Study of a Woman* in New Haven (19.5 × 13.7 cm; New Haven, Yale Center for British Art), from the model's pose, the costume and the dating, could well be a preparatory study for it. Yet another version of this portrait exists – a copy or an autograph work – which came up for sale in London, in 1920 (Christie's, December 3, lot 114).
C. B.

Bibliography:
E. Marshall, published letter in *Notes and Queries*, 19 February 1876, p. 155; W. Armstrong, *Gainsborough and His Place in English Art*, London, 1899, p. 195; "Gainsborough's Portrait of his Wife and Daughter", in *The Times*, 20 October 1908; E. Waterhouse, "Checklist of Portraits by Thomas Gainsborough", in *Walpole Society*, XXXIII, 1953, p. 46, no. 2 ; E. Waterhouse, *Gainsborough*, London, 1958, pp. 69–70, no. 298; M. Davies, *National Gallery Catalogue. The British School*, 2nd ed. 1959, pp. 41–42, no. 5638.

The Impressionist Revolution

Started by Courbet and his disciples, and by Delacroix, the pictorial revolution which overtook art during the nineteenth century was to continue during the following century. The complete change in the artist's statute meant that he was no longer a simple artisan who carried out commissions. From then on, the artist was an independent agent, free to paint and above all, to choose the motifs and the place where he carried out his paintings. In 1874, the first group show of Impressionist painters organized by Degas in the studio of Nadar, the photographer, signals the effective birth of the movement.

Described as "impressionistic" by the critic Leroy, these artists wanted, like their predecessors (Courbet, Corot), to unmask the conventions which tended to turn painting into a faithful projection of reality. To achieve this, they abandoned the artificial lights in their studios to work outdoors. This approach, *in situ*, allowed them to capture the instantaneous and fugitive nature of light. This method, which had already been tried by the Barbizon painters, necessitated new techniques: as undertaking a painting in this way meant that it was now subjected to light vibrations, the painter had to place paint directly on the canvas with quick little brushstrokes, the mixing of colours no longer carried out on the palette, but directly on the canvas. This principle of "division" and of the optical mixing of colours already recommended by Delacroix is the basis of the Impressionist revolution.

Considered subversive, the movement was under attack from virulent critics: they were reproached for leaving their pictures unfinished, imprecise, slapdash. And so painters such as Manet, Pissarro, Sisley, Bazille, Degas, Renoir, Guillaumin, Morisot, all gathered around Monet and, refusing to exhibit in the official Salon, made up an Independent Artists' Society. United in the notion that light submits every object to its own variations, these painters gave up the values on which, until then, the act of painting had been based: outline, modelling, chiaroscuro, perspective. However, each of them took different paths. Monet, who followed Boudin's advice and painted in the open air, soon became the leading light of the movement. The series representing the Saint-Lazare railway station, the Rouen cathedral, the haystacks, a bend in the Seine, views of London and Venice, as well as the waterlilies in his garden in Giverny, make up as many themes and motifs, which Monet immortalized by capturing an instant's luminousness, at any hour, and regardless of its quality. His landscapes can be compared to those of Sisley and Bazille. On the other hand, Manet, Degas and Caillebotte's works represent indoor scenes, in which different social classes are shown. The research carried out by the Impressionists on the visual perception of light was to reach a pinnacle with a small band of artists grouped around Signac and Seurat. Basing themselves on optical studies carried out by Chevreul and Charles Henry, these two artists wished to create a rational definition and a scientific method concerning the optical divisions of colour. It was in that context of theoretical experiments that the Neo-Impressionist movement came about.

Alongside Signac and Seurat, were painters such as Pissarro, Cross and Luce. Their technique was based on pointillism or division of colour: it was applied in small dots and the mix becomes exclusively optical. At the start of the twentieth century, Severini's first paintings were in the Neo-Impressionist manner, before he joined the Futurist movement.

*50 Jean-Baptiste Camille Corot (1796–1875)
Path Leading Towards a House in the Country, 1864

Oil on canvas.
H: 33 cm; W: 41 cm.
Signature lower left: *Corot.*
Written on the frame:
Donné à mon ami Camus le 22 décembre 1864. C. Corot
(Given to my friend Camus on December 22, 1864.
C. Corot).
GR 1.585

History:
Given by Corot to his friend Camus of Arras in 1864; Arras, sale of Camus collection, 1878, bought back by family; Paris, sale of the Patin collection, 1892, no. 9 (*Route de village*); Paris, sale Mme X., December 16, 1916, no. 7; M. Tinet's collection, bequeathed by the latter to his daughter, Mme Villiers; Galerie Hector Brame – Jean Lorenceau, 1971.

Bibliography:
Manuscript documentation of Alfred Robaut, Bibliothèque Nationale, Département des Estampes et de la Photographie, vol. V, fol. 273; A. Robaut, *L'œuvre de Corot. Catalogue raisonné et illustré*, Paris, 1905, vol. II, no. 975.

Jean-Baptiste Camille Corot (Paris, 1796 – Paris, 1875) was encouraged by his masters, the landscape painters Michallon (1796–1822) and Jean-Victor Bertin (1767–1842), to paint nature. It is there that he learned his best lessons. Three trips to Italy marked the evolution of his style. The first and longest (1825–1828) put him in contact, in Rome, with painters from all over Europe. The decisive phase of his training took place in the midst of naturally, harmoniously organized sites. He frequented a circle of artists who scorned historical landscapes but were committed to the creative depiction of light. He painted countless Italian views suffused with the feelings he would remember later, when he executed landscapes during his tireless hikes in the French countryside.
On return from his third trip to Italy in 1843, his art took a new direction against the mainstream. Possibly alarmed by the tendencies of the young forerunners of Impressionism, he became a lyrical landscapist inspired by Claude Lorrain and Watteau's Fêtes Champêtres (Souvenirs de Mortefontaine)*. His works, for a long time derided, nowadays receive justly merited acclaim. But the great Corot remains the painter of sometimes small landscapes that communicate an inner feeling, and the painter of* Figures*, often dressed in Arab garb, and for which he has no equal. Because of his immense success he was the painter most imitated by followers and also, unfortunately, by counterfeiters.*

In his manuscript notes, A. Robaut added to the title of the picture: *Smallholding at Saint-Lô*. There is no reason to doubt that the location is correct, but the date of 1855 which he gives in the corpus of *L'Œuvre de Corot* must be put back. The artist actually only returned to the Normandy town between 1862 and 1866 for an annual stay, after an absence of twenty-five years. It is therefore correct to date the painting to between 1862 and 1864, the latter year being that of Corot's gift, according to the inscription on the stretcher. The work is very typical of those which Corot painted during this period, in which he imbued these open air landscapes with a foggy atmosphere where the filtering sun brings a pearly luminosity with a success that is still Corot's secret.
This little painting, in spite of the modest nature of its scope, must be related by its handling to Corot's great masterpieces at this time, such as the *Church at Marissel* (1864; Paris, Musée du Louvre), the various landscapes at Mantes, views of the cathedral or of the bridge (Paris, Musée du Louvre; Reims, Musée des Beaux-arts, etc.) and the *Ponds in Ville-d'Avray* from the end of his career. The limited colour scheme, lightness of hand and simplification of the organization supported by the leaning tree seen on the right, bear witness to the special emotion felt by Corot when he painted a rural universe in this often-imitated manner of which he was the originator.
Corot was far removed from the concerns of his friends, the Barbizon School landscape painters, who were devoted to a pantheistic cult and overloaded their paintings in an unrequited metaphysical quest. Far away too are the "trowellings" of a Courbet, the apostle of Realism, building trees like rocks. His aim is not lesser, it is different. Corot, as an onlooker moved by woods, meadows and rustic cottages, was the minstrel of a peaceful nature in which man must find his happiness. His landscapes are usually inhabited. A shepherd, a girl cutting wood, a simple passerby, as in this picture, give a human dimension to his work. In his own words, he was happy to hum a little song, but his work, as his admirers knew, is a "miracle of the heart and spirit".
H. T.

COROT

51 Jean-Baptiste Camille Corot (1796–1875)
Algerian Woman

Oil on canvas.
H: 79 cm; W: 60 cm.
Lower left: stamp from the Corot sale.
GR 1.553

History:
Paris, Corot sale, 1875, no. 178, bought by Jean Dollfuss; Paris, sale at Galerie Georges Petit of the Dollfuss collection, 1912, no. 11, bought by antique dealer Florine Ebstein-Langweil; given by the latter to her daughter, Berthe, wife of painter André Noufflard (1885–1968); sale Berthe Noufflard, 1970; sale at Hector Brame Gallery, 1972.

Exhibitions:
Paris, Salon d'Automne, *Portraits du XIXe siècle*, 1912, no. 61; Paris, Galerie Rosenberg, *Camille Corot. Figures et paysages d'Italie*, 1928, no. 42; Paris, Galerie Hector Brame, *Corot*, 1957, no. 25; Bern, Kunstmuseum, *Corot*, 1960, no. 83; Paris, Musée Jacquemart-André, *Chefs-d'œuvre dans les collections françaises*, 1961, no. 38; Paris, Musée du Louvre, *Figures de Corot*, 1962, no. 65; Marseille, Musée Cantini, *Daumier et ses amis républicains*, 1979, no. 98; Paris, Musée du Grand Palais – Ottawa, Musum of Art – New York, Metropolitan Museum of Art, *Rétrospective Camille Corot*, 1996.

The *Algerian Woman* is one of Corot's best-known figure paintings. It apparently owes its title only to the North African garment worn by the model. As time went on Corot demonstrated an increasing interest in interpreting the human figure. He used various approaches, and his intentions are often difficult to comprehend. Early on, he was inspired by figures met by chance on his travels, such as the many picturesque Italian figures he brought back from his stays in Rome. He depicted these people in small paintings full of tenderness, which fit into the portrait tradition.

In 1845 he began conveying new feelings inspired by his female models, which he painted nude or dressed in reinvented costumes where Antiquity, the Orient and medieval Italy meet in a curious blend. These seated or standing figures are in pensive or even melancholic poses, endowing them with an abstract, timeless character. The *Algerian Woman*, which was painted during the last decade of Corot's life, is one of the "figures" series' most significant examples. The painter feared painting outdoors, the way he used to do, but he achieved some of his finest works in the studio. They have acquired a monumentality that he had not yet sought.

Many contemporary paintings make it possible to recognize the model who sat for the *Algerian Woman*. They include the *Sibyl* (1870; New York, Metropolitan Museum of Art), *Albanian Woman* (1872; New York, The Brooklyn Museum), *Woman with the Yellow Sleeve* (circa 1872; private collection) and the problematic *Woman with Pearl* at the Louvre. The latter has turned out to be a copy painted by a student of an original which has disappeared (photograph at the Prints Department of the Bibliothèque Nationale). It echoed the *Algerian Woman* owned by the collector Jean Dollfuss, the first individual to have bought a Corot after the artist's death. These works were similarly inspired and are almost the same size. The composition is also the same, with the half-length model standing out against a dark but vibrant background. The faces express the same melancholy. Nevertheless, each of these figures possesses her own identity. All of them demonstrate Corot's inventive vigour. The artist revitalized his work by varying the presentation and constantly changing the technique.

In this series, the *Algerian Woman* stands out strongly because of its greater modernity, which is made possible by a nimble, allusive stroke and a very particular search for tonality. The artist's concern for modulating values in a very limited range can be perceived. Here, the master of silvery symphonies has pushed the experiment to the point where colour is eliminated, replaced by variations of more or less tinted whites, browns and ochres. His virtuosity shines through in this risky exercise. The painting reflects the desire for dreamlike escape. The choice of an exotic costume, for example, eloquently expresses a yearning for lost happiness symbolized by the evocation of a far-off world. The line is uninterrupted, which is often the case with Corot. The book slipped between the woman's fingers expresses meditation awakened by thought of the other. It is known that the old artist was soothed by reading ancient writers, a feeling which is communicated when his paintings are contemplated.

H. T.

Bibliography:
Manuscript documentation of Alfred Robaut, Bibliothèque Nationale, Département des Estampes et de la Photographie, vol. XXV, fol. 44; A. Robaut, *L'œuvre de Corot. Catalogue raisonné et illustré*, Paris, 1905, vol. III, no. 1576; C. Bernheim de Villers, *Corot peintre de figures*, Paris, 1930, no. 273; J. Meier-Graefe, *Corot*, Munich, 1913, repr. p. 96; D. Baud-Bovy, *Corot*, Geneva, 1957, p. 29; G. Bazin, *Corot*, 3rd ed. Paris, 1973, p. 115; *André et Berthe Noufflard. Leur vie, leur peinture, une évocation par leurs filles et leurs amis*, Paris, 1982, p. 272.

COROT

52

Gustave Courbet (1819–1877)
Bacchante

Oil on canvas.
H: 65 cm; W: 81 cm.
GR 1.549

History:
Paris, Alexandre Dumas; Paris, sale at the Galerie Georges Petit of Emile Pacully's collection, May 4, 1903, no. 2 (note saying that, according to Mme Courbet, this is a youth work painted at the time of *Amants dans la campagne*); Paris, Lair-Dubreuil, auctioner; Kneinberger, Henri Hase, expert, sale for 3,400 francs; Amsterdam, Mulder's House, bought by Mme van Pierop, circa 1915; Amsterdam, collection of Louis Ph. van Nierop Fils; New York, Knoedler; London, Lefevre Gallery; London, Reid and Lefebvre, July 3, 1973.

Exhibitions:
Paris, Rond Point de l'Alma, 1867, no. 102; Paris, Ecole des Beaux-Arts, *Gustave Courbet*, 1882, no. 31; Paris, Bibliothèque Nationale, *Un siècle de vision nouvelle*, 1955, no. 61; London, Alex Reid & Lefevre, *The 19th and 20th Centuries: French Paintings*, 1968, no. 8; Tokyo, Lefevre at Takashimaya, *Marsterpieces of Modern French Paintings*, March 1971, no. 2; Tokyo, Bridgestone Museum of Art, *Gustave Courbet*, 1989, p. 1127, no. 6, repr. p. 50; Ornans, Musée Gustave Courbet, *Courbet. L'Amour*, 1996, no. 18, p. 61.

Jean Désiré Gustave Courbet (Ornans, 1819 – La Tour-de-Peilz, 1877) was born into a family of wealthy farmers. His parents sent him to Besançon to study philosophy at the Collège Royal, where he learned the basics of drawing. He decided to settle on art as a career and moved to Paris in 1840. He was a frequent visitor to Steulen's studio before enrolling in the Académie Suisse, where he worked from live models and copied paintings at the Louvre by masters such as Velázquez, Veronese, Zurbarán, Rembrandt, Hals, Géricault and Delacroix. Very early on, Courbet revealed his ability to master various genres, but his early years were especially marked by portraits of the people around him and self-portraits.

A free thinker and a politically committed artist, Courbet was one of the painters who best conveyed the mood of the Second Empire. He became friends with Corot, Daumier, Baudelaire, Proudhon and, later, Boudin, Monet and Whistler. The Burial*, which was rejected by the 1850 Salon, triggered a huge scandal and ushered in a long series of quarrels set off by the painter and his work. The public, already offended by his choice of topics, called the realism of his nudes indecent.*

Courbet is first and foremost a sensual artist. His paintings' depth and complexity make him one of the greatest poets of the nineteenth century. The years after 1850 were as glorious as they were productive. In 1855, Courbet said he was "in a position to translate the mores and the ideas of my era, according the way I see them, and to be not only a painter but, even more so, a man, to make, in a word, living art. That is my goal".

Hungering after fame, Courbet kept himself in the limelight by creating one sensation after another. However, not too much importance should be accorded to the painter's eccentricities and thundering statements, which make up a considerable part of his legend. Asserting his talent in the face of one and all – the public, the regime and critics – he became an indispensable figure on the Paris scene, a favorite subject for caricaturists, leading his career with an innate sense of public relations. Unfairly accused of participating in the destruction of the Vendôme column, the Council of War sentenced Courbet to six months' imprisonment and a 500-franc fine after a hateful trial that caused his mother to die of sorrow. Released in March 1872, he returned to his studio to try and recover paintings that had been stolen from him. In 1873, when the earliest symptoms of dropsy were appearing, the trial was reopened and Courbet was sentenced to paying for the rebuilding of the Vendôme column at a cost of 323,000 francs. His property was confiscated.

It is often forgotten that he helped save the Louvre when revolutionaries set the Tuileries on fire during the Paris Commune in 1871. In the end, Courbet's persona got the better of his art. Forced into exile, he left for Switzerland. With his father at his bedside, he died in La Tour-de-Peilz on December 31, 1877. His body was moved to Ornans in 1919.

Courbet was a forerunner of modern art: he painted the way he wanted, without caring about whether anyone liked his work, and was the first artist to work entirely with a knife. He had an unquenchable thirst for freedom. He was fond of saying, "I start where others leave off."

Courbet painted nudes with an unprecedented desire for expression. He treated the subject with realism, which aroused the public's and critics' indignation, giving his paintings a lively tension. This *Bacchante* embodies the grace and voluptuousness that Courbet saw in the female body. The palette exalted all the emotion he felt. Though based on the contrast between green and red in the foreground and sinks into the shadows in the woods in the background, the chromaticism remains warm. Courbet painted swiftly. He enjoyed working the paint with a knife, often transforming pure tones, giving the trees a soft, coppery hue, a languid woman an alabaster body and her legs light shadows. Realistic details such as the earring, the bunch of grapes and the grape leaf recalling the presence of Bacchus punctuate the scene. Light creates and defines each parcel of space, a process which enhances the clearing on

Bibliography:
Ch. Leger, *Courbet et son temps*, Paris, 1948, p. 33, fig. 2; *Les amis de Courbet*, Paris, 1955, no. 16; *The Times*, April 20, 1968; S. Williams, *Antique Weekly*, November 23, 1965, repr.; "The Pick of Courbet", in *Illustrated London News*, December 1968, repr.; *The Studio*, December 1968, repr.; *Art and Antiques Weekly*, March 6, 1971, p. 9, repr.

the right. Painting outdoors one day with Max Claudet, Courbet said about his method of working, "you're surprised that my painting is dark and black; I'm doing the same thing as light, illuminating the high, prominent features". Black expresses depth, the muted life that rises to the surface of the sometimes massive vegetation and rocks. Courbet enjoyed protected, secret places. Here he depicts the forest in Franche-Comté that he loved so much. Like a sacred offering to nature, the diagonal of the woman's body gives the work dynamism. In the letter to his students (July 25, 1861) Courbet wrote, "the beautiful is contained in nature, and meets itself in reality in the widest variety of forms... Like truth, beauty is relative to the time in which one lives and to the individual capable of conceiving it." The themes closest to the painter's heart – nature and woman – are simple pleasures.

Baudelaire considered Courbet a fanatic of "positive, immediate outdoor nature" and infinite tenderness suffuses this work: the half-closed eyes, the head resting on a cushion of moss, the body offered to the viewer's gaze, the hand letting go of a cup of wine, the beautiful woman who seems to be overcome by slumber and the world of dreams. Women slowly being overcome by sleep is a recurring theme in Courbet's work. The body's abandonment to sleep becomes an ode to freedom. What was sometimes considered indecent in these nudes was none other than the full expression of flesh quivering with sensuality and exhilaration.

F. K.

53

Eugène Boudin (1824–1898)
The Beach at Trouville, 1868

Wood.
H: 21 cm; W: 35 cm.
Signed and dated lower right:
E. Boudin 68.
GR 1.631

History:
Thinet collection; bought by Hector Brame; Galerie Hector Brame – Jean Lorenceau, March 8, 1971.

Exhibitions:
Paris, Salon d'Automne, *Rétrospective Boudin*, 1931; Paris, Galerie Charpentier, *Cent tableaux de Boudin*, 1945; Paris, Galerie Hector Brame, *Eugène Boudin. Peinture, pastels, aquarelles*, 1956, no. 15; Paris, Galerie Schmit, *Eugène Boudin. Vingt scènes de plage*, 1965; Osaka, Museum of Art – Hiroshima, Museum of Art – Chiba, Sogo Museum – Shizuoka, Prefectoral Museum of Art, *Eugène Boudin*, 1996; Bogota, National Museum of Colombie – Medellín, Cultural Foundation, *Eugène Boudin*, 1998.

Eugène Boudin (Honfleur, 1824 – Deauville, 1898) was a sailor's son. At the age of twenty he opened a stationery shop in Le Havre, where passing artists exhibited their work. This is how he met Isabey, Troyon, Couture and Millet, who encouraged him with their advice. In fact since childhood he had been trying to depict the world around him, the cloudy skies, waves and ships.
A scholarship offered by the town of Le Havre allowed him to study in Paris for three years, which he spent mostly copying Flemish and Dutch landscape painters in the Louvre. In 1858 he met the young Monet, who would never forget his debt to this older painter who taught him how to concentrate on the subject by awakening him to the feeling of a moving nature.
Success was slow in coming but, in 1868, Boudin finally achieved well-deserved fame. His years of poverty over, he renewed his inspiration by constant trips across France and Holland and to Venice. Trusting his instinct and sharp rapid vision, he was the very example of the painter of movement, depicting water, clouds and atmospheric subtleties. He paved the way for Impressionism by fixing the unfixable.

"Monsieur Boudin has really created a genre of seascapes which are his very own, and which consist of painting on the beach an exotic *beau monde* which the high life brings together in the summer in our seaside towns." It is in these terms that the critic Castagnary welcomed the work Boudin submitted to the Salon of 1869 (*Salons*, Paris, 1892, vol. I, p. 374). The Second Empire's smart set made summer vacationing on the banks of the Channel *de rigueur*. The Empress, Princess Mathilde, and the Duke de Morny were joined by financiers, senior civil servants and those who conformed to fashion out of snobbery. They all met at newly discovered Trouville, Deauville and Dieppe. Boudin recorded this society not to moralize, even less to caricaturize, but simply to depict these upper crust gatherings that were gaily coloured by the shimmering of crinolines in the seaside climate's pearly light.
Eugene Isabey, his follower, and the young Claude Monet, his fellow countryman, whom he met in 1858, lured Boudin to this coast, which he painted from then on in continually different versions. How many landscape painters of this period have been called the precursors of Impressionism, the movement being only the result of the inevitable evolution of the art of painting? However, with Boudin the statement is accurate because of his friendship with Monet, aged seventeen, and because of the direct influence that they exercised on one another.
A brilliant little picture like this beach scene reveals the artist's ultimate aims before the dawn of Impressionism. The nimble strokes try to realistically express a play of lively colours juxtaposed by black dashes under the light of a changing sky. Realism is only allusive in a sketch, but there is no recourse to abstract meaning. Therefore pure painting is discovered in a physical realization. Boudin carried out innumerable studies, sketches, pastels and watercolours on the Normandy beaches. For some, these exercises would not have consisted of any more than a repertoire for a work to be done in the studio. For him they were practise pieces, since it is certain that the paintings comparable to this one were executed on the spot, as their spontaneous character demonstrates.
H. T.

54 Frédéric Bazille (1841–1870)
Fisherman with a Net, 1868

Oil on canvas.
H: 137.5 cm; W: 86 cm.
Signed and dated lower right:
F. Bazille. July 1868.
GR 1.653

History:
Artist's family; Mme Rachou-Bazille's collection; Jean Davray's collection, after 1959; Paris, sale Palais Galliéra, June 23, 1961.

Exhibitions:
Paris, Salon d'Automne, *Rétrospective Bazille*, 1910, no. 15; Montpellier, *Exposition internationale. Rétrospective Bazille*, 1927, no. 19; Liège, *Exposition internationale de l'Eau*, 1939; Paris, Galerie Wildenstein, *Frédéric Bazille*, 1950, no. 40; Montpellier, Musée Fabre, *Frédéric Bazille*, 1959, no. 28; Chicago, Art Institute of Chicago, *Frédéric Bazille and Early Impressionism*, 1978, no. 32, repr. p. 76; Montpellier, Musée Fabre, *Frédéric Bazille et ses amis impressionnistes*, 1992, pp. 108, 109, no. 19; New York, The Brooklyn Museum – Memphis, Dixon Gallery and Gardens, *Frédéric Bazille: Prophet of Impressionism*, 1992–1993; Paris, Musée du Grand Palais – New York, Metropolitan Museum of Art, *Les origines de l'impressionnisme*, 1994–1995, no. 10, ill. 153.

Certainly influenced by his frequent visits to the Hôtel Bruyas, Frédéric Bazille (Montpellier, 1841 – Beaune-la-Rolande, 1870) decided to become a painter early in life. On his parents' insistence, he enrolled in medical school but never completed his studies. He learned drawing with Bausan père et fils, sculptors in Montpellier, before moving to Paris in 1862, where he met Monet and Renoir at Charles Gleyre's studio.
During that period, Bazille painted many portraits of artists he felt close to, including Renoir, who shared his studio for a while. Under Monet's influence, Bazille left the studio and began painting outdoors, making trips to Fontainebleau forest and Honfleur, where he met Boudin and Jongkind, and often visiting his family's estate in Méric. He regularly submitted works to the Salon, which sometimes accepted them, sometimes did not. Cut to the quick, Bazille launched the idea of organizing an exhibition of the rejected works, which unfortunately he never lived to see. At the outbreak of the Franco-Prussian War in 1870, the painter enlisted in a regiment of Zouaves and was killed at the battle of Beaune-la-Rolande on November 28.

After the 1868 Salon, Frédéric Bazille left Paris to spend the summer at the family estate in Méric. Pursuing his experiments with outdoor painting, the artist drew inspiration from the Languedoc countryside for two scenes: *Fisherman with a Net* and *Village View* (Montpellier, Musée Fabre).
Fisherman with a Net is set on the banks of the Lez river. In the centre, a nude man is preparing to throw the net, while in the background another figure is sitting on the grass. This is one of the first Impressionist works that features nude figures posing outdoors. A briskly-sketched, non-detailed preparatory pencil study (Paris, Musée du Louvre, Département des Arts Graphiques, Fonds d'Orsay, RF 5259, fol. 64) demonstrates that Bazille worked on balancing the composition in order to obtain a better grasp of the motif. Bazille also displays his predilection for plastic precision in the rendering of each component of the landscape and in the anatomical study of the bodies, whose treatment demonstrates that he was still under the influence of the academic tradition.
In the slow development of the work, the artist studied each variation of light, which he rendered with painstaking accuracy. He reconstructed the effects of sunlight filtering through foliage, creating bright bands of light on the grass and subtle bluish reflections indicating the water's movement. Painted with bold strokes, this work illustrates Bazille's desire to paint lighter, brighter scenes.
The jury of the 1869 Salon rejected the painting, preferring *Village View*. "The jury massacred paintings by four or five artists we get along with very well. They accepted only one of my paintings: *The Woman*", Bazille wrote on April 9, 1869. Obviously, the somewhat eclectic choice of heroic nudity transposed to a scene from contemporary life fell short of the standards established by the academic system. The jury's rejection deeply affected Bazille. In response, that same year he painted *Summer Scene* (Cambridge, Fogg Art Museum), a larger format where a group of bathers appears on the banks of the Lez. *Fisherman with a Net*, which G. Poulain has described as an "indispensable and fruitful experiment", remained hanging in a prominent place in the artist's studio, as his painting *Studio on Rue de la Condamine* shows (Paris, Musée d'Orsay).
Ch. D.

Bibliography:
G. Poulain, *Bazille et ses amis*, Paris, 1932, no. 40; G. Sarraute, "Peintre de l'été", in *Arts*, June 1950, no. 40; F. Daulte, *F. Bazille et son temps*, Geneva, 1952, p. 180, no. 35; D. Cooper, *Great Private Collections*, New York, 1963, p. 255; K. Swiler Champa, *Studies in Early Impressionism*, New Haven-London, 1973, p. 89, fig. 126; J. P. Marandel, *F. Bazille and Early Impressionism*, Chicago, 1978, p. 77, no. 32; D. Pitman, *The Art of Frédéric Bazille 1841–1870*, The John Hopkins University, 1989, pp. 86–88; F. Daulte, *Frédéric Bazille et les débuts de l'impressionnisme. Catalogue raisonné de l'œuvre peint*, Paris, 1991, p. 169, no. 38.

F. Bazille Juillet 186

55

Paul Cézanne (1839–1906)
The Sea at L'Estaque, 1876

Oil on canvas.
H: 42 cm; W: 59 cm.
Signed lower right:
P. Cézanne.
GR 1.905

History:
Paris, sold by Galerie Georges Petit (Victor Choquet), July 1–4, 1899, no. 2; Paris, Bernheim-Jeune; Paris, Gaston Bernheim de Villers; New York, Sam Salz; New York, Mrs. Richard J. Bernhard; New York, Wildenstein and Co. Inc; London, Sotheby's, June 30, 1981, no. 8.

Exhibitions:
Paris, 6 rue Pelletier, *3ᵉ exposition de peinture*, April 1877; Paris, Galerie Bernheim-Jeune, *Rétrospective Paul Cézanne*, June 1926, no. 57; Paris, Musée de l'Orangerie, *Cézanne*, 1936, no. 35, repr.; New York, Metropolitan Museum of Art, *Paintings from Private Collections*, 1960, no. 8; Washington, National Gallery of Art – San Francisco, M. H. de Young Memorial Museum, *The New Painting. Impressionism 1874–1886*, 1986, no. 17; Tübingen, Kunsthalle, *Cézanne Gemälde*, 1993, no. 19; Marseille, Musée Cantini, *L'Estaque, naissance du paysage moderne*, 1994; London, Royal Academy of Arts, *From Manet to Gauguin. Masterpieces from Swiss Private Collections*, 1995–1996, no. 4; Paris, Musée du Grand Palais – London, Tate Gallery – Philadelphia, Philadelphia Museum of Art, *Cézanne*, 1996, no. 44; Basel, Kunstmuseum, 1997–1999, on permanent loan.

Paul Cézanne (Aix-en-Provence, 1839 – Aix-en-Provence, 1906) attended law school in Aix-en-Provence before leaving to study painting in Paris in 1861. The following year he regularly attended the Académie Suisse, where he met Guillaumin and Pissaro. The artist struck up a friendship with the Impressionists, whom he met in the company of Zola at the Café Guerbois. From 1863 to 1870, Cézanne divided his time between Paris and Aix. All the paintings he submitted to the Salon during this period were rejected. In 1863 he took part in the Salon des Refusés, and from 1874 to 1877 displayed his work at the Impressionists' exhibitions. In 1882 the painter left Paris for Aix, where he was to remain for the rest of his life, with the exception of a few rare journeys. In 1895 Ambroise Vollard held a major exhibition of Cézanne's works in his gallery on the rue Lafitte. From that moment on, Cézanne's fame among artists and enthusiasts continued to grow until his death in 1906.

In 1870, during the Franco-Prussian War, Cézanne spent several months in L'Estaque, a small fishing village on the Gulf of Marseilles. He returned there to spend part of the summer of 1876, when Victor Choquet, an "understanding and clear-sighted art lover", commissioned him to paint a view of the bay. Zola, moved by the landscape's beauty, described the scenery at L'Estaque in his short story *Naïs Micoulin*: "The area is splendid. Rocky arms reach out from both sides of the gulf, while the islands, in the open sea, seem to block the horizon; and the sea is nothing more than a huge pool, a lake whose colour is an intense blue when the weather is fine." A letter to Pissarro dated July 2, 1876, demonstrates that Cézanne carefully observed the motif: "I've started two small motifs with the sea for Monsieur Choquet, who had talked to me about it. It's like a playing card. Red roofs overlooking the blue sea [...]. The sun is so frightfully hot and bright it looks to me as if objects turn into silhouettes, not just black and white ones but blue, red, brown and purple, and peel away from the background. I may be wrong, but it seems to me as if they are the exact opposite of the model."

Cézanne developed a complex construction of space in the *Sea at L'Estaque*, introducing varying levels of depth. He sought to render the plasticity of coloured masses, differentiating each surface with a specific handling. In the foreground, which is brought right up to the viewer, he portrays a close, composite world in motion where each tree, each house becomes a "peeled-away silhouette". In the background, the sea and the islands look like immutable elements. Cézanne's methods changed in the blazing sunlight. He gave up the traditional modelling technique in favor of flat surfaces and contrasts between warm and cold colours. Likewise, he used small, diagonal brushstrokes to obtain a lumpy, thick texture in the foreground and a smoother one in the background. Cézanne was already making his break with Impressionism. In 1878 and 1883, fascinated by this motif, he returned to L'Estaque to paint works characterized by a more rigorous geometric pattern (Liège, Musée d'Art Moderne; Paris, Musée Picasso; Baden, Stiftung Langmatt Sidney and Jenny Brown).
Working in L'Estaque around 1908, artists such as Braque and Dufy pursued Cézanne's experiments, developing a style that was to climax in Cubism.
Ch. D.

Bibliography:
Album Cézanne, Paris, 1914, pl. 39; *L'Art moderne à la Collection Bernheim-Jeune*, Paris, 1919, pl. 24; L. Venturi, *Paul Cézanne. Son art, son œuvre*, Paris, 1936, p. 63, no. 168, repr.; J. Rewald, *Correspondance de Paul Cézanne*, Paris, 1937, pp. 126–127, letter XXXIV; B. Dorival, *Cézanne*, Paris, 1948, pl. 35; L. Guerry, *Cézanne et l'expression de l'espace*, Paris, 1950, p. 83; J. Rewald, *The History of Impressionism*, New York, 1961, p. 375, repr.; J. Rewald, "Choquet and Cézanne", in *La Gazette des Beaux-Arts*, July-August 1969, fig. 8, pp. 44, 82, no. 2; A. Gatto and S. Orienti, *L'opera completa di Cézanne*, Milan, 1970, no. 172, repr.; G. Adriani, *Cézanne Gemälde*, Tübingen, 1993, pp. 93–96.

56

Edouard Manet (1832–1883)
Woman with a Black Hat

Pastel on canvas.
H: 54 cm; W: 45 cm.
GR 1.557

History:
Paris, Pierre Auguste Renoir; Paris, Ambroise Vollard; New York, Mr. and Mrs. L. M. Rogers; London, Christie's, The L. M. Rogers collection, June 27, 1972, no. 107.

Exhibitions:
New York, *American Friends of the Hebrew University*, 1867; New York, Wildenstein & Co. Inc, 1962, no. 32; Philadelphia, Philadelphia Museum of Art, *Edouard Manet*, 1966, no. 180; Martigny, Fondation Gianadda, *Manet*, 1996, no. 94.

Bibliography:
Th. Duret, *Manet and the French Impressionists*, London, 1910, p. 272, no. 49; Th. Duret, *Histoire de Manet et de son œuvre*, Paris, 1919, p. 292, no. 49; A. Tabarant, *Manet. Histoire catalographique*, Paris, 1931, p. 501, no. 74; P. Jamot and G. Wildenstein, *Manet*, Paris, 1932, p. 131, no. 450, ill. 246, repr.; A. Tabarant, *Manet et son œuvre*, Paris, 1947, p. 447, no. 529, repr.; Ph. Paul and S. Orienti, *The Complete Painting of Manet*, New York, 1967, p. 118, no. 384, repr.; D. Rouant and D. Wildenstein, *Manet: Pastels, aquarelles et dessins*, Geneva, 1975, p. 34, no. 87, repr.

Born into an upper-middle class Parisian family, Edouard Manet (Paris, 1832 – Paris, 1883) was drawn to an artistic career at a very early age. In 1850 he joined Thomas Couture's studio, where he remained for six years. He rounded out his training with trips to Germany, Holland and Italy and frequent visits to the Louvre, where he copied paintings by Titian and Velázquez. Turned down by the 1859 Salon, he displayed his work at the official exhibition for the first time in 1861.
Two years later Manet's Luncheon on the Grass *sparked an outcry at the Salon des Refusés. His* Olympia *produced the same effect at the 1865 Salon.*
In 1867, Manet organized an exhibition of his own works in a shed near Courbet's. The show touched off a scandal, but a group of artists and writers marked him out as the leader of the new school. In 1874, he discovered open-air painting in Argenteuil. The artist's palette became brighter after meeting Monet, but he refused to join the ranks of the Impressionists – especially since his paintings were beginning to win favor in official circles.
Recognized and respected, Manet was a very ill man towards the end of his life. The artist went into seclusion in Rueil, where he painted many portraits and still lives until his death in 1883.

Towards the end of his life, Manet was frail and confined to his home in Rueil, where he received visits from friends and a few society ladies whose portraits he enjoyed painting. In his biography of the painter, Théodore Duret wrote that "pastel enabled Manet to do relatively easy work that distracted him with the company of pleasant women who came to pose" (Duret, 1919, p. 131). The Rau collection canvas belongs to a long series of women's portraits that Manet painted between 1879 and 1882. The artist found that pastel held out many possibilities, especially when it came to rendering light and shadow. He was able to capture his model's features, while at the same time the velvety medium helped him convey the look and texture of a powdery face. Briskly drawn without idealization, this portrait is handled like an effigy. The bright face crowned by an elegant hat stands out against an unfinished grey scumble background. Whether he painted society women or friends and acquaintances such as Isabelle Lemonnier, Mery Laurent and Madame Guillemet, Manet attached little importance to rendering his models' psychological traits, instead focusing on each one's elegance and appearance. During these late years, the artist seems to have been striving after the social success he had always hoped for.
Ch. D.

*57

Edgar Degas
(Hilaire Germain Edgar de Gas, known as Degas, 1834–1917)
Two Young Girls Looking at an Album, circa 1884

Pastel on dyed paper.
H: 41 cm; W: 74 cm.
Signed lower left in red:
Degas.
GR 1.674

History:
First sale of Degas's studio, May 6–8, 1918, no. 166, repr. p. 91; Paris, Monteux collection; Geneva, Galerie Motte.

Exhibitions:
Zurich, Kunsthaus – Tübingen, Kunsthalle, *Degas. Die Portraits*, 1994–1995; Geneva, Palexpo, *La Fondation pour l'écrit. Salon international du livre et de la presse. Le livre et la presse dans la peinture*, 1996; Basel, Kunstmuseum, on permanent loan.

Bibliography:
Catalogue de la Première Vente Atelier Degas, 6–8 mai, 1918, no. 166, p. 91; P. A. Lemoisne, *Degas et son œuvre. Catalogue raisonné*, Paris, 1946–1949, fig. 779, p. 443.

Edgar Degas (Paris, 1834 – Paris, 1917) was the first child of a wealthy, cultivated bourgeois family whose name was de Gas. He received a classical education. When his mother died in 1847, his father, an art and music-loving banker, decided to show him the Louvre, introduce him to works by his friends Louis Lacaze and Edouard Valpinçon and bring him to the print cabinet at the Bibliothèque Nationale, where the young Edgar made his first copies. In 1855 he registered at the Paris Ecole des Beaux-Arts, where he made the acquaintance of Léon Bonnat and Fantin-Latour. The same year he also met Ingres, who advised him, "Draw lines, young man, many lines from real life and from memory, and that is how you will become a good painter". From that moment on, the line was the young artist's constant concern. He was struck by the art he saw during frequent visits to his family in Naples, Rome and Florence, especially works by Mantegna and Veronese. Back in Paris the young, talented socialite was a frequent visitor to certain coteries, studios and literary cafés in Montmartre. In 1859 he must have met Manet at the Louvre and, through him, Renoir, Monet and Zola. Degas remained critical but well-disposed towards the Impressionists' open-air painting, taking part in their exhibitions from 1874 to 1886. He was a studio painter who enjoyed capturing instinctive expression and the unaware movements of young girl's bodies. While searching for studio secrets and age-old techniques, Edgar Degas discovered various processes, especially for pastel.
Failing vision forced him to gradually give up painting, and he began devoting himself to wax modelling. Declining strength forced him to give up all of his artistic pursuits shortly before his death.

The pastel *Two Young Girls Looking at an Album*, which dates from around 1884, illustrates the artist's interest in scenes painted directly from real life. Edgar Degas liked depicting women in natural poses, and consequently his paintings are far from traditional studio works. He was a sharp observer and merciless analyst who closely watched the everyday movements of dancers (1872), laundry women (1876) and milliners (1882). Here he painted two friends absorbed in looking over a family album. Perhaps it is a photo album, the sort of which were very popular in the 1880s. Indeed Degas, himself a photographer, had carefully studied Muybridge's early photographs in 1879. The technique in this pastel is thin and the stroke smooth. The artist used few colours to draw the composition, limiting himself to fiery pink for the dresses, red-ochre for the hair and back of the chair and blue, white and orange for the background's broadly-hatched sfumato. Only the black pencil line accentuates shapes and movements. In his 1884 pastels, women's faces are often concealed by abundant, auburn-coloured hair. Here it is not the girls' hair, pulled back in a bun, that hides their faces, but simply the position of their bodies. As is often the case with Degas, the face is not his main concern. The movement of the arm, which is the work's main subject, can also be found in several sketches and preparatory pastels. Degas, who traced his drawings to correct them better, even said, "No art is as unspontaneous as mine. What I do is the outcome of thought and study. I know nothing about inspiration, spontaneity and temperament. The same subject must be redone ten or a hundred times. Nothing in art, not even movement, must look like an accident."
Degas, who greatly admired Ingres, aspired to doing modern portraits nurtured by precision and realism. Here, the truncated painting does not show the left arm of the young girl on the right, but merely the hand holding the album. This slight, intentional "shift", which Degas had been using since the *Lowering of the Curtain* in 1880, forces the eye to focus on the composition's movement. The artist, who mastered all painting media, gave pastel its *lettres de noblesse*. With his nimble pencil and innovative techniques, such as the addition of paint, successive fixings and humidification, Edgar Degas captured and gracefully conveyed fleeting sensation and vibration, and stalked the intensity of the vulnerable, briefly-glimpsed instinctive or learned move.
F. K.

58

Edgar Degas
(Hilaire Germain Edgar de Gas, known as Degas, 1834–1917)
Self-portrait, 1900

Pastel on dyed paper.
H: 47.5 cm; W: 32.5 cm.
Oval stamp, lower left: *Atelier Ed Degas*.
GR 1.577

History:
Paris, Galerie Drouant-David; Dr Robert Ducroquet's collection; London, Christie's, November 28, 1972, no. 104A, repr.

Exhibitions:
London, Royal Academy of Arts – Tokyo, Sezon Museum of Art – Nagoya, Matsuzakaya Museum of Art, *From Manet to Gauguin. Masterpieces from Swiss Private Collections*, 1995–1996; London, National Gallery, 1996; Chicago, Art Institute of Chicago, *Degas: Beyond Impressionism*, 1996–1997.

Bibliography:
Ph. Brame, *Catalogue raisonné*, supplement in preparation.

During the autumn of his life Edgar Degas painted a handful of final self-portraits. The one in the Rau collection, which can be dated to the early 1900s, came before a series of photographic self-portraits he began making in 1912, when he was suffering from the first signs of blindness. Here he is seen posing naturally in front of a mirror. He is dressed in his work clothes, a white frock and blue cap. Degas is in his Montmartre studio at 37 Rue Victor-Massé, the secret sanctuary where he kept his works for twenty years before being chased out by a demolition crew in 1912. The artist was a studio painter who found all the pictorial richness of a rolling landscape in the grey walls around him.
His self-portraits were often a pretext for affirming his own identity. The one in the Rau collection is the counterpoint to a large pastel of a bathing woman, a work that is especially representative of his female nudes. Degas painted countless variations on the theme of women washing, drying or combing themselves. In this way he reaffirmed a paradoxical idea of Ingres that can be found in all of his paintings, that a model's back could express more than a frontal view of the face. Degas's friend Edmond Duranty recalled this idea during the second Impressionist exhibition in 1876 in his book *La Nouvelle Peinture*: "With a back, we want to reveal a temperament, an age or a social status."
Degas tirelessly sought the perfect technique, ceaselessly repeating what he called his "initiatives". In his art he was forced to come to terms with his failing vision. From 1892 to 1910 he used almost nothing but pastel, a medium that allowed him to immediately observe its effects. In the Rau collection self-portrait, warm colours take the place of drawing. The green-dyed paper matches the soft ochre, yellow, white and grey tones. The black line accentuates the whole. Two scarlet curves on the eyelids mark the eyes, like a pair of prominent wounds. Degas put a tragic accent on the approaching blindness that would force him to give up his work.
His *Self-portrait* poses the question he was never able to answer: painting's quest and its symbol of life.
The sadness and anguish emanating from this portrait of an old, embittered man convey both the artist's disillusionment and still-fertile creativity.
F. K.

59

Claude Monet (1840–1926)
Woods and Undergrowth, W 58, 1865

Oil on canvas.
H: 81 cm; W: 59 cm.
Signed lower left: *Claude Monet.*
GR 1.844

History:
Paris, Daussyl; Paris, Galerie Bernheim-Jeune, 1923; London, Independent Gallery, 1929; Bradford-on-Avon, Great Britain, Esher's collection, 1936; London, Arthur Tooth and Sons, no. 2872; Great Britain, Mr. and Mrs. Clifford Curzon's collection, 1952; London, Christie's, November 29, 1982, no. 7.

Exhibitions:
London, Arthur Tooth and Sons, *Monet*, 1936, no. 24; London, Royal Academy of Arts, *Landscape in French Art*, 1949–1950, no. 231; Edinburgh, Royal Scottish Academy – London, Tate Gallery, *Claude Monet. The Early Years*, August-November 1957, no. 3, pl. 16F; London, Royal Academy of Arts – Tokyo, Sezon Museum of Art – Nagoya, Matsuzakaya Museum of Art, *From Manet to Gauguin. Masterpieces from Swiss Private Collections*, 1995–1996; Vienna, Österreichische Galerie, Schloss Belvedere, *Claude Monet*, 1996; Basel, Kunstmuseum, on permanent loan, 1997–1999.

Bibliography:
D. Wildenstein, *Claude Monet. Biographie et catalogue raisonné*, Lausanne-Paris, 1974, vol. I, p. 142, no. 58, repr.

In 1858 Claude Monet (Paris, 1840 – Giverny, 1926) met Eugène Boudin, who encouraged him and introduced him to outdoor painting. He studied at the Académie Suisse before going back to Le Havre, where he worked with Boudin and Jongkind. Back in Paris in 1862, he enrolled in the Gleyre studio, where he met Bazille, Renoir and Sisley. In 1863 he began painting landscapes of Fontainebleau forest, in the Barbizon school tradition, before going to Normandy. Shortly afterwards, in 1865, the Salon accepted his first painting. During the Franco-Prussian War of 1870, he stayed with Pissarro in London.
He lived in Argenteuil from 1872 to 1878, a period which was marked by the actual birth of Impressionism. In 1874 he helped initiate the group's first exhibition at Nadar's. He was deeply affected by the death of his wife, Camille, and went through a dark period in Vétheuil from 1878 to 1883, when he withdrew to Giverny, where he bought a house in 1890. In the meantime he had painted his great same-subject series, including Haystacks *in 1890 and* Rouen Cathedral *in 1892–1893. Aside from trips to Norway in 1895, Madrid in 1904 and Venice in 1909, he remained in Giverey, where he worked on the* Water Lilies *series until his death.*

In the spring of 1865 Monet moved to the small village of Chailly-en-Bière, located a few kilometers from Barbizon on the edge of Fontainebleau forest. At the time, artists came to the forest in search of a refuge away from civilization. Monet stayed with Father Barbey at the Lion d'Or hotel. As during his first stay in Chailly in 1863, the artist worked outdoors, painting many landscape studies.
The traditional composition of a forest road can be found in the Rau collection work, which dates from Monet's second stay. At the time, he greatly admired the works of Corot, Courbet and Daubigny. The use of greens and browns here shows how much he owed to the Barbizon masters, but the artist demonstrates greater freedom in the overall handling, especially in the way he rendered the foliage with a nimble superimposition of strokes. This work preceded and undoubtedly paved the way for the ambitious *Luncheon on the Grass*, which Monet began painting during the summer of 1865. Monet sought to transfer the same contrasts of light he achieved in studies painted outdoors to the monumental work, but it was through integrating the figure into the landscape that he would attempt to deal with the problem of light and colour in *Luncheon on the Grass*.
He may have been inspired by the preceding generation's depiction of a docile nature, but he nevertheless broke with the spirit of Barbizon. He emptied his work of romantic and moral connotations, focusing his interest on the reality of what he saw. Like Bazille, Pissarro and Sisley at the same time, Monet inherited a great landscape painting tradition. However, the attention he paid to light provided his work with a modern character that foreshadowed the innovations of the 1870s.
Ch. D.

60 Claude Monet (1840–1926)
The Wooden Bridge, W 195, 1872

Oil on canvas.
H: 54 cm; W: 73 cm.
Signed lower left: *Claude Monet*.
GR 1.805

History:
Bought from Monet by Edouard Manet, 1872; Paris, Mrs. Manet's collection, 1883; Paris, Decap; Paris, sale X (Decap) at Drouot, April 15, 1901, no. 15; Paris, Barret-Decap's collection; Paris, sale at Drouot of Maurice Barret-Decap's collection, December 12, 1929, no. 7; Paris, Henri Canonne's collection, circa 1931; Paris, Jacques Canonne's collection, circa 1961; London, sale at Sotheby's of Mrs. Jacques Canonne's collection, April 29, 1964, no. 50; Los Angeles, Mr. Norton Simon's collection, circa 1968; London, sale at Christie's of Norton Simon's collection, November 30, 1971, no. 24.

Exhibitions:
Paris, Orangerie, *Monet*, 1931, no. 25; Tokyo, Bridgstone Museum of Art – Nagoya, City Art Museum – Hiroshima, Museum of Art, *Monet*, 1994–1995, no. 18; Chicago, Art Institute of Chicago, *Claude Monet*, 1995, no. 29; Vienna, Österreichische Galerie, Schloss Belvedere, *Claude Monet*, 1996; Washington, The Phillips Collection, *Impressionists on the Seine: A Celebration of Renoir's "Luncheon of the Boating Party"*, 1996; Basel, Kunstmuseum, on permanent loan, 1997–1999.

In early 1872 Monet moved to Argenteuil, a small holiday resort where Parisians came to sail. The bridge over the Seine was one of the first motifs he painted. It enabled vacationers to reach the resort by the road. The bridge had been destroyed in 1870 when the French retreated from the advancing Prussian army. Monet discovered the wooden structure during its rebuilding, and painted two versions of it from different angles. One of them shows a still-traditional perspective view. The Rau collection painting shows the view from the banks of the small Gennevilliers river of the Argenteuil basin. It is one of Monet's most daring compositions. The framing of the first arch of the bridge, which is reflected in the Seine with perfect symmetry, forms a window opening out on to the Argenteuil basin. The landscape's familiar elements can be found here, including the rowboat rental building, the outline of a manor house and a factory smokestack. Although the artist focused his attention on the rigourous construction of space, the painting offers a panorama of modern life, with an omnibus and the silhouettes of a few figures livening up the bridge.
This view of the landscape brings to mind popular, contemporary engravings and illustrations, but the composition was inspired by Japanese prints. The painting's construction is based on a bit of landscape that becomes fundamental. Likewise, following the example of Hiroshige's views of Tsuten and Kyobashi bridges, he carefully painted the wooden bridge's structure. Monet sought to capture subtle variations in light. He used cold colours to evoke the harshness of winter. A few briskly painted pink nuances in the sky indicate that the day is coming to an end.
This work, which is painted with broad and smooth strokes, inaugurated the Argenteuil period, one of Impressionism's most fertile. The modern motif of the highway bridge can be found several times in paintings by Sisley, Renoir and Caillebotte. Monet himself used it again in 1874, but by that time the adoption of pure, divided tones had already transformed his technique.
Ch. D.

Bibliography:
Inventory after death of Edouard Manet's collection, June 18, 1883 (in P. Jamot and G. Wildenstein, *Manet*, Paris, 1932); A. Alexandre, *La collection Canonne*, Paris, 1930, p. 12, repr.; D. Wildenstein, *Claude Monet. Biographie et catalogue raisonné*, Lausanne-Paris, 1974, vol. I, p. 202, no. 195, repr.; A. Bellony-Rewald, *Le monde retrouvé des impressionnistes*, Paris, 1977, p. 117, repr.; J. Isaacson, *Claude Monet. Observation et réflexion*, Neuchâtel, 1978, no. 35, repr. p. 93; L. Rossi Bortolatto and J. Bailly-Herzberg, *Tout l'œuvre peint de Monet, 1870–1889*, Paris, 1981, p. 92, no. 60, repr.; *The New Painting Impressionism 1874–1886*, San Francisco-Washington, 1986, fig. 14; D. Skeggs, *Monet et la Seine. Impression d'un fleuve*, Paris, 1988, p. 74, repr.; J.-J. Lévêque, *Les années impressionnistes, 1870–1889*, Paris, 1990, repr. p. 220.

Claude Monet

61

Claude Monet (1840–1926)
View of Amsterdam, W 303, 1874

Oil on canvas.
H: 61 cm; W: 101.5 cm.
Signed lower left: *Claude Monet*.
GR 1.612

History:
Paris, Ernest May's collection; Paris, Galerie Paul Rosenberg; Paris, sale at Drouot of Alfred Baillehache's collection, June 5, 1909, no. 14; Paris, Guirault; Paris, Georges Bernheim; Argentina, Elvira Santamarina de Lezica-Alvear's collection, circa 1962; New York, sale at Parke-Bernet, April 6, 1967, no. 21; Basel, Galerie Beyeler; New York, Stephen Hahn, circa 1968; Basel, Galerie Beyeler, 1970; London, Sotheby's, December 6, 1978, no. 209; London, Christie's, April 2, 1990, no. 15 (withdrawn).

Exhibitions:
Buenos Aires, Museo Nacional de Bellas Artes, *Impressionismo francés en las colecciones argentinas*, 1962, no. 31, repr.; Basel, Galerie Beyeler, *Impressionnistes: Monet, Renoir, Sisley, Degas, Pissarro, Cézanne*, October-November 1967, no. 13, repr.; Tokyo-Osaka-Fukuoka, *Claude Monet*, 1973, no. 3, repr.; Amsterdam, Rijksmuseum Vincent van Gogh, *Monet in Holland*, October 1986 – January 1987, no. 31, repr.; London, Royal Academy of Arts – Tokyo, Sezon Museum of Art – Nagoya, Matsuzakaya Museum of Art, *From Manet to Gauguin. Masterpieces from Swiss Private Collections*, 1995–1996; Charlottenlund-Kobenhavn, Ordrupgaardsamlingen, *Impressionism, the City and Modern Life*, 1996, no. 43, fig. 14.

In 1871 Monet followed Daubigny's advice and for the first time went to the Netherlands, where he painted mostly Zaandam landscapes. D. Wildenstein argues that he did not paint his views of Amsterdam until his second trip three years later, between January and April 1874. The winter landscape in the Rau collection is part of this group. Monet was fond of the local architecture's picturesqueness and character. He painted the site of Kamperhoofd twice. Here the point of view, precisely identified by Wildenstein, shows the corner of the Waalseilandsgracht and the Prinsendrikkade. The Schreijerstoren (Weeping Tower) can be made out behind the trees in the background.
A stylistic evolution noticeable in relation to the Zaandam works has made it possible to date this work to 1874. Monet had just come into contact with the light of the north, which enriched his style. He followed the example of Dutch artists by trying to suggest a special atmosphere, managing to simply render the slightest atmospheric variations with colours and a precise stroke, which is broken up and becomes sparser in the sky and on the water. It takes shape against the bright background of the canvas, which the artist has cleverly allowed to show through. The sober colours also help create an effect of diffuse light. The watered-down, grey-blue tones ensure the landscape's admirable harmony, handling the delicate distance in a way that brings to mind van Goyen's misty backgrounds.
Monet was looking for new motifs and varied effects. In Amsterdam he pursued the pictorial experiments he had been conducting in Argenteuil since 1872. The use of a suggestive touch and the size – the largest in the Amsterdam series – makes it possible to compare this work with those painted in Le Havre in 1873 and Argenteuil in 1874 (*Regatta Boats in Argenteuil*; Paris, Musée d'Orsay). It helps measure how far Monet had come since his Zaandam stay. While his style was asserting itself, his eye seemed more sensitive to the atmospheric "envelope", which later turned out to be one of his main concerns.
Ch. D.

Bibliography:
Bulletin de la Vie Artistique, Paris, February 15, 1926, p. 53; D. Wildenstein, *Claude Monet. Biographie et catalogue raisonné*, Lausanne-Paris, 1974, vol. I, no. 303, repr. p. 247.

62

Claude Monet (1840–1926)
Flood, W 642, 1881

Oil on canvas.
H: 60 cm; W: 100 cm.
Signed and dated lower right:
Claude Monet 1881.
GR 1.509

History:
Bought by Monet through Durand-Ruel, February 1881; Geneva, Motte sale, June 16, 1972, no. 49.

Exhibitions:
Paris, 251 Rue Saint-Honoré, *7ᵉ exposition des artistes indépendants*, 1882, no. 71; Brussels ?, *La Libre Esthétique*, 1901, no. 349; London, Grafton Galleries, *Pictures by Boudin, Manet*, 1905, no. 106; Paris, Galerie Durand-Ruel, *Paysages par Cl. Monet et Renoir*, 1908, no. 6; Paris, Galerie Durand-Ruel, *Monet*, 1914, no. 39; New York, Galerie Durand-Ruel, *Monet*, 1915, no. 14; Paris, Orangerie, *Monet*, 1931, no. 64; London, Tooth, *Monet*, 1939, no. 33; Zurich, *Monet*, 1952, no. 53; London, Royal Academy of Arts – Tokyo, Sezon Museum of Art – Nagoya, Matsuzakaya Museum of Art, *From Manet to Gauguin. Masterpieces from Swiss Private Collections*, 1995–1996; Basel, Kunstmuseum, on permanent loan, 1997–1999.

Bibliography:
M. O. Maus, *Trente années de lutte pour l'art*, Brussels, 1926, p. 259; M. Malingue, *Claude Monet*, Paris, 1943, p. 101, repr. p. 147; O. Reuterswärd, *Monet*, Stockholm, 1948, p. 137, repr.; D. Wildenstein, *Claude Monet. Biographie et catalogue raisonné*, Lausanne-Paris, 1974, vol. I, no. 642, repr. p. 391; J.-J. Lévêque, *Les années impressionnistes, 1870–1889*, Paris, 1990, repr. p. 426.

In December 1878 Monet moved to Vétheuil, a small village located on the right bank of the Seine. On September 5, 1879 his wife Camille died, and he entered a very dark, depressed period. However, during the harsh winter of 1879–1881 the spectacle offered by the Seine's thawing triggered a burst of activity. The next year, at the end of January 1880, a period of cold and snow was followed by a sudden thaw, causing a spectacular rise in the water level which culminated in mid-February.
Monet did five paintings of the flood. The one in the Rau collection is striking because of its austerity and tragic aspect. It is a panorama of the Lavacourt plain. In the background a few houses can be made out on the Vétheuil bank. Monet, adopting a point of view used frequently by the Impressionists, organized his painting into horizontal bands. He rejected classical arrangement, seeking asymmetry on the left by painting a group of trees emerging from the waves. The special handling of each surface and the artist's impassioned technique make this painting a powerful work. Monet used spirited strokes of colour to render a full, tumultuous sky and, similarly, energetic commas and elongated strokes to recreate the river's impressive flow, creating the illusion of relief with rich textural effects. Lastly, a remarkable luminosity bathes the entire work and is mirrored in the surface of the swiftly moving waters in a contrast of juxtaposed colours.
This very personal technique, which was developed in Vétheuil, characterizes the seascapes that were painted shortly afterwards in Fécamp and Etretat. There may be a relationship between the depiction of nature's unleashed elements and the tormented emotions being felt by the artist at the time. Monet, who was above all fascinated with studying atmospheric phenomena, filled his work with a dramatic tension that was closer to Paul Huet's romantic landscapes than the tranquil Port Marly flood scenes painted by Sisley in 1876.
In February 1881 the art dealer Durand-Ruel bought this and approximately fifteen other works. The purchase was a turning point in Monet's life. From then on, Durand-Ruel's moral and financial support would enable the artist to definitively forego exhibiting at the Salon. Monet broke away somewhat from the group of Impressionists to achieve greater independence, starting out on the road to new innovations in painting.
Ch. D.

63

Claude Monet (1840–1926)
The Port-Coton Pyramids, W 1087, 1886

Oil on canvas.
H: 65.5 cm; W: 65.5 cm.
Signed and dated lower right:
86 Claude Monet.
GR 1.564

History:
Bought by Monet through the Galerie Boussod, Valadon et Cie, May 1887; Paris, Dupuis, 1887; Boussod, Galerie Valadon et Cie, 1888; Paris, Gallimard's collection, 1889; Paris, Paul Rosenberg, circa 1924; London, Sotheby's, November 29, 1971, no. 19.

Exhibitions:
Brussels, *6ᵉ exposition des XX*, 1889, no. 1; London, Goupil, *Monet*, 1889, no. 1; Paris, Rosenberg, *Monet*, 1924, no. 13; Chicago, Art Institute of Chicago, *Claude Monet*, 1995; Vienna, Österreichische Galerie, Schloss Belvedere, *Claude Monet*, 1996; Basel, Kunstmuseum, on permanent loan, 1997–1999.

Bibliography:
J. Rewald, "Theo van Gogh, Goupil and the Impressionists", in *Gazette des Beaux-Arts*, January-February 1973, p. 75, Appendix I [98]; D. Wildenstein, *Claude Monet. Biographie et catalogue raisonné*, Lausanne-Paris, 1979, vol. II, no. 1087, repr. p. 199; D. Delouche, "Monet et Belle-Ile en 1886", in *Bulletin des Amis du Musée de Rennes*, 1980, no. 4, repr. p. 42, fig. 5; D. Delouche, *Monet à Belle-Ile*, 1992, pp. 60–61, repr.

On September 12, 1886, Monet landed at Belle-Ile-en-Mer. He spent a short amount of time in the harbour town of Palais before moving in with a fisherman in the hamlet of Kervilahouen. He was full of wonder at the wild coastal landscape, which he described as "sinister, diabolical, but superb". On September 18 he wrote to Alice Hoschedé, "I must become familiar with this nature, the sea is utterly beautiful. The rocks are a mass of grottos, points and extraordinary needles" (Wildenstein, 1979, vol. II, letter 688). The painter embarked upon a period of relentless daily work, made even more difficult by bad weather. The *Port-Coton Pyramids* belong to a group of six works painted by Monet of the same motif. He noticeably varied the sizes and framing and paid attention to changes in weather and light: "To really paint the sea, it must be seen every day, at all times and at the same place [...] that is why I redo the same motifs up to four and even six times" (ibid., letter 730). This square version of the *Pyramids* – one of two works with this layout – demonstrates a search for balance in the format and in the powerful construction of space. The view overlooking the sea raises the horizon quite high, while the jagged, rocky isles form the frame. This composition is partly derived from Japanese art. The contrast between the rocky outlines and the surface of a stormy sea brings to mind Hokusai's drawings and a print by Hiroshige entitled *The Rocks of Bonoura*. The work, which was painted on a clear day, offers contrasting values between the various elements. Monet was bedazzled by a sea "incredible in colour", and tried to convey the richness and density with his brush. His varied, divided stroke recreated the intensity of the ocean's greens, blues and mauves, which he contrasted with the dark masses of the reefs. He also introduced a relationship between the depths of the foreground and the wide, white-fringed horizontal bands slipping towards the horizon. At a time when Seurat was methodically developing the Divisionist technique, Monet was expanding Impressionism's possibilities by stressing its spur-of-the-moment character. At Belle-Ile, Monet's instinct and persistence in painting the same motifs grew stronger, foreshadowing the large series he did several years later.
Ch. D.

64

Claude Monet (1840–1926)
Houses in the Snow in Norway, W 1395, 1895

Oil on canvas.
H: 61 cm; W: 84 cm.
Stamp of the signature lower right and reverse.
GR 1.664

History:
Giverny, Michel Monet; Paris, sale at Palais Galliéra, December 3, 1975, no. ZB (withdrawn); London, Sotheby's, April 2, 1979, no. 38.

Exhibitions:
Paris, André Weil, *Centenaire de Cl. Monet*, 1940, no. 31; Stavanger, Rogaland Kunstmuseum – Paris, Musée Rodin – Copenhagen, Ordrupgeard, *Manet en Norvège*, 1995–1996; Vienna, Österreichische Galerie, Schloss Belvedere, *Claude Monet*, 1996; Basel, Kunstmuseum, on permanent loan, 1997–1999.

Bibliography:
D. Wildenstein, *Claude Monet. Biographie et catalogue raisonné*, Lausanne-Paris, 1979, vol. III, no. 1395, repr. p. 183.

From the beginning of his career, Monet was fascinated by landscapes in the snow. Later, in 1895, he took advantage of the presence in Norway of Jacques Hoschedé, the eldest son of his wife, Alice, and set out to discover the snowy landscapes of Scandinavia. He arrived in Christiania on February 1, and two weeks later moved into an artists' inn in Sandviken. At first, fog and snow interfered with his search for a motif, but he was soon filled with wonder at the landscape's beauty. He wrote to Blanche Hoschedé, "it is possible to see the most beautiful effects only here. I am talking about effects of snow that are absolutely stupefying" (Wildenstein, 1979, vol. III, letter 1276).
The motif Monet chose was not far from the hamlet of Bjorngaard. Two houses occupy the landscape in the middle of a "white immensity". The artist tried to paint a series, but was forced to adapt his working methods to the weather in order to capture the fleeting aspects. In a letter dated March 12 he wrote, "I am working ceaselessly despite all these changes, despite the snow, but I never manage to finish anything. I have to limit myself to painting aspects once or twice. It is impossible to find the same effects again, especially at this time of winter" (ibid., letter 1282).
Unlike the other two versions of houses in the snow (*Norwegian Landscape*; Paris, Musée Marmottan), the one in the Rau collection was painted in foggy weather. The hill in the background, which can be seen in the other two paintings, has vanished in the mist. The motif's simplicity contrasts with the colourful harmony of the highly admired snow effects. The luminosity of a pink-tinted winter sky provides the snow with bluish reflections which underscore the elongated impasto. Monet had to interrupt the series when warmer weather started melting the snow. He wrote, "I have to give up on a beautiful motif where I had painted three canvasses, because there is no longer any snow on the roofs" (ibid., letter 1284). The artist began painting other motifs, including the large Mount Kolsaas series.
On March 29, at the end of his stay, Monet was visited by Prince Eugene of Sweden and several painters, all of whom wanted to see his work. In his last letter to Alice he wrote, "everyone here is full of admiration. All the newspapers are talking about my work. They are not very demanding, but, I must admit, I am touched by their expression of admiration, which seems so heartfelt" (ibid., letter 1290). As soon as he was back in Giverny, Monet admitted his satisfaction to Durand-Ruel: "I am not unhappy with what I have brought back" (ibid., letter 1291). On May 10, 1895, at Durand-Ruel's gallery, he exhibited eight Norway landscapes next to a series of twenty paintings of Rouen cathedral.
Ch. D.

65

Auguste Renoir (1841–1919)
Head of a Woman or *Woman with a Rose*

Oil on canvas.
H: 35 cm; W: 27 cm.
Signed lower right, one-third of the way from the bottom: *Renoir*.
GR 1.682

History:
Dollfuss collection; Paris, sale at the Galerie Georges Petit of the Jean Dollfuss collection, March 2, 1912, no. 58; Paris, Stettiner's collection; Paris, Rosenberg's collection; chosen in 1941 by Marshall Goering for his collection; recovered in Germany; London, Christie's, July 3, 1973.

Exhibitions:
Paris, Rue Le Pelletier, *Deuxième exposition des impressionnistes*, 1876, no. 217; Paris, *Chefs-d'œuvre des collections privées françaises retrouvés en Allemagne*, 1946, no. 44; London, Royal Academy of Arts – Tokyo, Sezon Museum of Art – Nagoya, Matsuzakaya Museum of Art, *From Manet to Gauguin. Masterpieces from Swiss Private Collections*, 1995–1996, no. 59; Tübingen, Kunsthalle, *Renoir Retrospektive*, 1996, no. 81; Basel, Kunstmuseum, on permanent loan, 1997–1999.

Bibliography:
F. Daulte, *Auguste Renoir, figures, 1860–1890*, Lausanne, 1971, no. 167, repr.; B. Dunston, *Painting Methods of the Impressionists*, New York, p. 57, repr.

Auguste Renoir (Limoges, 1841 – Cagnes-sur-Mer, 1919) was born into a poor family that moved to Paris when he was a young child. He began earning a living as a painter on porcelain, eventually making enough money to strike off on his own. Renoir entered the atelier Gleyre, where he met Monet, Bazille and Sisley and worked outdoors with them. At first he was influenced by Courbet, Fantin-Latour and Diaz, but in 1869 the artist set out in a new direction. His brushwork became brisk and was made up of small, juxtaposed strokes, and his vision emphasized the interpretation of light. Impressionism was born.
Renoir tackled every genre throughout his long and highly varied career – nudes, figures, landscapes, portraits and still lives. His work never turned stale or predictable. Sometimes the artist neglected draftsmanship to interpret the reflection of light. At other times he again took up the line, fulfilling his search for colour with bright reds, blues and greens. Renoir and Monet are considered the greatest two Impressionist painters.

This female head was one of fifteen paintings Renoir put on display at the second Impressionist exhibition in 1876. At the time, the artist painted a number of portraits and half-length figures, earning him a sound reputation as a portrait painter with the middle class. The woman who sat for this painting may have been Marguerite Legrand, known as Margot, who died in 1879 at the age of twenty-three. One of Renoir's favorite models, she can also be found in *Le Moulin de la Galette* (1876; Paris, Musée d'Orsay) and the *Cup of Chocolate* (Mrs. Edsel Ford, Grosse-Pointe Shores). Renoir paid close attention to his models' features, trying to capture the calm and gentleness of their faces. He adopted a fairly unusual method to achieve this aim, using short, brisk and tightly-knit brushstrokes to render iridescent flesh tones, silky hair and the background. In this portrait the painter captured, as usual, the model's heart-warming look, but he also introduced a bit of a dreamlike quality that adds to her charm. The rose in her hair and the pendants, the only small touches of coquetry, brighten up her face, providing it with special relief. In short, this portrait could very well be considered a statement of what was called the "Renoir type".
H. T.

*66

Auguste Renoir (1841–1919)
Portrait of Henry Lerolle, circa 1895

Oil on canvas.
H: 46 cm; W: 35 cm.
Signed upper left: *Renoir*.
GR 1.671

History:
Painted for Henry Lerolle;
Paris, Charpentier Gallery, sold by the model's heirs, June 17, 1960, no. 101bis;
London, Christie's, March 27, 1973, no. 50.

Exhibition:
Tübingen, Kunsthalle, *Renoir Retrospektive*, 1996, no. 27.

The relationship between Henry Lerolle (1848–1929) and the world of artists, musicians and writers makes him one of the late nineteenth and early twentieth-century's most significant figures. He was a painter who studied under Lamothe, was a follower of Ingres and taught Degas, and is an all too-forgotten representative of post-Impressionism. His most memorable works are religious (the churches of Créteil and Saint-François-Xavier in Paris). He devoted his life as much to music as to painting, not as a performer or composer but as a patron. In his salon composers from Debussy's generation – Ernest Chausson was his brother-in-law – met the painters Degas, Puvis de Chavannes, Besnard and Maurice Denis as well as the writers Gide, Claudel and Valery, among others.
This splendid portrait, which was painted around 1895, was originally lined with a rose garland on the left, but old photographs do not make it possible to tell whether this rather incongruous feature was a tapestry or a bouquet. Between 1960 and 1973 it was decided to eliminate this insignificant detail. Cutting out the garland in no way detracted from the painting, which was originally 51 centimeters wide. Renoir painted these down-to-earth portraits several times. They are almost like the precious little secrets of his friendships and admirations (*Copy of the Portrait of Wagner from 1882*, 1893; Paris, Musée de l'Opéra).
The Rau collection portrait may be dated from around 1895.
It shows the model's head and shoulders, which was one of the artist's favourite formulas. The natural portrait was painted from real life, and the process further adds to the instantaneous feeling. Expressive impasto structures the face, and the background is a frottage. The various browns give the figure a severity belied by his soft eyes, and he seems to be having a conversation with the painter. The work bears out Renoir's rank as a great portrait painter, continuing in the tradition of his classical predecessors while at the same time breathing life into his figures.
H. T.

67 Camille Pissarro (1830–1903)
View of L'Hermitage, Jallais Hill in Pontoise, 1867

Oil on canvas.
H: 70 cm; W: 100 cm.
Signed lower right:
C. Pissarro.
GR 1.519

History:
Lord Ivor Spencer Churchill's collection; Paris, Mme Balsan's collection.

Exhibitions:
Paris, Galerie Manzi-Joyant, *Camille Pissarro: exposition rétrospective des œuvres*, March 1914, p. 29, repr.; Paris, Musée du Louvre (Orangerie), *Centenaire de la naissance de Camille Pissarro*, February-March 1930, no. 36, repr.; London, Royal Academy of Arts, *French Art*, 4 January – 5 March 1932, no. 422; Jerusalem, The Israel Museum – New York, Jewish Museum, *Camille Pissarro: Impressionist Innovator*, October 1994 – July 1995, no. 27, repr.; London, Royal Academy of Arts – Tokyo, Sezon Museum of Art – Nagoya, Matsuzakaya Museum of Art, *From Manet to Gauguin. Masterpieces from Swiss Private Collections*, 1995–1996, no. 41; Basel, Kunstmuseum, on permanent loan; Tokyo, Isetan Museum of Art – Fukuoka, Mitsukoshi Museum of Art – Mle, Prefectoral Art Museum – Yamaguchi, Prefectoral Art Museum, *Camille Pissarro and the Pissarro Family*, 1998; Basel, Kunstmuseum, on permanent loan, 1998–1999.

Jacob Abraham Camille "Pizarro" (Saint Thomas, 1830 – Paris, 1903) was born on the Caribbean island of Saint Thomas, a Danish dependency where his parents owned a thriving hardware shop in the port town of Charlotte-Amélie. At the age of eleven (1841), he left to study in France. Five years later he began studying business while taking up drawing at the same time. In 1855, the year of the Universal Exhibition, Pissarro moved to Paris, where he discovered Delacroix, Courbet, Daubigny, Ingres and above all, Corot.
He first studied painting in the studio of Anton Melbye, then at the Ecole des Beaux-Arts, and on-and-off at the Académie libre (Rue Cadet) and the Académie Suisse, where he met Monet (1859), Cézanne and Guillaumin (1861). In 1866, he became a frequent visitor to Bazille's studio and met Renoir and Sisley, painters with the same tastes and affinities who later formed a group that came to be known as the Impressionists (1874). Pissarro was always one of the movement's catalysing forces. Loyal to the core, he was the only painter who took part in every Impressionist exhibition and unreservedly supported artists as different from each other as Degas, Cézanne, Gauguin, van Gogh and Seurat. Receptive to new ideas and gifted with a highly flexible mind, his work developed, his style grew more authoritative and he became something of an elder statesman. Other artists sought him out for advice, which he offered with kindness and simplicity. "He was such a good mentor", said Mary Casatt, "that he could have taught stones to paint."
The circle of Paris painters widened and Pissarro frequently saw Manet, Fantin-Latour, Zacharie Astruc and Emile Zola. When Prussia invaded France in 1870, he left for London, where he found Monet, who introduced him to his future dealer, Durand-Ruel. During that stay, in 1871, he married his longtime companion Julie Vellay. They were to have eight children. After the war, Pissarro returned to the environs of Paris, where he spent the rest of his life, living in Pontoise for a long time. Towards the end of his days he lived in Eragny-sur-Epte.
Pissarro had an inquisitive mind and was always looking for new techniques. From 1885 to 1890, he was an adept of Seurat's and Signac's Pointillisme, returning to "his Impressionism" the richer for the experience. Pissarro had a large family to support and was beset by financial woes that, however, affected neither the quality of his work nor his cheerful personality. Cézanne said that "Pissarro was humble and colossal, and he had something like the dear Lord about him". Despite an eye disorder diagnosed in 1888, he mastered water-colours, drawings, etchings, oils and lithography equally well. At the end of his life he was somewhat better off financially and travelled to England, the Netherlands and throughout France, discovering the attraction of cityscapes. His last series were views of Paris, Rouen and Le Havre, but interior scenes account for most of his work.

The *View of L'Hermitage, Jallais Hill in Pontoise* (1867) belongs to a series of large landscapes Pissarro painted northeast of Pontoise, where he lived from 1866 to 1868. All of them show the hamlet where the hermitage is located, nestled at the foot of a tall hill named Le Jallais. The scene is viewed from a high point. The level foreground contrasts with the steep hill in the background. Pissarro emphasized structure, underscored by the almost geometric roofs painted with broad, even strokes. Painted directly on the canvas, this landscape heralded the start of the artist's pre-Impressionist period, a direction encouraged by Daubigny and Monet. Still under the influence of Corot, Pissarro divided the surface into horizontal strips and a geometric order.
The art of Cézanne, with whom Pissarro worked for a while, echoes this type of composition. The fields on the hillside are drawn in such a way as to create a uniform area that further accentuates the painting's flatness and authoritatively orders the composition. This method of organization underscores a sense of continuity, the evenness of the spaces between the elements accentuating the colours and values. This process provides an optical perception of volume and space. The brightness prevents us from making out specific details, while the

Bibliography:
M. Hamel, "Camille Pissarro: exposition rétrospective des œuvres", in *Les Arts*, no. 147, March 1914, p. 26; L. R. Pissarro and L. Venturi, *Camille Pissarro, son art, son œuvre*, Paris, 1939, p. 57, no. 10; "The Churchill Collection", in *The Times*, June 27, 1928, repr.; J. Rewald, *Pissarro*, Paris, 1939, no. 14, repr.; "C. Pissarro", in *Apollo*, November 1992, p. 287, no. 1, repr.

simplified drawing of the characters – their faces are blurred – and the handling of the grass and foliage in the foreground foreshadow the painter's interest in chromatic and optical effects.
At the 1860 Salon, Zola called Pissarro the ideal representative of the "naturalist" landscape. About Le Jallais he wrote, "it is the modern countryside. You sense that man has been there, digging into the soil, cutting it up, saddening the horizon. And this glen, this hill are so simple, so heroically stark. Nothing would be more commonplace if it were not so big. The painter's temperament has created a rare poem of life and force from ordinary truth" (E. Zola, "Mon Salon, III: les naturalistes", in *L'événement illustré*, May 19, 1868). This painting bears witness to Pissarro's mastery of execution and composition, accurate powers of observation and subtle sensibility.
F. K.

68

Camille Pissarro (1830–1903)
The Road from Saint-Germain to Louveciennes, 1870

Oil on canvas.
H: 38.5 cm; W: 46.5 cm.
Signed and dated lower left:
C. Pissarro 1870.
GR 1.626

History:
Henri Rouart, Paris; Paris, sale at Galerie Manzi-Joyant, December 9–11, 1912, no. 260; Bremen, Senator H. Rodawald; New York, Sam Salz.

Exhibitions:
Paris, Galerie Durand-Ruel, *L'œuvre de Camille Pissarro*, April 7–30, 1904, no. 8; New York, Wildenstein & Co, *Camille Pissarro*, 1965, no. 5; London, Royal Academy of Arts – Tokyo, Sezon Museum of Art – Nagoya, Matsuzakaya Museum of Art, *From Manet to Gauguin. Masterpieces from Swiss Private Collections*, 1995–1996.

Bibliography:
Th. Duret, *Les peintres impressionnistes*, H. Floury, Paris, 1923, repr.;
Ch. Kunstler, *Camille Pissarro*, Paris, 1930, repr.;
L. R. Pissarro and L. Venturi, *Camille Pissarro, son art, son œuvre*, Paris, 1939, no. 74.

In 1869, Camille Pissarro left Pontoise for Louveciennes without giving a genuine reason, but he probably went there to paint with Monet, Sisley and Renoir, all of whom were living nearby and represented a new generation of landscape artists. Pissarro depicted the landscape around Louveciennes, showing the predilection for roads that he had already displayed in previous works (*Road to Louveciennes*, 1870; Paris, Musée d'Orsay; *Coach at Louveciennes*, 1870; Paris, Musée d'Orsay and the *Road from Versailles to Louveciennes*, 1870; Zurich, Bührle Foundation). The *Road from Saint-Germain to Louveciennes* (1870) is part of that series. Seen here just as it leaves the village, the road from Saint-Germain is the continuation of the route from Versailles where the Pissarro family lived. The "straight highway" (as this painting was entitled the first time it was sold in 1912) lined by trees and houses fades into the background, two pedestrians walk behind a canvas-covered wagon and a woman on the right shoulder comes towards the viewer.
At the time he painted this work, Pissarro was establishing a pictorial dialogue with Monet and moving towards a new style. He chose smaller formats, a range of ochre, pink, green and blue tones that enhanced his already-bright palette and a freer technique. Pissarro used a palette-knife to make broad, fresh, increasingly supple strokes (for example, the kerbstones in the foreground). Air circulated more lightly and space grew brighter.
Although there was a great amount of affinity between Pissarro and Monet, the two artists had no direct influence on each other's work. Each developed his own style. At the time he painted this picture, Pissarro was fourty (Monet ten years younger) and had already mastered his technique. Although Pissarro and Monet painted the scene from the same point of view (in 1869 and 1870), they achieved very different results. However, both artists were working towards what later came to be known as Impressionism: putting impressions of the landscape on canvas. Perhaps understandably, this was deemed ludicrous and absurd at the time: by definition, impressions are impossible to depict because they belong to the immaterial realm. The practice of open-air painting continued gaining ground and its exponents boldly asserted new techniques. They were emerging their studios armed with tin tubes of colours, which were mass-produced since 1820, and unsized canvases. Material reasons explain the choice of small formats: they were easier to carry.
Shortly after Pissarro painted this work in late September 1870, the Prussian advance compelled the family to flee Louveciennes. Leaving furniture and art works behind, they found refuge with their friend Ludovic Piette in Montfoucault and finally reached London in early December, where they met Monet, who had also gone into exile in England. When Pissarro returned at the end of June 1871, he found a ransacked house. Few of his works from this period survive, the Prussians having destroyed most of them during the war. Soldiers used his paintings to walk across the courtyard without getting their feet wet on rainy days. This work, then, is a rare example of the studies on reflections the artist painted at the time.
F. K.

69

Camille Pissarro (1830–1903)
The Courthouse at Pontoise, 1873

Oil on canvas.
H: 33 cm; W: 40.7 cm.
Signed lower right:
C. Pissarro.
GR 1.1033

History:
M. Rondest, sale at L'Isle-Adam, September 8, 1929; Paris, Galerie Etienne Bignou; Glasgow, Art Gallery; New York, Millicent Rogers, Christie's, May 11, 1995.

Exhibitions:
Taos, Harwood Foundation of the University of New Mexico, *Late 19th-Century Paintings from the Collection of Millicent Rogers*, 1948; New York, Wildenstein & Co, Inc, *Camille Pissarro*, 1965; Jerusalem, The Israel Museum – New York, Jewish Museum, *Camille Pissarro: Impressionnist Innovator*, October 1994 – July 1995, p. 116, no. 42, repr.

Bibliography:
L. R. Pissarro and L. Venturi, *Camille Pissarro, son art, son œuvre*, Paris, 1939, vol. I, p. 108, no. 211, vol. II, pl. 42.

Camille Pissarro returned to Pontoise in April 1872, where he remained until 1883. He was very familiar with the lively, friendly town, where many fairs and markets were held, and the nearby countryside offered a wide variety of landscapes. In the *Courthouse at Pontoise*, painted in 1873, a group of strollers chats on Saint John's square and, a little further away, carriages await their passengers. Although the courthouse overlooks the scene and occupies the centre of the work, it is not the primary feature. This is a landscape painting, and as usual Pissarro introduced human figures. Indeed, he is probably the only Impressionist who gave them such a prominent role. They create a landscape-like mood and provide the scene with a sense of intimacy. Pissarro did not artificially apply portraits on landscapes; he gave the figures natural poses and expressive faces. Included in a structured composition, they move to the rhythm of the colours. Pissarro's richly-nuanced palette features a full range of brown, ochre, green, pink and blue tones that create an illusion of movement, which is visible in the foreground's windswept grass and the clouds skidding across the sky.
The accuracy of the details also breathe life into this autumn scene, which doubles as a study on the effects of vibrating light and the instability of the landscape. In this sense it is an Impressionist work, painted on the eve of the group's first exhibition at Nadar's in 1874. Pissarro's oeuvre reconciles reality with the artist's feelings.
F. K.

70

Camille Pissarro (1830–1903)
Portrait of Jeanne, 1898

Oil on canvas.
H: 56 cm; W: 47 cm.
Initialled on back.
GR 1.621

History:
Mme A. Bonin, Paris (Jeanne Pissarro, the artist's daughter); London, Sotheby's, March 28, 1973, no. 23.

Exhibitions:
Paris, Orangerie, *Centenaire de la naissance de Camille Pissarro*, February-March 1930, no. 121; Brussels, Palais des Beaux-Arts, 15 June – 29 September 1935, no. 58; Basel, Kunsthalle, September-October 1949, no. 1822; London, Matthiessen Gallery, 1950, no. 27; London, Lefevre Gallery, *19th and 20th-Century French Paintings*, September-October 1956, no. 8, repr.; Jerusalem, The Israel Museum – New York, Jewish Museum, *Camille Pissarro: Impressionnist Innovator*, October 1994 – July 1995, no. 122; Tokyo, Isetan Museum of Art – Fukuoka, Mitsukoshi Museum of Art – Mle, Prefectoral Art Museum – Yamaguchi, Prefectoral Art Museum, *Camille Pissarro and the Pissarro Family*, 1998.

Bibliography:
L. R. Pissarro and L. Venturi, *Camille Pissarro, son art, son œuvre*, Paris, 1939, no. 1065, repr.; *The Times*, September 26, 1956, repr.; *The Observer*, September 30, 1956, repr.

Camille Pissarro painted this portrait of his daughter, Jeanne, around 1898, when he was in the autumn of his years. The father of eight children, he had three daughters: Jeanne-Rachel, nicknamed Minette, who was born in 1865 and died at the age of nine; Adèle-Emma, who was born in 1870 and perished fifteen days later; and Jeanne-Marguerite Eva, affectionately called Cocotte, who was born in 1881. One of Pissarro's five sons died during his lifetime: Félix, nicknamed Titi (1874–1897), was also an artist and signed his works "Jean-Roch". When Pissarro painted this portrait, the other members of his family were still alive: Lucien (1863–1944), Georges Henri (Manzana, 1871–1961), Ludovic-Rodolphe (Rodo, 1878–1952), Jeanne (Cocotte, 1881–1948), Paul-Emile (1884–1972) and his wife Julie (1838–1926).
At the time, Jeanne was seventeen years old. The bearing of her head is proud and wilful and her gaze seems plunged in deep thought. An orange blossom pinned to her corsage barely brightens up her austere, dark clothing. Pissarro's treatment of the painting's surface is supple and self-assured. The flowing technique provides glimpses of the brush's movements – for example, in the broad strokes of the background – and on some parts of the forehead thick impasto covers the highly-wrought surface. The chromatic range is limited but lighter than usual, with clear, bright patches standing out in contrast. For a long time Pissarro rejected the use of black, which the Impressionists considered a "non-colour", but in this portrait he employed deep black for the clothes, which brings out the young woman's flesh tones.
Pissarro regularly painted his family and friends, executing several portraits of Jeanne in 1893, 1897, 1898 and 1899. All show her as a young woman, perhaps to ease painful memories of the first Jeanne's death, perhaps to keep her memories fresh in the painter's mind.
The intense interplay between light and shadow helps modulate the background and sets the figure off in a bright light. But the painting's most important aspect lies in Pissarro's revelation of his own feelings: the mysterious young face reflects a father's affection for his child.
F. K.

71

Alfred Sisley (1839–1899)
Effect of Snow at Marly, 1876

Oil on canvas.
H: 50 cm; W: 61 cm.
Signed and dated lower right:
Sisley 76.
GR 1.154

History:
Paris, Auguste Renoir; Paris, Durand-Ruel, June 25, 1892; Paris, Gardin's collection, December 9, 1893; Paris, sale at Palais Galliéra, June 17, 1970, no. L; Zurich, Marianne Feilchenfeldt, 1971 or 1972.

Exhibitions:
London, Royal Academy of Arts – Tokyo, Sezon Museum of Art – Nagoya, Matsuzakaya Museum of Art, *From Manet to Gauguin. Masterpieces from Swiss Private Collections*, 1995–1996; Washington, The Phillips Collection – San Francisco, Fine Arts Museum – New York, The Brooklyn Museum of Art, *Impressionists in Winter: Effets de neige*, 1998–1999.

Alfred Sisley (Paris, 1839 – Moret-sur-Loing, 1899) was a British citizen by birth, but lived nearly his whole life in France. Brought up in an upper-middle-class family, young Alfred's childhood was carefree and happy. At the age of eighteen, his parents sent him to London to study business. During his stay in the British capital, the young man visited museums, especially admiring the works of Turner, Constable and Bonington, neglecting his business apprenticeship.
In the spring of 1862, he returned to France with the desire to become a painter. Sisley's parents gave him permission to study in the studio of Charles Gleyre, which had a good reputation but was, in fact, mediocre. He became friends with Monet, Renoir and Bazille. In March 1863, they were working outdoors in the Ile de France countryside, especially near Fontainebleau. In 1866, Sisley met Marie-Adélaïde Eugénie Lescouezec, with whom he was to spend the rest of his life. The couple had two children, Pierre and Jeanne.
The year 1870 was a turning point in his life and work: for the first time, he used bright colours and juxtaposed strokes. It was also the year of the Franco-Prussian War. Paris was under siege and the Empire collapsing. Sisley's infirm father died, depriving the painter of financial support. This was the start of the darkest period in his life. He was constantly short of money and had trouble selling his works. The critics ignored him and the public scoffed at his works.
Sisley's character changed because of these misfortunes: the affable, sociable man became gloomy, anguished and mistrustful. Yet in spite of setbacks he painted frantically, and his work reflects the kindness still within him. Sisley untiringly studied the changing of the seasons and light, always returning to the same places to contemplate nature, which he held so dear. Unfortunately, he came down with throat cancer and stopped painting in 1897. Facing the ordeal with bravery and resignation, he died at the age of fifty-nine on January 29, 1899, on the verge of obtaining French citizenship. Throughout his entire life Sisley was beset by anxiety. As cruel luck would have it, during his lifetime, "No ray of glory ever shined on his art" (G. Geffroy), but success and recognition came right after his death. His works sold for record-breaking prices at the auction that was held to benefit his children.
F. K.

In 1872, Sisley painted his first wintry landscapes at Louveciennes. During the winter of 1875–1876, he again depicted many snowy scenes, sometimes from a window with a view of the village or countryside at his house in Marly or Louveciennes. Dated 1876, the Rau collection work is a meticulous exploration of the site; the painter was attracted to still-unblemished rural landscapes. *Effect of Snow at Marly*, which was painted from Sisley's window, shows the garden enclosure with the silhouettes of bare trees. In the background, a path runs alongside a few houses before vanishing into the forest.
As he often did, Sisley painted another, very similar version of this scene (F. Daulte, *Alfred Sisley. Catalogue raisonné de l'œuvre peint*, Lausanne, 1959, no. 195) in which the artist slightly shifted the viewpoint of the house on the left, transforming the balance of the masses and the landscape's depth. The hushed atmosphere, achieved with the help of a range of monochrome tones, is what is so striking about *Effect of Snow at Marly*. The blue-grey of the sky and trees, the white of the snow and the brown-ochre of the stone provide the whole scene with a remarkable unity. The flowing, light touch, similar to Monet's, is in perfect harmony with the stillness of the site. "He expresses his personality with grace, gentle colours, a quiet vision and an intimate form of expression", Durand-Ruel fittingly wrote in 1874 (quoted by L. Venturi, *Les Archives de l'Impressionnisme*, 1939, vol. 1, p. 28). *Effect of Snow at Marly* is considered one of Sisley's best works from the Impressionist period. A few weeks later, he painted the famous flood series at Port-Marly, which was to definitively establish his renown.
Ch. D.

Sisley . 76

72

Alfred Sisley (1839–1899)
The Small Meadow at By

Oil on canvas.
H: 60 cm; W: 73 cm.
Signed lower right: *Sisley*.
GR 1.85

History:
Paris, Feder's collection; Paris, sold to Durand-Ruel, June 25, 1892; Paris, Durand-Ruel's collection; London, Reld & Lefevre Ltd, April 1968.

Exhibitions:
Paris, Galerie Durand-Ruel, *Sisley*, 1902, no. 34; Paris, Galerie Durand-Ruel, *Sisley*, 1914, no. 55; London, Lefevre Gallery, *19th and 20th-Century Paintings and Drawings*, 1964, no. 21; London, Royal Academy of Arts – Tokyo, Sezon Museum of Art – Nagoya, Matsuzakaya Museum of Art, *From Manet to Gauguin. Masterpieces from Swiss Private Collections*, 1995–1996; Basel, Kunstmuseum, on permanent loan, 1997–1999.

Bibliography:
F. Daulte, *Alfred Sisley. Catalogue raisonné de l'œuvre peint*, Lausanne, 1964, no. 21, repr.

In 1880, Sisley moved to Veneux-les-Sablons in the Seine-et-Marne. He worked on the left bank of the Seine west of Saint-Mammès, along the path that follows the river to By. The shore is covered with woods at this spot, which lies on the edge of the Fontainebleau forest. The artist painted very dense landscapes during this period, when his style and stroke were becoming rich and varied.
In the Rau collection painting, Sisley used small, juxtaposed hatchings to suggest the meadow's tall grass and an abundance of comma strokes to render the trees' thick foliage. He modulated the different planes and managed to blend each tone in with the whole, depicting no more than a thin slice of sky in the middle of the branches. Although the site is located near the river bank, Sisley focused on the landscape's vegetation, as if exploring a mysterious aspect of nature. Twenty years after discovering open-air painting at Barbizon, the artist tried to revive the spirit of that "school of nature" by making allusions to works by Diaz and Dupré from around 1850.
The Rau collection work belongs to a group of By landscapes that Durand-Ruel sold to the director of the Union Générale bank, Jules Feder, who had helped the art dealer to patronize painters like Sisley. Consequently, for several months Durand-Ruel purchased most of Sisley's production. Afterwards, the artist moved to Moret-sur-Loing, lived in increasing seclusion and, like Monet, repeatedly painted the same motifs.
Ch. D.

73 Alfred Sisley (1839–1899)
Saint-Mammès, la Croix-blanche, 1884

Oil on canvas.
H: 54.3 cm; W: 65 cm.
Signed and dated lower right:
Sisley 84.
GR 1.1032

History:
Paris, Galerie Georges Petit; Paris, New York, Wildenstein & Co. Inc; Washington D. C., Mrs. Aila Mellon-Bruce.

Exhibitions:
San Francisco, The California Palace of the Legion of Honor, *French Paintings of the 19th Century from the collection of Mrs. Mellon-Bruce*, June-July 1961, no. 59, repr.

Bibliography:
F. Daulte, *Alfred Sisley. Catalogue raisonné de l'œuvre peint*, Lausanne, 1959, no. 510, repr.

Sisley is the least-known Impressionist painter, yet he cared so much about depicting the changing effects of light on nature that he unquestionably fits the label best. Observing the same landscape from different angles, at different times of day and in different seasons, Sisley conveyed his feelings with a sensibility that is always fresh and new. In 1880, the Seine near its confluence with the Loing became his subject of predilection. Sisley never tired of painting the river's banks at Saint-Mammès, the hillsides of La Celle and the *Croix-blanche* château.
Saint-Mammès, la Croix-blanche is part of this "perpetual series". Sisley always planted his easel on the same bank. He enjoyed working outdoors, painted directly on the canvas without doing a preparatory sketch and made very few touch-ups in the studio. The composition is rigidly structured: the alignment of white houses, themselves structured by windows and chimneys, strengthens the painting's verticality; the rising road accentuates the position of the poplars, echoing the opposite bank of the Seine by creating an aerial perspective. The vast, tranquil sky covers much of the canvas. In a letter to the critic Adolphe Tavernier, Sisley wrote, "the sky cannot be merely a background. On the contrary, its planes help to provide depth (for the sky is layered with planes just as the ground is) and its form, its arrangement in relation to the painting's effect or composition, provides movement." This painting's soft, shadowless light is a perfect example of Sisley's attraction to autumn landscapes. His chromatic palette of tender, transparent pink, mauve, violet, green, blue and Gary tones painted with small strokes lets patches of the canvas show through, especially in the sky. Sisley played with paint, colours and light. He considered texture decisive in the development of his work. The artist told his friend Tavernier that he was in favour of "a variety of techniques in painting. That is not in step with contemporary opinion, but I think I am right, especially when it is a matter of rendering the effects of light. For as the sun softens some parts of the landscape, it brightly illuminates others, and these effects of light, which appear almost tangibly in nature, must be rendered tangibly on the canvas". The paste is thick in the foreground, becoming more fluid in the sky, and the brushstrokes order the forms. Sisley depicted each element with a specific technique, painting the trees with a flexible line, the houses with bolder strokes.
This work, which Sisley painted in his mature period, bears witness to the artist's feelings about nature. Nature's radiance is evident in the lush vegetation overrunning the riverbanks, the silvery poplars whose foliage seems to be rustling in the wind and the sky offering its crystalline reflection to the water. No one knew better than Sisley, who cared so much about "the beloved nook of painting", how to express vibrations, reflections, movement, the rustling of the wind, the quivering of light, which make and unmake forms. "Sisley sets down fleeting moments of the day, observes a passing cloud and seems to paint it in mid-flight. On his canvas, the lively air moves and leaves still tremble and rustle", wrote Mallarmé in 1876 ("The Impressionists and Edouard Manet", in *The Art Monthly Review*, 1975, pp. 153–154).
It is about time for this painter of light to at last receive the recognition he is due. Pissarro wrote of him, "He is a beautiful and great artist. In my opinion, he is a master on a par with the great painters. I have once again seen works by him of a rare scope and beauty" (letter to his eldest son Lucien, January 22, 1899).
F. K.

Sisley

74

Gustave Caillebotte (1848–1894)
The Snow-covered Rooftops

Oil on cardboard.
H: 59 cm; W: 72 cm.
GR 1.517

History:
Paris, private collection; London, Sotheby's, July 1, 1970, no. 57; London, Sotheby's, December 3, 1971, no. 28.

Exhibitions:
Charlottenlund-Kobenhavn, Ordrupgaardsamlingen, *Impressionism, the City and Modern Life*, 1996, no. 58, fig. 24; Washington, The Phillips Collection – San Francisco, Fine Arts Museum – New York, The Brooklyn Museum of Art, *Impressionists in Winter: Effets de neige*, 1998–1999.

Bibliography:
M. Berhaut, *Gustave Caillebotte, sa vie et son œuvre. Catalogue raisonné des peintures et pastels*, Paris, 1978, p. 119, no. 108, new ed. revised and augmented, Paris, 1994, p. 108, no. 95, repr.

The heir to a large fortune, Gustave Caillebotte (Paris, 1848 – Genevilliers, 1894) supported the Impressionists by organizing their exhibitions and purchasing their works. His teacher, Bonnat, introduced him to Degas, who in turn acquainted him with the Impressionists. Caillebotte assembled a collection that included several of their masterpieces. His bequest to the French government sparked a famous controversy.
He was also a painter whose works were not rediscovered until the 1970s. His early style was very naturalistic. Caillebotte was interested in indoor scenes similar to those painted by Degas, but he also painted the streets of Paris and views from a balcony or a window. He demonstrated a remarkable sense of composition characterized by surprising perspective effects. From 1880, the artist's technique became fully Impressionist. His landscapes and boating scenes, at Argenteuil and Genevilliers, are very similar to works by Renoir. At the end of his life, Caillebotte painted less to devote more time to one of his other passions: sailing.

Caillebotte painted several views of the roofs of Paris in 1878. He presented two of them at the 1879 Impressionist exhibition, including one of snow-covered rooftops (Paris, Musée d'Orsay). According to Mrs. Berhaut, the Rau collection painting dates from the same period. Caillebotte painted it from the motif in snowy weather. Unlike his other cityscapes from the same period, the artist chose a point of view from which no window or facade can be seen. It was not until 1886 that he painted views from a higher angle (*Paris in the Snow*; Geneva, Petit Palais). Here, he focuses attention on two rooftops and several chimneys in the foreground. The architectural forms in the background and the right-hand side have dissolved. However, on the right the urban landscape opens up, veiled in smoke up to the chimneys. As the broad strokes indicate, the work was painted briskly. The juxtaposed brushstrokes are thick. This technique is a far cry from the smooth, small strokes Caillebotte customarily used in 1878. In many places, for example on the rooftops, he let the canvas show through to suggest different thicknesses of snow. Giving the zinc rooftops the ochre colour of the cardboard was a bold move. Caillebotte also broke with the realistic tones he customarily used to paint snow with touches of blue juxtaposed with white. All these features make him an Impressionist artist.
At the same time, the painting has a special sense of structure. Instead of dissolving the two rooftops' architectural forms, the snow makes them appear more prominent and underscores the separation between the zinc sheets. Caillebotte already painted them in the *View of Rooftops* displayed at the 1879 Impressionist exhibition (Berhaut, 1978, no. 105). Their diagonal lines offset the rooftops' horizontal surfaces, which otherwise would have been too overwhelming. The dark, vertical forms of the chimney bases stand out against the rooftops. Higher up in the sky, the somewhat disquieting black and grey vertical lines of the chimneys themselves respond to the white horizontal rooftops.
Caillebotte was extremely skillful at rendering the motionless state that things take when they are covered or surrounded by snow. The prevailing silence is barely disturbed by the garlands of smoke on the right. It should come as no surprise that the Impressionists were, for the most part, uninterested in this theme. They preferred snow-covered scenes in the countryside, where the lines fade, making it easier to do a study of light. What is more, motifs with too many lines hardly appealed to them. However, Cézanne and Gauguin were exceptions. The composition of Gauguin's *Paris in the Snow* (Amsterdam, Rijksmuseum Vincent van Gogh) reveals that his vision was quite different from Caillebotte's, but Cézanne's *View of Paris, Rooftops* is similar due to its respect for geometric structure. The horizontal surface of a zinc roof stretches out in the foreground. In this regard, it would not be far-fetched to speak of a connection between the two artists. Mrs. Berhaut has suggested applying Maurice Denis's description of Cézanne's work as "ordered Impressionism" to Caillebotte. In any case, the expression suits the Rau collection work, in which painting from the motif led to a very orderly composition. Despite the works by Gauguin and Cézanne, the subject is now associated with Caillebotte.
F. de V.

75

Mary Cassatt (1844–1926)
Louise Feeding Her Child, 1899

Pastel on brown paper.
H: 72.4 cm; W: 53.4 cm.
Signed lower left: *Mary Cassatt*.
GR 1.949

History:
Bought from the artist by Mrs. d'Alayer de Costermore, April 1899; France, Alayer's collection; London, Sotheby's, December 2, 1986, no. 11, repr.

Exhibitions:
Manchester-Paris, Galerie Durant-Ruel, *Group of French Impressionists*, 1907–1908, no. 44; London, *Marie Cassatt*, 1953, no. 9; Tokyo, Isetan Museum – Hiroshima, Museum of Art – Osaka, Takashimaya Art Gallery, *Les femmes impressionnistes: Morisot, Cassatt, Gonzales*, 1995, no. 47; London, Royal Academy of Arts – Tokyo, Sezon Museum of Art – Nagoya, Matsuzakaya Museum of Art, *From Manet to Gauguin. Masterpieces from Swiss Private Collections*, 1995–1996; Chicago, Art Institute of Chicago – Boston, Museum of Fine Arts – Washington, National Gallery of Art, *Mary Cassatt Retrospective*, 1998–1999.

Mary Cassatt (Pittsburgh, 1844 – Le Mesnil-Théribus, 1926) was born in the United States and settled in France at a young age to pursue her artistic career. After discovering the classical masters in Italy, Spain and Belgium, she frequented Chaplin's studio in Paris. Noticed by Degas, Cassatt soon became acquainted with the Impressionists and joined their circle. In 1879, she took part in the group's fourth exhibition, and displayed her work at the first Impressionist show in New York in 1886. Under the influence of Renoir and Degas, Cassatt became a prominent member of the Impressionist movement, producing many pastels, drawings and engravings featuring intimate subject matter until the end of her life. Aside from her career as an artist, she played a leading role in popularizing French Impressionism in the United States.

Critics have often hailed this pastel depicting a noble image of motherhood as a genuine masterpiece. Women and children play an essential role in Mary Cassatt's work and were her main source of inspiration. The artist sought to grasp the deep-seated feelings that sustained her models as if guided by a profound intuition of motherly love. She composed and recomposed the theme of motherhood, varying the forms and the means of expression.
In this painting, a sturdy woman seated in profile is looking down at her child. The model, who has been identified as Louise Fissier de Fresnaux, posed several times for the artist. She can also be seen in a similar composition in a drypoint engraving where the artist used a more linear technique. Towards the late nineteenth century, Cassatt used pastels increasingly often to depict childhood scenes.
This work, which dates from 1899, displays her outstanding, confident draftsmanship and rich, surprising tones. The bright bodice and the delicate modelling of the light tones, which are heightened by a few discreet black outlines, stand out against the background's mauve nuances. The search for feeling combined with subtle chromatic harmonies make this pastel one of the most representative works by Cassatt, an artist with a strong personality who contributed an original feminine sensibility to Impressionism.
Ch. D.

Bibliography:
C. Mauclair, "Un peintre de l'enfance, Miss Mary Cassatt", in *L'Art décoratif*, vol. VIII, no. 47, August 1902, p. 179, repr.; G. Geffroy, "Femmes artistes, un peintre de l'enfance, Mary Cassatt", in *Les Modes*, vol. IV, February 1904, p. 5, repr.; A. Mellerion, "Mary Cassatt", in *L'Art et les Artistes*, vol. XII, November 1910, p. 70, repr.; A. Segard, *Un peintre des enfants et des mères, Mary Cassatt*, Paris, 1913, p. 68, repr.; *Good Housekeeping Magazine*, vol. LVIII, February 1914, p. 152, repr.; E. Valerio, *Mary Cassatt*, Paris, 1930, p. 9, pl. 12; *La Renaissance*, vol. XIII, February 1930, pp. 55–56, repr.; F. Watson, *Mary Cassatt*, New York, 1932, p. 35, repr.; A. Bresskin, *Mary Cassatt. A Catalogue Raisonné of the Oils, Pastels, Watercolors and Drawings*, Washington, 1970, p. 138, no. 311, repr.

76

Max Liebermann (1847–1935)
Playtime at the Amsterdam Orphanage, 1876

Oil on canvas.
H: 45 cm; W: 72 cm.
Signed and dedicated lower left: *à Mr. Backer / Souvenir affectueux / de M. Liebermann.*
GR 1.565

History:
Kept in a private collection in Breslau until 1945; Cologne, Galerie Abels, March 22, 1973.

Exhibitions:
Berlin, Nationalgalerie, Staatliche Museen Preußischer Kulturbesitz, *Max Liebermann in seiner Zeit*; Munich, Haus der Kunst, 1979–1980, no. 27, pp. 194–195, repr.

Bibliography:
Kunst und Kunst, June 1923, repr.; W. Rainer, "Die Tugend der puren Malerei", in *Stuttgarter Zeitung*, no. 208, September 8, 1979, repr.

From 1866 to 1868, Max Liebermann (Berlin, 1847 – Berlin, 1935) studied in the city of his birth under Karl Steffeck, who introduced him to a sober brand of realism. Afterwards, and until 1872, he took classes with Thumann and Pauwels at Weimar's School of Fine Arts. The Goose Pluckers *of 1873 was the first in a long series of paintings depicting the labours of farm and factory. In 1872, he met Munkácsy in Dusseldorf. Liebermann lived in Paris from 1873 to 1878, visiting Barbizon where he met Daubigny, Corot and, most importantly, Millet.*
He subsequently moved to Munich, where the realism of Jesus Among the Doctors, *painted in 1879, was deemed blasphemous and triggered a public outcry. In 1884, the artist settled permanently in Berlin, becoming a member of the city's academy in 1898. He co-founded the XI group in 1892 and the Berlin Secession in 1898, of which he was president from 1899 to 1911, and the Deutscher Künstlerbund in 1904.*

Max Liebermann spent the summer of 1876 in Haarlem, where he painted copies of works by Frans Hals, before moving into the Amsterdam orphanage for a few months. In his work on the artist (1914, p. 112), E. Hancke writes that Liebermann was so struck by the orphan girls' dresses in black and red, the colours of the city of Amsterdam, that he wanted to use them as a pictorial theme. The city orphanage was located in the old Saint Lucien's cloisters, founded in 1520, rebuilt in 1634, and decorated with paintings by seventeenth-century Dutch masters such as Jacob Backer, Jürgen Ovens and Abraham de Vries.
Liebermann obtained permission to set up his atelier inside the orphanage and painted numerous studies, all of a similar nature. The first (formerly in the Bode collection; Hancke, 1914, p. 114, repr.) is now in the Nationalgalerie in Berlin. It is very similar to the Rau collection painting, although slightly larger. The dedication, written in French in the bottom left-hand corner of this picture, takes on a clear meaning only when it is understood that *Mr. Backer* was Jonkheer Jacob Back (Utrecht, 1820 – Amsterdam, 1905), director of the orphanage from 1855 until his death. Liebermann and Back communicated in French, which was still the international language in artistic circles at the end of the nineteenth century. The chain of events can then be easily reconstructed. The artist first painted the piece now in Berlin. It must have pleased the director of the establishment, and to thank him for his hospitality Liebermann gave him a slightly smaller version in which he put more detail into the young girls' faces, giving the work a more finished look. He painted these two studies in 1876.
In 1881 Liebermann reworked the theme of the young orphan girls in the courtyard, adding some very interesting light effects, in a study now in the Bremen Kunsthalle (*Max Liebermann*, 1979–1980, fig. 327) and a painting sold at Christie's on June 28, 1977 (no. 36, repr.). The composition differs to some extent in that the perspective is shifted to the left. All these innovations culminated in the painting of 1881–1882, now in the Frankfurt Städelsches Kunstinstitut, whose composition and technique are more finished.
Ph. L.

à Mr. Backer
souvenir affectueux

77

Paul Signac (1863–1935)
The Sea. Saint-Briac. The Guérin Guard. Saint-Lunaire. Opus 211, 1890

Oil on canvas.
H: 65 cm; W: 81.5 cm.
Signed and dated lower left:
P. Signac 90.
Inscription, lower right:
Op. 211.
GR 1.520

History:
Paris, given to Arsène Alexandre; Paris, Georges Petit's, A. Alexandre's collection, May 18–19, 1903, no. 59; Paris, Bernheim-Jeune; Paris, Marcel Norero; Paris, Drouot's, M. Norero's collection, February 14, 1927, no. 91; New York, J. Stonborough's collection, 1940; New York, Parke Bernet's, October 17, 1940, no. 59; New York, Wildenstein Institute; Zurich, Marianne Feilchenfeldt.

Exhibitions:
Brussels, Musée de Peinture (now Musée d'Art Moderne), *Salon du cercle des XX*, 1891; Paris, *Salon de la Société Nationale des Artistes Indépendants*, 1891, no. 1114; Copenhagen, *Exposition d'art francais du XIXe siècle*, 1914, no. 193; Cologne, Wallraf-Richartz-Museum – Lausanne, L'Ermitage, *Pointillismus: Auf den Spuren von Georges Seurat*, 1997–1998.

In June 1880, when he was seventeen, Paul Signac (Paris, 1863 – Paris, 1935) visited the La Vie Moderne *exhibition devoted to Claude Monet. That was when he decided to become a painter and adopt the Impressionists' technique. Signac was the oldest son of a wealthy family that did not oppose his wishes. He started working from real life in Montmartre, and soon discovered the pleasures of sailing at Asnières. In 1883 Signac, impassioned by a love of the sea that would remain with him for the rest of his life, purchased the first of the thirty-two boats he would own. It was named after three of the most fiery figures of the time*: Manet, Zola, Wagner. *His first seascapes at Port-en-Bassin in Brittany, where Seurat had painted before him, date from this period.*
In 1884 he played an active role with Redon, Cross and Angrand in founding the Société des Artistes Indépendants. That was when he met Georges Seurat, with whom he developed the theoretical foundations of Neo-Impressionism.
The year 1885 was marked by two encounters, with Camille Pissarro in April and Claude Monet at Giverny. He would remain friends with Monet for the rest of his life.
Paul Signac was very interested in the theories of Michel Eugène Chevreul, whom he had met at the Société des Indépendants. When Charles Henry (1859–1926) published his Introduction à une esthétique scientifique *in 1886, he was fascinated by the scientist's research on "the rhythms and measurement of lines and colours", becoming a leading advocate of Neo-Impressionism. Seurat, who was working in a similar spirit, completed the same yea,* Sunday Afternoon on the Island of La Grande Jatte *(Chicago, Art Institute of Chicago), which was the concrete expression of these scientific theories and soon became the symbol of nascent Divisionism.*
Signac would be the link between Camille Pissarro, Georges Seurat and Theo van Rysselberghe and the Symbolist writers Félix Fénéon, Gustav Kahn, Maurice Maeterlinck and Emile Verhaeren. In 1899 he published an account of this period in a book-manifesto entitled D'Eugène Delacroix au néo-impressionnisme, *whose influence was felt as far as Fauvism and Cubism.*

This large painting belongs to a series of four works painted in Brittany in 1890 and exhibited in 1891 at the Brussels Salon des XX under the title *The Sea*. It was shown with *Opus 209* (United States, private collection), *Opus 210* (New York, private collection) and *Opus 212* (Moscow, Pushkin Museum). Until 1894 Signac gave his paintings the designation *Opus*, demonstrating his essentially Symbolist search for a parallel between the luminous waves of painting and the sound waves of music. The painter was an excellent sailor who identified with the sea and knew it perfectly. His grand-daughter, Françoise Cachin, recalled "that he loved quoting his beloved Stendhal's axiom: Nearness to the sea destroys smallness" (Cachin, 1971, p. 103).
In the Rau collection work he used an even, Pointillist technique consisting of fine, tightly-knit strokes more to accentuate the contrasts of light than the intensity of colour. He defined the painting's composition with the divided strokes, optic mixture and contrast of complementarities that he borrowed from Neo-Impressionism. Sobriety, simplification and the splitting up of strokes appear in his large beaches, contrasting with the blue sea and yellow grass. Signac expresses rhythm more than vision by contrasting these two dominant colours. The sharp observer in him recreated a luminous landscape with calm, harmonious lines evoking "the exquisite goldenness" of his seascapes, as Félix Fénéon described them in 1887. Signac was also intent on expressing the lines' decorative and synthetic values. That is undoubtedly why some people have seen in the Saint-Briac seascapes the influence of japonisme, which was highly esteemed by French artists at the time. Several prints by Hokusai and Hiroshige had been exhibited in Paris the same year.
F. K.

78 Henri de Toulouse-Lautrec (1864–1901)
Gabrielle the Dancer

Oil on cardboard.
H: 35 cm; W: 24 cm.
CR 1.978

History:
Paris, M. Le Garrec's collection; Buenos Aires, Antonio Santamarina's collection; London, Sotheby's, April 2, 1974, no. 25; London, Lady Baillie's collection; London, Sotheby's, December 4, 1974, no. 8A; London, Sotheby's, April 4, 1989, no. 19.

Exhibitions:
Buenos Aires, Galerie Viau, *Degas et Lautrec*, 1950, no. 21; Buenos Aires, *Toulouse-Lautrec*, 1964, no. 8; Hamilton, NY, Picker Art Gallery – Austin, Archer M. Huntington Art Gallery – Palm Beach, Society of the Four Arts Museum, *Impressionist and Post-Impressionist Works from a British Collection*, 1986–1987, no. 41, repr.; Norwich, Castle Museum, *Impressionist and Post-Impressionist Pictures from a British Collection*, 1987; Humlebaek, Louisiana Museum, *Toulouse-Lautrec*, 1994–1995, no. 37, repr.

Bibliography:
M. Joyant, *Henri de Toulouse-Lautrec*, Paris, 1927, vol. II, p. 253; *Magazine of Art*, February 1942, p. 56, repr.; M. G. Dortu, *Toulouse-Lautrec et son œuvre*, New York, 1971, vol. III, no. P600, repr.; G. M. Sugana, *Tout l'œuvre peint de Toulouse-Lautrec*, Paris, 1986, no. 550, repr.

Henri de Toulouse-Lautrec (Albi, 1864 – Malromé, 1901), who was born into a great aristocratic family, took his first painting classes at the Fontanes school in Paris. In 1878 two successive falls compromised an already frail health and left him handicapped.
Encouraged by Princeteau, he began devoting himself to drawing and painting. In 1882 he joined Bonnat's studio at the Ecole des Beaux-Arts before joining Cormon's, where he became friends with Emile Bernard, Anquetin and van Gogh. He was attracted to Impressionism's brightness before discovering Degas' works and Japanese prints.
In 1885 he settled in Montmartre and often went to balls and cabarets, where he painted continuously. From 1891 he did many colour posters and lithographs whose hallmarks are daring draugtsmanship and a bold lay-out. Alcohol abuse put an end to his career, and in 1901 he died at the age of thirty-seven.

Gabrielle was a familiar part of Toulouse-Lautrec's everyday world. In 1890 the artist began using her as a model in father Forest's garden, and the following year he painted a new portrait of her (Albi, Musée Toulouse-Lautrec; London, National Gallery).
However, the Rau collection painting is closer to a more ambitious work, *Au Moulin Rouge*, where Gabrielle accompanies arm-in-arm the clown Cha-U-Kao (Winterthur, O. Reinhardt collection). The same profile is seen wearing the same hat, but appears older and a bit sad. The portrait may not have been a preparatory study for the painting in the full sense of the term, but perhaps it helped the artist in his search for a physiognomy.
In a similar way, Toulouse-Lautrec painted the *Portrait of William Warner*, to which he returned in the *Englishman at the Moulin Rouge* (Albi, Musée Toulouse-Lautrec; New York, Metropolitan Museum of Art).
In the Rau collection work, he focused on the search for a lifelike expression. He went straight to the essentials with an exceptionally spur-of-the-moment technique. His brush applied a few strokes of colours that had been strongly thinned by gasoline. In this way he modelled the features of the face and painted the outlines.
Although Gabrielle looks more blonde in other works, this painting once again demonstrates Toulouse-Lautrec's attraction to red-headed women, which made it possible for him to juxtapose the flesh tones with those of the hair. The beige of the cardboard serves as a background value for the whole. The artist painted a candid portrait of this disenchanted woman, a model and, undoubtedly, prostitute who also posed in several brothel scenes (*Study for the Doctor's Visit*, Paris, Musée d'Orsay; *The Sofa*, New York, Metropolitan Museum of Art).
Ch. D.

79 Ignacio Zuloaga y Zabaleta (1870–1945)
Portrait of the Picador "El Coriano", 1897

Oil on canvas.
H: 80 cm; W: 60 cm.
Signed and dated lower left:
Souvenir à Madame Bulteau / I. Zuloaga.
GR 1.945

History:
Given to Mrs. Bulteau by the artist in 1895; collection of Maxime Dethomas; bought from Mrs. Dethomas in 1934 by an anonymous collector; London, Sotheby's, June 18, 1986, no. 228.

Exhibition:
Madrid, *Exposición National de Bellas Artes*, 1897, no. 1165.

Bibliography:
A. Alexandre, "M. Ignacio Zuloaga", in *Le Figaro illustré*, April 15, 1903, p. 7; J. M. de Cossío, *Los toros. Tratado técnico e histórico*, 1947, vol. II, p. 895, repr. p. 986; E. Lafuente Ferrari, *Ignacio Zuloaga*, San Sebastian, 1950, pp. 44, 181, 217, 218, nos. 64 and 70 (no. 10 of the "livre de raison" of the artist); re-ed. Barcelona, 1972, 1990, pp. 75, 76, 245, 492, nos. 64, 70.

Ignacio Zuloaga y Zabaleta (Eibar, 1870 – Madrid, 1945) was born into a family of renowned Basque country goldsmiths and gunsmiths. He was attracted to painting and in 1887 discovered the Spanish masters of the Golden Age at the Prado. They had a definitive impact on his painting. At the age of twenty, he went to Paris, frequented the studio of Gervex, who introduced him to the work of Courbet and Manet, and became a friend of avant-garde artists such as Degas, Gauguin and Rodin. He lived in Spain as much as in France, but it was in Paris that his portraits and paintings, inspired by everyday Andalusian life, were successful during the early years of the twentieth century. Exhibitions in Dusseldorf (1904) and New York (1909) crowned a reputation that had become international. His portraits would soon make him rich. In 1914, he permanently settled in the twelfth-century monastery at Zumaya (today the Zuloaga Museum), where he was the curator of major art collections. He died in Madrid in 1945 at the height of his fame.

What a wonderful rediscovery *Portrait of the Picador "El Coriano"* is. It was one of Zuloaga's earliest successes, but his biographers thought it lost. Antonio González "El Coriano", undoubtedly born in Coria del Rio, was a rather mediocre picador. He worked mostly with his brother, the somewhat successful torero Francisco González "Faico" (de Cossío, 1943, vol. III, p. 390). The young artist painted this work in 1897, at the height of his Andalusian period. The ostensibly dedicated portrait is irrefutable proof of the role played by Madame Bulteau in the Basque artist's Paris success. Unpublished documents have enabled Mayi Milhou (*Ignacio Zuloaga et la France*, 1981, pp. 51, 81–83) to establish that the Spaniard had links with Maxime Dethomas, whom he met at Gervex's studio, very early in his career. The young French painter introduced Zuloaga to Paris artistic circles and helped him successfully exhibit six *espagnolades* in 1895 at Le Barc de Bouteville's. In 1899, Ignacio married Maxime's sister, Valentine Dethomas. This event strengthened the friendship between the two artists, which made it possible for Zuloaga to enter the highly renowned salon of Augustine Bulteau, wife of novelist Jules Ricard. Later, he would often see his famous models there, Maurice Barrès and the Countess of Noailles.

Madame Bulteau was a cultivated, generous woman who had a real influence on Parisian newspapers, especially *Le Figaro*, which in 1903 helped launch Zuloaga's career by devoting a special issue to him. Maxime Dethomas, whom Madame Bulteau considered her "dear child", inherited the *Portrait of the Picador "El Coriano"*.

In spite of a few flattering articles in the press, Zuloaga never managed to make a living as a painter in Paris. He discovered Andalusia in 1892, staying a long time in Seville where he had many jobs and enrolled in Manuel Carmona's bullfighting school. He practised this sport for four years and developed a passion for it. He remained an *aficionado* throughout his life, became a friend of the greatest matadors and painted unforgettable portraits of them (*El Corcito, Belmonte, Domingo Ortega*). Rustic and down-to-earth Andalusian life, and encounters with gypsies, bullfighters, manolas, poets and farmers provided his powerful personality with typical subjects. He handled them with a broad, very colourful style inherited from the Spanish pictorial tradition of El Greco, Velázquez and Goya, but combined with the "modern" vision of nineteenth-century realist painters.

El Coriano is a simple half-length figure on a neutral background. It fixes the image of the picador, whose bitter mouth and fierce, sunburned features are painted with a remorseless, brisk stroke. The thick paint is spread on in large flat areas. The colour range is reduced to silvery greys and beige-ochre monochromes livened up by the intense pink of the embroidered bolero. It is a trademark of this artist, who said that his only teachers were "nature and museums".
O. D.

Souvenir à Madame Bulteau
I Zuloaga

80

Max Slevogt (1868–1932)
Portrait of Sada Yakko and a Japanese Child, 1906

Oil on canvas.
H: 131.2 cm; W: 110.2 cm.
Signed lower right: *Slevogt*, and inscribed with Japanese characters on right.
GR 1.932

History:
Given by the artist to Pr Peter Plesch; London, Christie's, December 3, 1985, no. 152.

Max Slevogt (Landshut, 1868 – Neukastel, Palatinate, 1932) studied classics in Wurzburg. In 1885 he became the student of Johann Herterich and Diez at the Academy of Fine Arts in Munich. For six months in 1889 he studied at the Académie Julian in Paris to complete his training. Afterwards he travelled to Italy and settled in Munich. In 1897 he exhibited in Vienna for the first time. In 1899 he exhibited at the Munich Secession where his Danaë *caused an uproar, whereas the painting was more successful in Berlin. He took part in the 1900 World Fair in Paris. The following year he moved to the German capital with Lovis Corinth and became a member of the Berlin Secession, signing the* Struggle for Art *manifesto in 1911. He travelled to Egypt shortly before the First World War. In 1915 he became a member of the Dresden academy, and from 1917 headed a studio at the Berlin academy.*

The model, Sada Yakko, was a Japanese actress and dancer who toured Europe in 1906–1907. She added the Japanese characters appearing on the right. They give her name and the date the work was painted, December 20, 1906.
Max Slevogt loved the theatre. He was not the only painter who concentrated on performing artists. In France, for example, Edgar Degas was painting dancers, Henri de Toulouse-Lautrec cabaret scenes and Seurat the circus. The *Clown in a Green Costume* by Macke is another example of modern artists' attraction to the living and ephemeral world of the performing arts. Slevogt painted other performers, notably Andrade, a baritone who was very famous in Germany (*Portrait of Andrade in Black*, 1903; Hamburg, Kunsthalle).
The prototype for all these portraits is the painting of *Lola de Valence* by Edouard Manet, an artist who was highly esteemed in Germany.
Slevogt's attraction to painting Japanese actors was also part of the ambient, late nineteenth-century "japonisme" which collectors of Japanese prints had made popular. Moreover, these works inspired the compositions of Manet, who showed several of them on the wall in the *Portrait of Emile Zola*. Slevogt, a faithful admirer of Manet, was inspired by these prints when he painted this work. His technique's extreme freedom is surprising today. The painter did not show the figures' feet nor the space around them, which creates the impression that they are close and moving. Sada Yakko seems to be walking towards the viewer to introduce him or her to this child, who may be her son.
The actress's spontaneous pose as well as the child's shy air are very simply yet expressively rendered. The colours – green, red, blue and yellow – stand out against the painting's light beige background. The clothes, which are painted with a few strokes of the brush, reflect the shiny fabrics of Japanese kimonos, with a splendid effect on Sada Yakko's belt. On her face is a hint of the very pale make-up characteristically worn by Japanese actresses.
Ph. L.

*81

Gino Severini (1883–1966)
Landscape at Civray, 1909

Oil on canvas.
H: 115 cm; W: 195 cm.
Signed in orange, lower right: *G. Severini.*
Pencil inscription on back: *Civray Vienna, G. Severini, 1909.*
GR 1.277

History:
Private collection; Paris, Donath's collection; Paris, Rosenberg's collection; Zurich, Marianne Feilchenfeldt's collection.

Exhibition:
Rotterdam, Museum Boymans-van Beuningen Museum, *Severini*, 1963, no. 4.

Bibliography:
D. Fonti (ed.), *Gino Severini. Catalogo ragionato*, Milan, 1988, p. 91, fig. 64.

Gino Severini (Cortona, 1883 – Paris, 1966) took his first drawing classes in Rome at the age of sixteen. The following year, 1900, he decided to become a painter. That was when he met Umberto Boccioni, who introduced him to Giacomo Balla. Balla was ten years older than Boccioni and Severini, and greatly influenced them during their formative years. He had recently returned from Paris and soon introduced his two students to Seurat's Divisionism, a revelation that would mark not only the work of the two friends, but nascent Futurism as well. For Gino Severini, the definitive choice was made, as he explained nearly half a century later: "I chose Seurat as teacher once and for all, and even today I have not changed" (Ecrits sur l'art, *Paris, 1987). He arrived in Paris in October 1906, and soon met not only his countryman Amedeo Modigliani but the entire Lapin Agile circle, including Suzanne Valadon, Francis Carco, Max Jacob, André Salmon, Pablo Picasso, Juan Gris, Maurice Utrillo, Félix Fénéon and Guillaume Apollinaire.*
On February 20, 1909, the newspaper Le Figaro *published the first* Manifesto of Futurism, *written by F. T. Marinetti and co-signed by Boccioni, Carrà and Russolo. This artistic and literary movement exalted the* future *and modern society's new myths, such as the machine and speed. Although Boccioni invited him to sign, Severini did not really become interested in Futurism until 1910. He went through a brief Cubist period from 1916 to 1921, represented mainly by still lives, before returning to Futurist painting, to which he added his Pointillist touch and subtle palette. His many writings on his life, his friends and the painting of his time are a priceless testimony. Severini was an all-around artist who, during his mature years, did frescoes, decorative panels and mosaics in Switzerland and Italy.*

Landscape at Civray, which was painted during the summer of 1909, belongs to Gino Severini's early period. The artist applied proven chromatic solutions stemming from Pointillism to a traditional organization. The Florentine critic Piero Pacini considers it "the most significant work from his stay in Poitou [...] to be compared to some of the landscapes Seurat painted between 1880 and 1890. It constitutes a spontaneous, emotional encounter with a restful, natural but surprise-filled environment". Severini's work would always remain influenced by Seurat, from whom he drew the ordered, precisely arranged composition. It should be pointed out that at the time, artists from the same generation, such as Picasso, Braque and Léger, were experimenting with considerably bolder innovations.
In any case, Severini perfectly mastered this painting's architecture and luminous problematic. The foreground, which stands out significantly, is enhanced by the trees on the sides, which gradually invade the perspective by lining up in successive curtains that change into a fleecy sky.
This painting marks the culminating point of Gino Severini's search to apply Impressionist theories, from which he naturally very quickly tried to free himself. The artist drew upon Chevreul's discoveries by using warm yellow and red tones in the foreground, which move out towards the viewer, and cold blue and violet tones in the background, which recede into the painting's depth. In the same spirit, the broader Pointillist strokes at the bottom become increasingly small as they move to the top of the painting, ending up as tiny dots in the sky. Gino Severini described this work as "a veritable colour poem that gave the most ordinary landscape a definitive, grandiose expression" (ibid.).
Faithful to spontaneous, outdoor art, he was still interested in the effects of light. Here, the summer sun stretches its wide, coloured shadows across the ground and heightens the relief of the clouds with an underlying mauve reflection. Severini wrote about how essential Impressionism was to his work: "Today I realize that anyone who has not understood Impressionism well cannot create anything sound and really new in modern art" (ibid.).
The painter made the most of his teachers' lessons, developing in *Landscape at Civray* the harmony of a moment of sunny calm. Gino Severini's airy touch, bright palette, pure, delicate tints and rather unreal range of colours used to express depth are the hallmarks of his work.
F. K.

véritable poésie de la couleur qui donnait au paysage le plus banal une expression grandiose définitive" (*ibid.*).
Fidèle à cet art de l'instant et de plein air, l'artiste s'intéresse encore aux effets de la lumière ; ici le soleil estival étend ses larges ombres colorées au sol et souligne le relief des nuages par un reflet mauve sous-jacent. Severini a écrit combien l'apport de l'impressionnisme était pour lui essentiel : "Je me rends compte aujourd'hui que celui qui n'a pas bien compris l'impressionnisme ne peut rien construire de solide et de vraiment neuf sur le plan de l'art moderne" (*ibid.*).
Tirant parti des leçons de ses maîtres, le peintre développe dans *Paysage à Civray* l'harmonie d'un moment de calme ensoleillé. Sa touche désinvolte, sa palette claire, son chromatisme assez distant de la réalité pour en exprimer toute la profondeur, ses teintes pures et délicates constituent la signature picturale de Gino Severini.
F. K.

Symbolism and Nabis

Symbolism came to the fore in Europe from 1885 onwards, as a reaction to Impressionism and Naturalism. Although artists such as Blake, Füssli and Friedrich are not described as Symbolist painters, their works foreshadow Symbolist aesthetics. Like them, the Symbolist artists wanted to explore hidden worlds and to express a subjective vision, based on dreams, the imaginary, medieval legends, silence and anguish. Their creative approach wanted to distance itself from observation and the pure transcription of reality. United in a common inspiration, the Symbolists did not, however, create a uniform style. Each one went his own way, finding inspiration in different models such as Neo-Classicism or Gauguin's synthetism. One must also note the close ties between Symbolist painting and literature; the latter, thanks to numerous articles, was an important factor in the dissemination of Symbolist painting.
And so it was that, around 1890, a group of French artists came together under the name of Nabis. Taken from Hebrew, the word "Nabi" means "prophet" and denotes the second generation of Symbolist artists. Just like their predecessors, they violently reacted against Impressionism, and introduced themselves as disciples of Gauguin and Sérusier. They also evinced a profound admiration for the works of Redon and Puvis de Chavannes. The best definition of Nabi is probably that given by Maurice Denis, for whom painting "is essentially a flat surface covered in colours assembled in a certain order". Denis, Bonnard and Sérusier, the main leaders of the group, were later joined by Vuillard and Vallotton. Arabesques, a taste for the decorative, for symbolization, are among the chief characteristics of their style. From an iconographical point of view, the Nabis had a fondness for indoor scenes and the evocation of Parisian life. However, some of their compositions were inspired by mythology and a dreamlike imaginary. Their art was widespread among a number of different outlets such as posters, wall papers, postcards, or playing cards, book illustrations, or else theatre sets.

82

Odilon Redon (1840–1916)

Rose in a Vase

Oil on canvas.
H: 33 cm; W: 28 cm.
Signed lower left:
Odilon Redon.
GR 1.899

History:
Paris, Princess Bibesco;
Paris, Galerie Bernheim-Jeune.

Exhibitions:
Rotterdam, Museum Boymans-van Beuningen, *Vier Euwen Stilleven in Frankrijk*, 1954, no. 106; Paris, Galerie Framond, *Palette de fleurs*, 1955; Paris, Galerie Bernheim-Jeune, *Voici des fruits, des fleurs*, 1957, no. 48; Paris, Galerie Bernheim-Jeune, *Odilon Redon*, 1963, no. 18.

In his youth, Odilon Redon (Bordeaux, 1840 – Paris, 1916) had an encounter that changed the course of his life: he met Rodolphe Bresdin, who introduced him to engraving and taught him how to look beyond nature's appearances. The Impressionist movement left him dissatisfied, although he did take part in their last exhibition (1886). At first, Redon developed his talent with black and white charcoal drawings that had fantastic themes. His goal was to "use the logic of the visible to reveal the invisible as much as possible". The Symbolist writers Huysmans and Mallarmé, who were interested in the same theme, were his earliest supporters. Redon's work achieved a fairly wide distribution through his lithographs, which influenced the Nabis generation. In the 1890s, he returned to colour by way of pastels. Shortly afterwards, Redon experienced a revival of interest in oil painting, which he had abandoned. His works during that period were primarily mythological scenes. After 1900, at age sixty, he began receiving commissions for decorative paintings.

Redon managed to provide his subject with a monumental dimension despite this painting's small size. A vase containing a rose and a few leaves is set fairly high in relation to the lower edge of the canvas and stands out against a non-descript green-grey surface. The leaves stand out against a bare, dark background. The flowers open up towards the light, which comes from the painting's left. Redon painstakingly painted the rose but simplified the leaves to the point that they seem unreal. The few delicate, harmonious colours set off the red heart of the rose. The touch of ochre on the vase's inner rim responds to the vivid flower like a distant echo. Redon contrasted the tones of the two sides of the leaves, which helps give them a fantastic aspect.
This work can be dated to the early part of the artist's career, in any case before 1870, a period when he painted other, similar still lives. A thinly-painted *Rose in a Vase* (Algiers, Musée des Beaux-Arts) features a comparable composition. A *Celeriac* (Paris, Musée d'Orsay) is also very similar. The synthetism, realism and technique of that painting and the canvas in the Rau collection are reminiscent of Manet's style. In his critique of the 1868 Salon, Redon acknowledged Manet as a master of the still life: "Mr. Manet, who seems especially gifted for the still life, should limit himself to that genre, which is not inferior when treated with such talent." However, the liberties Redon took with reality in the Rau collection painting show that he was interested in moving beyond naturalistic depiction. He was enthusiastic about Romanticism right from the beginning of his career. At the 1868 Salon, the artist again declared his admiration for Bresdin.
His mature style was a blend of imagination and reality. In the early twentieth century, Redon continued doing paintings and pastel drawings of flowers, especially wildflowers, that were now filled with mystery. One example is *Woman Amidst Flowers* (New York, Mrs. H. Harris Jonas collection), where a simple bouquet takes on an enchanted allure.
F. de V.

ODILON REDON

83 Odilon Redon (1840–1916)
Apollo's Chariot

Oil on canvas.
H: 60 cm; W: 73 cm.
Signed lower right: *Odilon Redon*.
GR 1.663

History:
New York, Adelaide Milton de Groot; New York, Metropolitan Museum of Art; New York, sale at Sotheby's of the Parke-Bernet collection, October 25, 1972, lot 9, repr.; Japan, Pola's collection, circa 1973; London, Sotheby's, December 5, 1979, no. 25, repr.

Exhibition:
Kamakura, Prefectural Museum of Modern Art – Nagoya, Aichi Art Gallery, *Odilon Redon*, 1973, no. 16.

Bibliography:
K. Berger, *Odilon Redon, Phantasie und Farbe*, Cologne, 1964, p. 193, no. 156; *World Collectors Annuary*, 1972, vol. XXIV; J.-J. Lévêque, *Les Années de la Belle Epoque, 1890–1914*, Paris, 1991, repr. p. 570; A. Wildenstein, *Odilon Redon: catalogue raisonné de l'œuvre*, Paris, 1994, vol. II, p. 60, no. 868, repr.

In this work, Odilon Redon painted a patch of sky set ablaze by Apollo and his quadriga. The course of the Sun is drawing to a close: its couriers are coming back down to Earth. At the end of his life, Redon was passionate about the theme of Apollo, painting ten works on the subject between 1905 and 1914. Delacroix's ceiling in the Louvre's Apollo gallery was probably the source of his interest. "It is the triumph of light over darkness," he wrote. "It is the joy of broad daylight opposed to the bleakness of the night and its shadows, and like the joy of a happier sentiment that comes after anguish" (O. Redon, *A soi-même. Journal (1867–1915)*, Paris, 1961, p. 175). The emotion he felt before *Phaeton's Fall*, a watercolour by Gustave Moreau which he saw at the 1878 World's Fair, probably also fuelled his passion for the myth of Apollo. Describing the work, he wrote, "There is a grandeur, an excitement and, in a way, a fresh astonishment in the brightness of these billowy clouds, in the bold divergence of the lines, in the harshness and mordancy of the vivid colours."
Did Redon use some of the figures he admired in the preceding works? The Sun god and his chariot seem to be made of an incandescent material. The clouds around them take on all sorts of warm tones, from red-ochre to mauve. They exalt the turquoise blue that dominates the canvas. The god's passage cleaves the clouds into a V-shape, opening them up as his fiery mount streaks through. The play of shadow and light delicately models the horses, and a brown outline traces their contours. The air around them is still light before the Sun's passage. The thin, yellow clouds let the turquoise blue show through where it does not emerge. Following in his forerunners' footsteps, Redon gave the sky a bright colour that fills the viewer with joy.
In his other works, Apollo's chariot has not yet begun its descent; sometimes the artist chose to surround it with nothing but sky (New York, Metropolitan Museum of Art). The ether radiates peace and tranquillity, contrasting with the divine quadriga's speed.
In these paintings, including the one in the Rau collection, Redon still treated the sky in a realistic manner. In fact, he enjoyed painting studies of the sky from the motif. The ones he did in Peyrelebade, his family home in the Landes, are in the Musée d'Orsay, Paris. In other works, especially pastels, the sky takes on fantastic tones, and the compositions are filled with Python's corpse, a tall mountain or butterflies and flowers (Paris, Musée d'Orsay; Bordeaux, Musée des Beaux-Arts). In the early twentieth century, Redon revitalized mythological scenes with a breath of fresh air.
F. de V.

***84**

Ferdinand Hodler (1853–1918)
Portrait of a Lady, 1884–1890

Oil on canvas.
H: 55 cm; W: 46 cm.
GR 1.2

History:
Collection of the painter's daughter and heiress, Paulette Marquerat-Hodler; Bern, sale Kornfeld and Klipstein, June 20, 1973, no. 335, repr.

Between 1867 and 1870 Ferdinand Hodler (Bern, 1853 – Geneva, 1918) trained under Ferdinand Sommer (1812–1901), the painter of Swiss views. In 1872 he went to Geneva, where he studied under Barthélémy Menn (1815–1893), a student of Ingres and professor at the School of Fine Arts. In 1877 he went to Paris and in 1878–1879, Madrid. From 1890 he was recognized as the master of mural painting with the execution of major monumental commissions including the famous Retreat from Marignan *for the Swiss Kunsthaus in Zurich. Invited to exhibit in 1903 by the Vienna Secession, he received international recognition. Hodler was adopted by Germany, which did not keep him from taking a stand against his host country following the bombardment of Rheims cathedral in 1914. As a result he was excluded from all the German academies.*

Dr Huggler has dated this picture, whose sitter has not been identified, to around 1905, which is not appropriate for stylistic reasons. The *Portrait of a Lady* should be placed at the beginning of the artist's career, when he was painting portraits in a style that was, if not traditional, at least hardly innovative.
In a *Portrait of Berthe Jacques* (Küsnacht, private collection), painted in 1898, Hodler used a very pronounced line and visible brushwork, which demonstrate a more advanced stylistic effort. In the years after 1904 he painted mostly portraits of Valentine Godé-Darel, employing from then on a more modern technique, made up of small dashes of colour. On the other hand, in 1884 Hodler had done a drawing of a melancholy sitter, the *Beautiful Augustine in Thought* (Bern, Kunstmuseum; *Ferdinand Hodler (1853–1918)*, 1983, no. 11), similar to the *Portrait of a Lady*. Moreover, the smiling young woman in the Rau collection painting could well be this same Augustine Dupin whom Hodler met in 1884 and who was his companion until 1908, when he met Valentine Godé-Darel. Augustine died the next year, and Hodler, moved by her suffering, painted her on her death-bed.
He did a portrait of Augustine (Zurich, Kunsthaus; *Ferdinand Hodler (1853–1918)*, 1983, no. 23) in 1887 which shows the massive, thick-featured face of a woman who is much older than the woman in the 1884 drawing and a long way from the *Portrait of a Lady*. Did she change so suddenly or is the sitter for the Rau painting a different woman? In this case, the casual clothing and largely decolleté, open blouse suggests it was a close friend. In any case the portrait must have been painted during the years 1884–1890.
These identification and dating problems in no way detract from the work's outstanding quality. A lack of ornamentation characterizes this portrait, which is painted exclusively in brown tones. It expresses the unity which Hodler spent his entire life trying to capture. The artist focused all his attention on the face, extraordinary in its sweetness, liveliness and spontaneity, which enhances the almost uniform background.
Ph. L.

*85

Gustav Klimt (1862–1918)
Old Woman, 1909

Oil on canvas.
H: 95.3 cm; W: 47 cm.
Signed lower right:
Gustav / Klimt.
GR 1.532

History:
Collection of US architect Frank Lloyd Wright; London, Piccadilly Gallery, 1974; Paris, Félix Landau's collection, 1983.

Exhibition:
Zurich, Kunsthaus, *Gustav Klimt*, 1992.

Bibliography:
F. Novotny and J. Dobai, *Gustav Klimt*, Salzbourg, 1967, no. 162, repr. p. 346; *Tout l'œuvre peint de Gustav Klimt*, Paris, 1983, no. 148.

Gustav Klimt (Vienna, 1862 – Vienna, 1918) trained at the School of Decorative Arts in Vienna with Ferdinand Laufberger and J. Berger. His earliest works were ceiling decorations and theatre curtains (Karlsbad, Reichenberg, Bucharest and the Burgtheater in Vienna). In 1890 he painted the pendentives of the great staircase of the Kunsthistorisches Museum in Vienna. He was one of the principal representatives of Jugendstil, Austrian Art Nouveau, before taking an active part in the creation of the Vienna Secession, of which he was the first president from 1897 to 1905. In 1898 he took part in the Symbolist review Ver Sacrum, *and in 1900 exhibited in Paris, where he won a prize at the World's Fair.*

Novotny and Dobai indicate that Gustav Klimt dedicated a drawing similar to this picture to Madame Gustav Nebehay (*Gustav Klimt, 40 auserwählte Zeichnungen*, 1960, no. 30, repr.). The subject chosen by Klimt, an old woman whose face with closed eyes appears in a huge black veil, is not unusual in his work. Around 1907–1908 Klimt painted the *Kiss* (Vienna, Österreichische Galerie) and *Hope* (Vienna, private collection), two elongated, vertical compositions which, among many others, show people of whom only the face is treated in a figurative manner, the body being merely a pretext for the arrangement of geometrical decorative motifs.
The Rau picture was painted around 1909, when Klimt temporarily abandoned the decorative style which was familiar to him. Nebehay defined this phase his "sombre period". At the time, Klimt painted several pictures whose brown and black tones accentuate their tragic character, achieved by an austere technique full of reserve and emotion. The *Old Woman* could only be an old woman, but the composition as well as the figure's pose accentuate the model's contemplative look and self-effacing, time-worn face.
The pyramidal composition frequently found in Klimt's paintings gives a certain majesty to this early twentieth-century *Virgin Mary*. Her age and apparent slumber evoke death, a theme dear to late nineteenth-century Symbolist painters, such as Ferdinand Hodler and the German Expressionists. Soon afterwards, Klimt's austere search culminated in a painting, now in a private collection, exhibited in 1910 at the 9th Venice Biennial under the title *The Family* (*Tout l'œuvre peint*, 1983, no. 149). The composition depicts a mother and her two children, their faces surrounded by sombre draperies, their eyes closed.
Here Klimt is similar to Egon Schiele, who certainly drew inspiration from these two works to paint the *Dead Mother* (1910). He did not pursue this attempt at Expressionism any further. From 1910 he painted gayer themes again, such as the *Hat Decorated with Roses* of 1910, or meditative allegories, such as *Life and Death* (circa 1908–1911), with a more decorative style.
Ph. L.

GUSTAV
KLIMT

86

Paul Sérusier (1863–1927)
Spring at Pouldu, 1890

Oil on canvas.
H: 54 cm; W: 65 cm.
Signed and dated lower right:
P. Sér. 90.
GR 1.17

History:
Galerie Druet, no. 3488;
former Leplant's collection.

Exhibition:
Paris, Musée du Grand Palais,
Les Indépendants à la Belle Epoque, 1895–1901, 1966.

Bibliography:
M. Guicheteau and P. H. Boutaric, *La vie et l'œuvre de Paul Sérusier*, 1976, no. 14, repr.

Paul Sérusier (Paris, 1863 – Morlaix, 1927) distinguished himself at the 1887 Salon with a work that was significantly influenced by Naturalism. His encounter with Gauguin in Pont-Aven the following year was decisive. Back at the Académie Julian, where he was in charge of collecting student's fees and providing for the studio's needs, Sérusier spread the ideas of synthetism and helped found the Nabi group, becoming the movement's main theorist. In 1891, he took part in the group's first exhibition at Le Barc de Boutteville's. In 1893 he began decorating the Théâtre Libre and Lugné-Poe's Théâtre de l'Œuvre. He travelled to Italy several times with Emile Bernard and Maurice Denis, and moved towards allegorical and religious subjects discovered at the art school in Beuvron. His theosophical leanings were buttressed by a desire to spread the ideas of Father Didier Lenz. In 1908 he began teaching at the Académie Ranson and writing the ABC de la peinture, *an essential theoretical work published in 1921. In 1914, he went into almost total seclusion in Châteauneuf-du-Faou in Brittany, where he lived with a former student whom he had married.*

In June 1890, Paul Sérusier went to Brittany for the third time. In 1888, he had met Gauguin in Pont-Aven and painted the famous *Talisman*. In October 1889 he joined Gauguin in Le Pouldu, to which the latter had fled from Pont-Aven, a crowded resort. At the time, Le Pouldu was isolated, proffering the image of a rural, idyllic Brittany evoked by Pierre Loti in his novels. During the summer of 1890, Sérusier joined a small group of artists in Marie Poupée's inn that included Gauguin, Meyer de Haan, Laval and Filiger.
He discovered Le Pouldu's landscapes of vast fields and rolling hills, offering obvious subjects to artists using synthetist methods. Gauguin's influence on Sérusier, who painted this work at the beginning of his stay, was essential. The works by Gauguin that had been exhibited at the café Volpini in 1889 made a powerful impression on the artist. Gauguin's style won him over, and the same year he wrote to Maurice from Le Pouldu, "I am living between Gauguin and de Haan [...] I am not working much but learning a great deal; my drawing especially is changing. The colours are more subdued because of a more divided, enriching handling of tone."
Sérusier was always trying to redefine nature's role in his painting. He expressed his feelings, drawing an outdoor sketch before painting in the studio. He chose his subject from the countryside surrounding Le Pouldu, recreating a landscape by synthesizing shapes in order to meet the decorative needs of the whole. He simplified the vegetation and shadows on the ground, establishing an intelligent relationship between the flat colours and the perspective obtained by aligning the trees and painting a darker background. These relationships introduce a feeling of strangeness, while the presence of a Breton figure accentuates the landscape's tranquil atmosphere, adding a somewhat melancholic note. Sérusier assimilated Gauguin's technique, using small, even strokes. However, he chose a more limited range of pigments and strove for the measured exaltation of subdued tones to attenuate his colours' brightness. The artist was still under Gauguin's influence, but kept his own sensibility, introducing a certain moderation and a more even design.
Ch. D.

87

Félix Vallotton (1865–1925)

Max Rodrigues-Henriques in the Studio of His Stepfather, Félix Vallotton, 1900

Oil on parquet.
H: 51 cm; W: 69 cm.
Signed and dated lower right;
F. Vallotton 1900.
GR 1.570

History:
Max Rodrigues-Henriques; Paris, Galerie Jacques Rodrigues-Henriques; Switzerland, private collection, May 1, 1973; Zurich, Mme Marianne Feilchenfeldt, September 5, 1973.

Exhibitions:
Zurich, Kunsthaus, *Félix Vallotton*, 1938, no. 46, pl. VII; New York, Palais de La France, *Exposition internationale*, 1939; Vienna, Institut français, *Nabis*, 1949; Bern, Kunsthalle, *Die Maler der Revue Blanche*, 1951, no. 134 (wrongly titled *André Rodrigues*); Paris, Musée National d'Art Moderne, *Félix Vallotton*, 1955, ill. 174, pl. 69; Winterthur-Bremen-Düsseldorf-Paris, Musée du Petit Palais, *Félix Vallotton*, 1978–1979, no. 46, fig. 32; Lausanne, Musée Cantonal des Beaux-Arts, *De Vallotton à Dubuffet: une collection en mouvement*, 1996–1997.

Bibliography:
Ch. Fegdal, *Félix Vallotton*, 1931, pl. 14; Marina Ducrey and the artist's heirs, *Catalogue raisonné de l'œuvre de Félix Vallotton*, being prepared.

Félix Vallotton (Lausanne, 1865 – Paris, 1925) arrived in Paris from Switzerland at the age of seventeen. He lived off sales of his early drawings and did a few portraits, chiefly woodcuts. He gradually made a name for himself through his illustrations for various magazines, including the famous Revue Blanche. *His friend Edouard Vuillard introduced him into the Nabis group, whose members at the time included Paul Sérusier, Maurice Denis, Pierre Bonnard and Emile Bernard. He was interested in their pursuits, and participated in their Paris exhibitions, starting in 1893 at Le Barc de Bouteville's; then in 1894, at the Paris offices of* La Dépêche de Toulouse; *in 1897–1898, at Ambroise Vollard's; and in 1899, at Paul Durand-Ruel's. After coming into contact with this group, his style became more flexible and asserted itself chiefly in his landscape paintings.*

Félix Vallotton traded his bohemian lifestyle for a bourgeois one when he married Gabrielle Rodrigues-Henriques in Paris in 1900. His wife had three children from a former marriage, and her fortune enabled the artist to lead a certain lifestyle. The painter left the Latin Quarter in June, moving into an apartment building at 6 Rue de Milan, near the Gare Saint-Lazare. The upper floor was reserved for his studio.
The works depicting his everyday life that he painted until 1904 attest to the stability and equilibrium the marriage brought him. Indoor scenes became more important than landscapes, which had been his favourite subjects. His literary talent also developed. He gradually gave up newspaper and magazine criticism (including for *La Gazette de Lausanne*) to devote himself entirely to writing novels (*La vie meurtrière*, *Les soupirs de Cyprien Morus*) and plays (*Un rien*, *L'homme fort*). This interest in letters led him to maintain steady relationships with figures in Paris literary circles, such as Stéphane Mallarmé, Octave Mirbeau, Jules Renard, Félix Fénéon, and Max Rodrigues-Henriques (1884–1927), his wife's oldest son, shown in this painting seated in front of an easel, painting a landscape.
Félix Vallotton portrayed the modest room that served as his studio. Its only decoration was a fireplace, a big Mediterranean rug and paintings on the walls. Several plastic elements echo each other in this composition, including the palette to the right of the fireplace – symbol of the painter – and the box of paints on the floor, the easel in the centre and its reflection on the left; and the partly opened room and closet doors. A matching pair of Veronese green lampshades add an especially lively touch. Vallotton's two favourite genres, the interior scene and the landscape, appear in the same painting, which is organized in bundles. The rug, painting, doorframe and mantelpiece concentrate space.
This work's precise organization of pictorial space makes it particularly representative of Félix Vallotton's technique during this period, when he was breaking with the Nabis movement. The artist used a smooth line to convey volumes with a new emphasis.
F. K.

F. VALLOTTON

88

Pierre Bonnard (1867–1947)
Saint-Tropez Bay, 1914

Oil on canvas.
H: 46.5 cm; W: 54 cm.
Signed lower right: *Bonnard*.
GR 1.36

History:
Paris, Bernheim-Jeune; Paris, Bernard Dorival; L.-G. Braathon; London, Sotheby's, December 5, 1962, no. 140; Zurich, Marianne Feilchenfeldt, 1968.

Exhibitions:
Marseille, Hôtel de la Région – Paris, Musée du Luxembourg – Lisbon, Fundação Arpad Szanes Viera da Silva, *Peintres de la couleur en Provence 1875–1920*, 1995–1996, repr. p. 261; Florence, Palazzo Corsini, *Bonnard, Vuillard, Denis, Vallotton... I Nabis alle origini dell'arte moderna*, 1998; Montreal, Musée des Beaux-Arts, *Le temps des Nabis*, 1998.

Bibliography:
J. Dauberville and H. Dauberville, *Bonnard. Catalogue de l'œuvre peint*, Paris, 1965, vol. II, no. 791, repr.

Pierre Bonnard (Fontenay-aux-Roses, 1867 – Le Cannet, 1947) studied law before entering the Ecole des Beaux-Arts in 1887. However, the Académie Julian is where he met Maurice Denis, Sérusier and Ranson, with whom he formed the Nabis group.
Very early on, Bonnard displayed a predilection for intimate, decorative scenes and lithography. After 1900, he made frequent trips to Vernon, in the Seine valley, where he met Monet, who lived in nearby Giverny. From 1914 to the post-war years, the painter went through a period of crisis and uncertainty. Bonnard travelled to southern France increasingly often, eventually settling in Le Cannet, where he purchased a house in 1925. That is where he painted remarkably complex, rich works until the end of his life.

In June 1909, Bonnard stayed at Saint-Tropez for the first time. He was deeply impressed by the legendary light of southern France, comparing it to something out of the *Thousand and One Nights*. Afterwards he went to the Côte d'Azur nearly every year, buying a villa there in 1925. During the winter of 1914 the artist rented the Villa Joséphine at Saint-Tropez, where he painted this view of the bay.
Bonnard began moving away from the Nabis aesthetic around 1900, setting out in his own direction and eventually returning to the use of bright colours around 1911. The Rau collection work is an example of the colourful, lavish landscapes the artist painted during this period. In the foreground, the dense vegetation's blend of warm hues contrasts with the cold tones of the sea, sky and trees. Bonnard's painstaking technique accentuates the foreground's richness, while the briskly painted background evokes the fluidity of the sea and sky. In 1914 Bonnard, attempting to order light in his works, arrived at a pictorial synthesis by combining a new construction of space with the harmony of powerful colours. In *Saint-Tropez Bay*, mauve and emerald green smooth the transition from orange-yellow to blue. In his search for balance, the artist reintroduced depth and perspective into this painting, which is composed of broad horizontal bands that a grove of pine trees in the centre provides with a sense of rhythm.
Bonnard closely followed the development of Cubism after the First World War, reconsidering the very meaning of his art and moving beyond the precepts of Impressionism in his handling of space. At the same time, his tones achieved a rare intensity.
Ch. D.

89

Pierre Bonnard (1867–1947)
Window Opened at Uriage

Oil on canvas.
H: 75 cm; W: 40 cm.
Signed towards the lower left: *Bonnard*.
GR 1.507

History:
Bought from Bonnard by a collector; Dr Emilio Jesi's collection; Geneva, Galerie Motte, 1971.

Exhibitions:
Mulhouse, *Bonnard*, 1951; London, Lefevre Gallery, 1954, no. 1; Turin, Galleria d'Arte Moderna, *La pittura straniera nelle collezioni italiane*, 1961, pl. 13; London, Royal Academy of Arts, *Pierre Bonnard*, 1966, no. 136, repr.; Munich, *Pierre Bonnard*, 1966–1967, no. 80, repr.; Paris, Musée de l'Orangerie, *Pierre Bonnard*, 1967, no. 86, repr.

Bibliography:
R. Huyghe, *Les contemporains*, Paris, 1949, pl. 9; G. Besson, *Bonnard*, no. 31, repr.; M. Vincent, *Catalogue du Musée de Lyon*, vol. VII, *La peinture des XIXe et XXe siècles*, 1956, p. 260; G. Melchiori, *La pittura straniera nelle collezioni italiane*, 1960; A. Vaillant, "Les plus beaux tableaux de Pierre Bonnard", in *Les Nouvelles Littéraires*, 12 January 1967, p. 8; J. Dauberville and H. Dauberville, *Bonnard. Catalogue de l'œuvre peint*, Paris, 1968, vol. II, no. 947, repr.

Pierre Bonnard spent the summer of 1918 at Uriage in the Isère, near the house where he had lived during part of his childhood. In 1913, the painter began introducing geometric shapes into his compositions with the aim of mastering increasingly intense colours. The open window motif enabled him to redefine a limited space and to introduce interacting lines and orthogonal planes. Following the example of Matisse who, in 1905 in Collioure, had chosen an open widow as the main motif of his painting, Bonnard was interested in the encounter between indoor and outdoor spaces.
In this painting, the window opens out onto a nearby, probably familiar landscape. The eye lands on the classical order of a facade surmounted by a triangular pediment. On either side of the building, tall trees capture the light. Below, a few briskly-painted silhouettes are the only human forms that appear. The artist structured his painting by using the window's architecture. The vertical lines underscore the wide, flat swaths of colour, whereas the horizontal line of the balcony creates a sense of depth towards the outside. Bonnard used the relationship between bold tones to contrast two qualities of light. He exalted the landscape's harsh brightness with strong greens and violets, whereas the softer harmonies of pinks and oranges create a bright, iridescent effect inside. Bonnard juxtaposed two separate spaces, as if he wanted to signify the duality of two worlds. Nevertheless, everything, right down to the thinned-out paint on the canvas, seems to suggest the fluidity of air in this motionless place.
Among the different versions on this theme, the painting in the Rau collection marks a turning point in Bonnard's work. The *aplais* of the tapestry and window form abstract elements that can be found in contemporary works by Matisse. This stylistic kinship indicates that the two artists shared similar concerns in response to the development of Cubism and the new experimentation with abstraction. Bonnard subsequently moved towards a more personal style, seeking to express the dissolution of objects in their environment with increasingly intense tones.
Ch. D.

Bonnard

***90**

Edouard Vuillard (1868–1940)
Self-portrait, 1889

Oil on canvas.
H: 28.6 cm; W: 25.1 cm.
Studio stamp, lower right: *Lugt 2497a*; dated on back: *89*.
GR 1.997

History:
Artist's collection; Paris, Galerie Rousso, 1973; Lausanne, Galerie Paul Vallotton; Switzerland, private collection; London, Christie's, December 4, 1990, no. 265.

Exhibition:
Lausanne, Galerie Paul Vallotton, *Hommage à Edouard Vuillard*, November 30, 1978 – February 3, 1979, no. 8, repr.

Bibliography:
A. Salomon, *Edouard Vuillard. Catalogue raisonné de l'œuvre peint*, being prepared.

Edouard Vuillard (Cuiseaux, 1868 – La Baule, 1940) led a calm, quiet life. In 1877 his family moved to Paris, where the young Edouard's parents enrolled him in a Marist school. His father died when he was fourteen, and Edouard was brought up by his mother. Vuillard was very close to this understanding, extraordinary woman and lived with her until she died.
He studied painting at the studio of Diogène Maillart before enrolling in the Académie Julian (Robert Fleury's studio) in 1886, where Maurice Denis, Bonnard, Roussel, Sérusier and Ibels formed the Nabis group. In 1887, Vuillard was admitted, after three failed attempts, to the Ecole des Beaux-Arts, where he joined the studio of the academic painter Jean Léon Gêrome. But he stayed only six weeks, preferring to sketch the works of Chardin, Vermeer, Rembrandt, Leonardo da Vinci, Titian, Raphael, Poussin and Le Sueur at the Louvre. Most of his paintings were still lives and self-portraits.
A friend of Maurice Denis's and Ker Xavier Roussel's future brother-in-law, Vuillard met Bonnard and Sérusier and took part in Nabis meetings. In 1891, he met Thadée Natanson, founder of the Revue Blanche, *to which he actively contributed. Vuillard followed the Nabis' tenets until 1900, producing posters, playbills (starting in 1890), decorative panels, easel paintings and prints. Enriched by these various decorative experiences, he created his own technique, simultaneously using oil, gouache and tempera, which gave his works the mat, refreshing quality of frescoes.*
At the same time, Vuillard travelled to the main cities of Europe, often brought by fellow painters and patrons, to visit museums. He painted interior scenes, drawing his subject matter from the people closest to him. In the early twentieth century, his style became more realistic. Success and honours were showered upon him. He exhibited regularly and, defended by several art dealers and patrons including Durand-Ruel, Vollard and Bernheim-Jeune, became a member of the Institut de France in 1937. A self-effacing man, Vuillard was reluctant to exhibit and sell his works and eschewed publicity all his life. "Silence keeps me," he often said.
His journal, which he kept from 1888 to 1940, is an invaluable source of information about his life and work.
F. K.

Vuillard was always interested in painting self-portraits. Like many artists from the eighteenth century on, he turned the self-portrait into a demonstration of style by pushing a telling image of his character to the forefront.
This is the most striking self-portrait of the many he painted during his youth, between 1888 and 1890. The twenty-eight year-old artist has depicted himself frontally with an apparent simplicity. He is staring intensely and wearing the wild beard that earned him the nickname "Zouave".
Unlike other self-portraits from the same period, here Vuillard imposes his image on the viewer in a face-to-face confrontation. However, this early work, where candour and discretion are mixed, does have something in common with other early self-portraits. The shy, withdrawn man does not let the least amount of emotion show.
This work, which is dated 1889, was painted during a period when Vuillard was inspired by old masters and Fantin-Latour, handling his subjects with grey tones. The dark blue suit matches the grey-blue background and the reddish-blond of the beard. The whole is handled as a great mass. The lighter-toned collar makes the face stand out from the suit. It is the only thing that gives a bit of relief to the whole. The painter used a special technique. In his search for an almost casual, unfinished, diaphanous effect in the background and suit, he has let the canvas show through. He has made the figure impalpable, focusing all attention on his penetrating look.
Vuillard used this process several times in his self-portraits, as in his *Self-portrait with Waroqui* (New York, Metropolitan Museum of Art), but introduces a different

meaning to the image here. The painter managed to give an immediate image of an absent man by using these devices, which could be defined as "modern" trademarks. The Nabis self-portraits from 1892 reveal the same frankness, but different methods, such as flat, harsh colours, are used. This portrait was painted at a time when the artist was still pondering the future of his art. Its hieratic quality and seriousness bring to mind the late Tintoretto self-portrait (Paris, Musée du Louvre).

This powerful image loaded with symbols thus fits into a long pictorial tradition, constituting one of the artist's exemplary early works.

Ch. D.

91

Edouard Vuillard (1868–1940)
The Chestnut Trees, Rue Truffaut, circa 1900

Oil on cardboard.
H: 42 cm; W: 36 cm.
Signed lower left: *E. Vuillard*.
GR 1.128

History:
Studio; Paris, Georges Maratier; Zurich, Mrs. Marianne Feilchenfeldt.

Exhibitions:
London, Malborough Fine Art, *Roussel, Bonnard, Vuillard*, May 5 – June 12, 1954, no. 64; Zurich, Kunsthaus, *Vuillard: Gemälde, Pastelle, Aquarelle, Zeichnungen, Druckgraphik*, September 17 – October 25, 1964, no. 148.

Bibliography:
A. Salomon, *Edouard Vuillard. Catalogue raisonné de l'œuvre peint*, being prepared.

In March 1899, Vuillard and his mother moved into 28 Rue Truffaut in the seventeenth arrondissement in Paris, where they would live until 1904. The painter extended his subject range by exploring his immediate surroundings. He used an atmospheric pictorial style, drawing some of his inspiration from urban landscapes, especially for his views of public gardens, a theme he would develop in a series of decorative panels commissioned in 1894 by the Natansons. The view from his Rue Truffaut studio does not have the same monumental character, but is a sketch of an everyday landscape.

The Rau collection painting is categorized among the series of Paris views, but its small size appears more like an originally designed landscape. The site is seen slightly from above, and the trees stand out against the building's facade. Relief is abolished. The foreground's void is the only thing that introduces a bit of depth into the composition. This method of handling space brings to mind some of the Nabis' works, where the influence of Japanese prints was essential. Vuillard sought deep, unexpected effects to recreate the site's atmosphere. The light on the facade in the background contrasts with the subdued tones of the green masses. The use of a multitude of greens of varying densities and shapes creates a harmony into which the cardboard's neutral background is perfectly integrated. The artist's preference for this material takes on special interest here. The oil paint he used on the unprepared surface makes infinite variations in the values' nuances and modulations possible. He obtained a dull, flat look that is close to glue painting and closely bonds with the cardboard. It gives the works tones a "surprising subdued resonance" (Chastel, 1946).

This work was painted around 1900, a turning point when Vuillard was moving towards new pictorial experiments. Its simplicity and decorative character make it clearly similar to great compositions such as the *First Fruits* (Pasadena, The Norton Simon Foundation), which was painted for Thadée Natanson in 1899. Furthermore, the flowering chestnut tree motif can be found several times in his major decorative works, such as the public gardens series and the 1895 stained glass project, but with a clear desire to stylize forms.

However, the freedom of execution shown here by Vuillard recalls how comfortable he felt in his everyday world. As in his indoor scenes, he penetrates the intimacy of a silent place.

Ch. D.

E. Vuillard

92

Edouard Vuillard (1868–1940)
Self-portrait, 1906

Oil on panel.
H: 41 cm; W: 32.5 cm.
Signed in red, lower right:
E. Vuillard.
GR 1.1021

History:
Artist's collection; New York, Sam Salz; New York, Donald S. and Jean Stralem.

Exhibitions:
Richmond, Virginia Museum of Fine Arts, *Paintings by the Impressionists and Post-Impressionists*, 1950; New York, MoMA – Cleveland Museum of Art, *Edouard Vuillard*, 1954, p. 103; Minneapolis Institute of Arts, *The Nabis and Their Circle*, 1962; New York, Wildenstein & Co. Inc, *Vuillard*, 1964, no. 32; Houston, Sakowitz, *Festival of the Arts*, 1965, no. 57; New York, Parke-Bernet Galleries, *Art Treasures Exhibition*, 1967; Philadelphia, The Pennsylvania State University, College of Arts and Architecture, *Edouard Vuillard 1868–1940. Centennial Exhibition*, 1968, no. 21; Toronto, Art Gallery of Ontario – San Francisco, Palace of the Legion of Honor – Chicago, Art Institute of Chicago, *Edouard Vuillard 1868–1940*, 1971–1972, no. 57, repr. p. 231; New York, Metropolitan Museum of Art, 1990; Lyon, Musée des Beaux-Arts – Barcelona, Fundació Caixa de Pensions – Nantes, Musée des Beaux-Arts, *Edouard Vuillard*, 1990–1991, p. 14, no. 101.

Bibliography:
Life Magazine, vol. XXXVII, no. 18, November 1, 1954, p. 74, repr.; S. Preston, *Edouard Vuillard*, New York, 1971, p. 120, repr. p. 121; A. Dumas and G. Cogeval, *Vuillard*, Paris, 1990, no. 101, p. 221, repr. p. 14.

During the last twenty years of his life, Vuillard was beset by dissatisfaction, doubt and disappointment. In the portraits, which accounted for a major share of his work during this period, he set new challenges for himself. He became the most highly sought-after portrait painter of the upper bourgeoisie, keeping pace with a relentless flow of commissions. Vuillard depicted the model as well as his or her environment, giving as much importance to the background as to the figure. The search for a certain kind of truth was crucial to him, and he believed that the surrounding space revealed as much about the sitter as anything else. "I don't do portraits; I paint people in their homes," he was fond of saying.
This *Self-portrait* depicts Vuillard at home in his studio, where he lived surrounded by many memories. Seated in a red velvet armchair, the liveliness of his penetrating, intense gaze is underscored by the warm, voluptuous chromatic palette of ochre, red and saffron tones. Here, the purpose of the self-portrait is not to show off the individual or his ego. On the contrary, the figure is discreet and self-effacing. It is therefore obvious that the topic is painting and its effects. Vuillard painted another self-portrait in 1912 (Zurich, Bührle Foundation). The composition is similar but the cold green chromatic scheme is completely different. The precisely-drawn face reveals a smooth pate – the painter was practically bald by the time he was thirty-five – and a bright red beard that earned him the nickname "Zouave". The window behind him lets in sunlight that illuminates his forehead, while on the right-hand side the juxtaposed brushstrokes do not reveal the exact outlines of the room's features. This part of the painting, which is almost non-figurative, may be an allusion to the artist's association with the Nabis, who sometimes pushed painting to the limits of abstraction. Despite the subject's nearness, there is a strong sense of depth and volume.
Vuillard developed a new conception of space, light and colour, and the work radiates a sense of calm and mystery. He did not paint portraits across from the model, but worked from memory. This *Self-portrait* is probably no exception. The most important thing was to reconstitute a memory, a timeless perception where past and present merge.
A patient, observant artist, Vuillard thought long and hard about his works in the silence of his studio before actually painting them. They depict "the ordinary and motionless existence of inner life" that Maeterlinck spoke about. Vuillard was part of a long European portrait tradition dating back to the seventeenth and eighteenth centuries, and his admiration for self-portraits by Rembrandt and seventeenth-century Dutch painters is well-known. Those masters were continuously reflecting upon their art, and Vuillard was probably consciously following their example. Driven by the desire to express all of his visual sensations, Vuillard perfectly illustrated a comment by his friend Mallarmé, who said, "I have never proceeded by anything but allusions."
F. K.

93

Edouard Vuillard (1868–1940)
Portrait of Monsieur André Bénac, 1936

Tempera on canvas.
H: 129.5 cm; W: 152.2 cm.
Signed and dated lower left:
E. Vuillard 1936.
GR 1.601

History:
Paris, Andre Bénac; Paris, Mrs. Candrelier-Bénac; Paris, Jacques Candrelier-Bénac; London, Christie's, July 3, 1979, no. 61.

Exhibitions:
Paris, Musée des Arts Décoratifs, *E. Vuillard*, May–July 1938, no. 212; Geneva, Palexpo, *La Fondation pour l'écrit. Salon international du livre et de la presse. Le livre et la presse dans la peinture*, 1996; Florence, Palazzo Corsini, *Bonnard, Vuillard, Denis, Vallotton... I Nabis alle origini dell'arte moderna*, 1998; Montreal, Musée des Beaux-Arts, *Le temps des Nabis*, 1998.

Bibliography:
W. George, "Vuillard et l'âge heureux", in *L'Art vivant*, no. 221, May 1938, p. 27, repr.; B. Dorival, *Les étapes de la peinture française contemporaine*, Paris, 1943, vol. II, p. 167; J. Salomon, *Vuillard, témoignage*, Paris, 1945, p. 122; C. Roger-Marx, *Vuillard et son temps*, Paris, 1945, pp. 107–108; C. Roger-Marx, "Vuillard, peintre de la vieillesse", in *L'Amour de l'art*, no. 6, November 1945, p. 152; C. Roger-Marx, *Vuillard*, Paris, 1948, p. 20; J. Salomon, *Vuillard admiré*, Paris, 1961, p. 182, repr.; A. Salomon, *Edouard Vuillard. Catalogue raisonné de l'œuvre peint*, being prepared.

In 1915, Vuillard started painting large portraits as commissions for the Paris high bourgeoisie. All of these late works, which are characterized by a painstaking realism, were often harshly judged in relation to his earlier paintings. The 1936 *Portrait of Monsieur André Bénac* illustrates what C. Roger-Marx called the "social nightmare", offering a reassuring view of an unadventurous society.

Mr. Bénac, a former member of the Council of State, an officer in the Legion of Honor, had himself immortalized in the familiar world of his office. Pointing out the seventy-eight year-old figure's friendly good-naturedness, C. Roger-Marx wrote, "There is goodness, clear-sightedness and something rather touching in those blinking little eyes, in those jowls, in the fat hand gently laid on the edge of the desk" (1945, pp. 107–108).

Vuillard was fond of portraying his models in their everyday setting. "I don't do portraits, I paint people in their homes," he told Maurice Denis in 1876, in keeping with the theories Duranty espoused in his manifesto, *La Nouvelle Peinture* in 1876. The over-abundant details and realistic depiction of the crowd of objects cluttering the desk in the foreground are striking. Eyeglasses, pens, an inkwell, magnifying glass, calender, telephone are randomly juxtaposed and, in a humorous touch, a popular comic book appears in this punctilious inventory of objects. The figure is set back in the middleground, integrated into his setting. In a different version of the portrait, the artist has tightened the frame around the model, eliminating all the picturesque details that distract the eye. He likewise dispensed with the window in order to obtain a closed space and focus attention on the elderly gentleman (London, sale at Sotheby's, April 7, 1976).

As usual, in the Rau collection painting Vuillard demonstrates great skill in structuring space by using a traditional perspective featuring several planes. An inventive opening to the outside allows a gentle winter light to bathe the entire room. "Here light illuminates the smallest details of the clothes, the slightest elements of a still life where purple abounds," adds C. Roger-Marx (1945, p. 107). The painter uses subtle reflections on the table, magnifying glass and richly carved Renaissance cabinet, juxtaposed with a myriad of colour touches. The glue paint technique, which was one of the artist's favourites, catches the light and confers the maturity of a fresco on his work.

Vuillard was attached to traditional concerns such as an interest in detail. He painted a completely classical work which has sometimes been labelled academic. This return to classicism illustrates the cultural context between the wars, which was characterized by a revival of order and the desire for formal stability. In 1938, the painting was among a splendid group of commissioned portraits presented at the Musée des Arts Décoratifs retrospective, which revealed Vuillard's late style.

C. Roger-Marx wondered about the value of this last period. He made a remarkable judgement that today has taken on its full meaning: "Instead of condemning such a body of work as a whole, it must be realized that with time the fuss will die down and the unity be redone" (1945, p. 108).

Ch. D.

94

Maurice Denis (1870–1943)
July, 1892

Oil on canvas.
H: 38 cm; W: 61 cm.
Signed and dated lower right:
MAVD 92.
GR 1.599

History:
Sold by the artist to Ambroise Vollard, 1892; Dr Ducroquet's collection; London, Christie's, November 28, 1972, no. 116.

Exhibitions:
Paris, Indépendants, 1892; Paris, Orangerie, *Maurice Denis*, 1970, no. 45; Lyon, Musée des Beaux-Arts – Cologne, Wallraf-Richartz-Museum – Liverpool, Walker Art Gallery – Amsterdam, Rijksmuseum Vincent van Gogh, *Maurice Denis*, 1994–1995, no. 33; Lausanne, Musée Cantonal des Beaux-Arts, *De Vallotton à Dubuffet: une collection en mouvement*, 1996–1997; Florence, Palazzo Corsini, *Bonnard, Vuillard, Denis, Vallotton… I Nabis alle origini dell'arte moderna*, 1998; Montreal, Musée des Beaux-Arts, *Le temps des Nabis*, 1998.

Bibliography:
G. Cogeval, "Le sacre du quotidien", in *Connaissance des arts*, October 1994, p. 95.

In 1888, Maurice Denis (Granville, 1870 – Paris, 1943) entered the Académie Julian, where he met Bonnard, Vuillard and Sérusier. The following year they formed the Nabi group. The "Nabi aux belles icônes" soon became the movement's theoretician. In 1890, he published the group's first manifesto. In 1893, he married Marthe Meunier, who was to become omnipresent in his work. Denis travelled several times to Italy, where he discovered the Italian primitives. He was a mystical artist who attempted to revive religious painting. In 1919, he founded the Ateliers d'Art Sacré with Georges Desvallières. He devoted a large share of his work to decoration, but was also a highly talented illustrator and a prolific author.

July was exhibited at the 1892 Salon des Indépendants with *April*, *September* and *October* under the title *Four Panels for the Decoration of a Young Girl's Bedroom*. The four paintings were designed as a cycle of the seasons in which *July* represents summer but winter is absent. In 1893, Gustave Geffroy described the group as "delicate gaiety, slow dances, obsessional gestures, frail hands picking flowers, pale dresses, a dark park, the pink countryside" (*La Vie Artistique*, 2nd series, 1893, p. 372).
Maurice Denis gradually turned towards a new aesthetic. Abandoning Pointillism, the painter depicted female silhouettes in a purely imaginary ornamental landscape, where the vegetation forms wide bands of colour. As in *April*, to which the Rau collection painting seems to correspond, picking flowers is a pretext for a repetition of supple arabesques, such as the silhouette bending over near the tree that, like an emblematic figure, illustrated a poem by Verlaine ("Ecoutez la chanson bien douce") in *Sagesse* and reappears in an 1894 cartoon for a stained-glass window, *Women at the Creek* (Saint-Germain-en-Laye, Musée Départemental du Prieuré).
The work contains a few Japanese-inspired details, such as the sinuous elements derived from engravings by Harunobu and Utamaro and the centering on the tree, which is used as a repoussoir in a composition with an approximative perspective.
Denis abandoned traditional iconography for more personal symbols and principals. In 1892, he began making use of themes based on Symbolist and Medieval epic poetry. In *July*, he introduced the image of a woman in a paradisiacal garden where pale, nuanced tones underscore a dreamlike atmosphere. Although *July* was clearly an attack on the Nabis' principles, Denis had already developed a very personal style. The decorative cycle is part of a long pictorial tradition, but for Jean-Paul Bouillon the modernity of a work like *July* heralded, "with a similar sensibility", *Composition II* and the *Joy of Living* by Matisse.
Ch. D.

95

Maurice Denis (1870–1943)
Mother and Child on a Yellow Bed, 1896

Oil on wood.
H: 33 cm; W: 41 cm.
Signed and dated upper right: *MAVD 96*.
GR 1.825

History:
Sold by the artist to Ambroise Vollard (?); Kunsthaus Lempertz, 1969, no. 4287; London, Sotheby's, April 4, 1974, no. 217, repr.

Exhibitions:
Lyon, Musée des Beaux-Arts – Cologne, Wallraf-Richartz-Museum – Liverpool, Walker Art Gallery – Amsterdam, Rijksmuseum Vincent van Gogh, *Maurice Denis*, 1994–1995, no. 70; Lausanne, Musée Cantonal des Beaux-Arts, *De Vallotton à Dubuffet: une collection en mouvement*, 1996–1997.

The year 1895 marked a spiritual and formal turning point in the work of Maurice Denis. Grief-stricken by the death of his first child in February 1895, the artist became a devout Catholic. He began enriching his themes and renewing his sources of inspiration. He painted many scenes of mothers with new-born children and visits to women who had just given birth, conferring a sacred character to depictions of family life. In this painting, Denis shows motherly love with a composition based on a Virgin with child motif. Once more, the artist tried to surround the image of mother and child with a sacred aura.
During his first journey to Italy, he was struck by the beauty of the Primitives and Renaissance paintings. Back in France, he set to work translating the new aesthetic values discovered during his long journey, gradually moving away from Nabi principles. Denis re-introduced a sense of depth while keeping a few archaisms. For example, in this work the high ground and the perspective of the bed hark back to the *Quattrocento*'s experiments. Wearing an immaculate dress, the mother presents her child like the Saviour in a closed space without details. The chromatic saturation of the background creates a tension that lends the painting an unreal quality.
The birth of Denis's second child in 1896 revitalized his home life. Guided by a deep, mystical faith, he continued to exalt the ideal of the Christian family in his paintings.
Ch. D.

Fauvism

The 1905 Salon d'Automne saw the first appearance of Fauvism. When he saw the works produced by a group of young painters, the critic Louis Vauxcelles cried: "Here is Donatello in the wild beasts' cage!" The start of the movement goes back to the formative years of such artists as Matisse, Manguin, Camoin and Marquet, in Gustave Moreau's studio, at the Beaux-Arts in Paris. The students followed their master's example, by directing their pictorial experiments towards principles totally different from those of academic traditions. Although their style was resolutely far from that of the Impressionist, the discoveries they made regarding colour and light were to be fundamental. But above all, they were influenced by van Gogh, Gauguin and the Neo-Impressionists. This movement might be defined as a new method of expression based on the autonomy of colour in relation to the subject: the canvas is not a mirror of nature, but a surface which allows colour to totally express itself.
As for the subjects, they are limited to indoor scenes or rather ordinary landscapes. And so it was by means of pure colour, applied with broad, flattened strokes, that the inner space of a picture is constructed. One of the great precursors in this field and soon to become the leading light of the movement was Henri Matisse. Alongside him Fauvism links up such artists as Braque, de Vlaminck, Derain, van Dongen, and Dufy, but equally Russian artists like Kandinsky and Jawlensky. In the 1906 Salon d'Automne, the group met with a genuine success. Although Fauvism played a primordial part in the search for chromatic values – especially for the Expressionist artists – it must be said that the unity of the group was relatively ephemeral. Around 1908, the powerful upsurge of Cubism broke up the movement, whose members then went their separate ways.

96

Albert Marquet (1875–1947)
The Old Marseille Harbour, 1916

Oil on canvas.
H: 60 cm; W: 73 cm.
Signed lower right: *Marquet*.
GR 1.921

History:
London, Sotheby's,
December 2, 1984, no. 76.

Exhibitions:
Christiana, Norway, 1917, no. 84; Marseille, Hôtel de la Région – Paris, Musée du Luxembourg – Lisbon, Fundação Arpad Szenes Viera da Silva, *Peintres de la couleur en Provence 1875–1920*, 1995–1996, repr. p. 303.

Bibliography:
F. Jourdain, *Albert Marquet*, Paris, 1959, p. 76, repr.;
M. Latour and J. Boissieu, *Marseille et les peintres du XIXe siècle à nos jours*, 1990, p. 80, repr.

In 1890, Albert Marquet (Bordeaux, 1875 – Paris, 1947) enrolled in the Ecole des Arts Décoratifs, where he became friends with Matisse. Afterwards, he frequented Gustave Moreau's studio at the Paris Ecole des Beaux-Arts. He copied the old masters and discovered the Impressionists at Durand-Ruel's. In 1897, he painted his first landscapes in Arceuil and the Luxembourg Garden, and in 1900 he was admitted to the salon of the Société Nationale des Beaux-Arts. He exhibited at the Salon des Indépendants from 1901 on and at the Salon d'Automne in 1903, and in 1905 was involved in the Cage aux Fauves *scandal.*
Marquet was a passionate traveller, discovering Naples with Manguin in 1908 and joining Matisse in Tangiers in 1913. He married Marcelle Martinet during a trip to Algiers in 1923. He sought out harbours on his many trips in France and abroad, but in the meantime drew inspiration from the quays of the Seine in Paris. Marquet made a last trip to Switzerland in 1946 before dying the following year in Paris.

Marquet spent time in Marseille for the first time during the winter of 1915–1916. He was fond of the city's site and picturesque quality, spending most of 1916 there and regularly returning during the difficult war years. He painted almost nothing but views of the harbour from the rooms and studios where he lodged.
The Rau collection view was painted at the very beginning of 1916, undoubtedly from a window of the Hôtel Beauvau where he stayed for a while before renting the writer Eugène Montfort's studio on the Quai de Rive-Neuve. In her work on the artist's travels, Marcelle Marquet, his wife, wrote, "Marquet was in his element in Marseille." He was interested in the harbour's tumultuous life, the streets, the liveliness of the quays, walking around with his sketchbook in hand. "He recorded all the gestures and poses he saw with an accurate line. He delighted in finding himself in the middle of people." The spectacle of the street fascinated him, as the group of onlookers watching the loading and unloading of cargo testifies. However, in his panoramas of the old harbour the artist seemed more concerned with depicting space and modulating values than with anecdote.
More than any other, this view shows a "ruthless geometry and implacable rigour" (Sembat, 1975–1976). Marquet set up an elaborate schema for structuring space. He went about it by creating a series of foregrounds and backgrounds connected to each other by an interplay of horizontal and vertical lines, with the rectilinear outline of the transporter bridge echoing the boats' slender masts. In the upper part of the work, traces showing changes the artist made in the course of painting reveal that originally the picture's composition was more frontal. The use of the transporter bridge to simplify the structure indicates a real search for balance.
Marquet did not discover the light of southern France in Marseille, but rather strove to convey its luminous atmosphere on harsh days. The purity of his forms suggests distance. He used neutral, subdued tones to create delicate nuances in the values of the sky and water. The systematic exploration of the port, organization of space and immediacy of feelings are more important than the site's symbolism of travel and escape. Marquet provided a poetic, contemplative vision of this closed world.
Ch. D.

marquet

97

Maurice de Vlaminck (1876–1958)
Fauve Landscape near Chatou, 1907

Oil on canvas.
H: 50 cm; W: 65 cm.
Signed in black paint, lower left: *Vlaminck*.
GR 1.35

History:
Basel, Ernst Beyeler, 1968.

Exhibitions:
Basel, Galerie Beyeler, *Présence des maîtres*, June-September 1967, no. 53, repr. fig. 53; Ingelheim am Rhein, Altes Rathaus, *Die Explosion der Farbe, Fauvismus und Expressionismus 1905–1911*, 1998.

Since 1900, Maurice de Vlaminck (Paris, 1876 – Paris, 1958) and André Derain had been sharing a studio in Chatou. In his own way, each of them contributed to Fauvism's full blossoming in Paris. "Each one plants his easel," Vlaminck said, "Derain facing Chatou, the bridge, the bell tower, the motif; me further away, attracted by the poplars. Of course, I finished first. I look at Derain's work. Solid, intelligent, powerful, already Derain. 'What about you?,' he says to me. My canvas pivots at the end of my arm. Derain looks, remains silent for a moment, nods his head and finally utters: 'It's beautiful.'" "That was the beginning of the entire Fauvist movement", asserted de Vlaminck, who continued, "What is fauvism? It's me [...] my way of rebelling and freeing myself at the same time, of refusing the school and indoctrination. My blues, my reds, my yellows, my pure colours without mixing tones. I undoubtedly contaminated Derain a little" (quoted by J. Leymarie, Le Fauvisme, *Geneva, 1987, p. 29). De Vlaminck had discovered van Gogh's work when he saw a retrospective exhibition of the artist's work at the Galerie Bernheim-Jeune in Paris during the spring of 1901. He was impressed by the unusual technique, and started furiously spreading his paints on the canvas, casting aside the line of the drawing. Painting became his "release": I was a tender, violent barbarian. I instinctively conveyed, without method, a truth that was not artistic, but human" (ibid., p. 36).*

This *Fauve Landscape near Chatou* fits in with a series of landscapes painted in the Ile-de-France, such as the *Gardens at Chatou* of 1904 (Chicago, Art Institute of Chicago), *Banks of the Seine at Chatou* of 1904–1905 (Musée d'Art Moderne de la Ville de Paris) and *View of Chatou* of 1906 (Tel Aviv Museum). It was done on the banks of the Seine near Chatou about 1907. The artist mainly used the three primary colours, red, yellow and blue. The paste is thick, and the wide, fat strokes heighten the contrasts. De Vlaminck squashed the tube directly onto the canvas, spreading the pigments on with a knife.

A dual treatment emerges from this painting. On the one hand, the colour could be independent of the motif, as the trees in the foreground on the right demonstrate. With this arrangement the artist asserted a personal pictorial language, Fauvism, where colour governs space and light. On the other hand, the painter takes the opposite approach by letting the bare canvas show, for example in the line of the two houses, and appropriates it as a value. About one of his Ile-de-France landscapes, de Vlaminck wrote, "I set myself up in bright sunlight. The sky was blue, the wheat seemed to tremble and shake in the torrid heat, yellow with the full range of colours, quivering as they were about to suddenly catch on fire. Vermilion was the only colour that could render the dazzling red of the tiles on the hillside facing me. The orange of the earth, the harsh, bitter colours of the greenery and walls and the ultramarine and cobalt of the sky were excessively harmonious in a sensual, musical order. The series of colours on the canvas, with all their power and resonance, were the only things that could, in being orchestrated with each other, convey the colourful emotion of this landscape" (Leymarie, 1987, p. 68). From 1908 on, de Vlaminck increasingly let the web supporting the work show through, which enabled him to structure his compositions and emphasize volumes.
F. K.

98

Raoul Dufy (1877–1953)
The Beach at Sainte-Adresse

Oil on canvas.
H: 76 cm; W: 97 cm.
Signed lower right: *Raoul Dufy*.
GR 1.912

History:
Geneva, Galerie Max Moos; Paris, sale at Drouot's, November 24–25, 1924, no. 50, repr.; London, Sotheby's, June 30, 1981, no. 32, repr.

Exhibitions:
Los Angeles-New York-London, *The Fauve Landscape*, 1990, fig. 24 p. 227, repr.; Sydney, Art Gallery of the New South Wales – Melbourne, National Gallery of Victoria, *The Fauves*, 1995–1996, p. 130, no. 43; Martigny, Fondation Pierre Gianadda, *Raoul Dufy, séries et séries noires*, p. 25, no. 5; Ingelheim am Rheim, Altes Rathaus, *Die Explosion der Farbe, Fauvismus und Expressionismus 1905–1911*, 1998; Lyon, Musée des Beaux-Arts – Barcelona, Museu Picasso, *Rétrospective Raoul Dufy*, 1999.

Bibliography:
M. Laffaille and F. Guillon-Laffaille, *Raoul Dufy, catalogue raisonné de l'œuvre peint*, supplement, Paris, 1985, fig. 1828 p. 23.

Raoul Dufy (Le Havre, 1877 – Forcalquier, 1953) was the eldest son in a large, music-loving family. At the age of fourteen he started working at a coffee import firm in the port of Le Havre. In 1892 he registered at the Municipal School of Fine Arts and took classes with Charles Lhuillier, who had been Cabanel's student and a great admirer of Ingres. One of his classmates was Othon Friesz (1879–1949). After performing his military service in 1898–1899, he obtained an annual grant of 1,200 francs from his native city, enabling him to register at the Ecole Nationale des Beaux-Arts in Paris. In 1900 he met his friend Friesz at the studio of Léon Bonnat (1833–1922), and the two former classmates moved into an apartment together in Montmartre.
From 1901 Dufy took part in the Salon des Artistes Français, but he preferred exhibiting at the more innovative Salon des Indépendants (from 1903 to 1936) and Salon d'Automne (beginning in 1906). At the time, his painting was influenced by Claude Monet and Camille Pissarro, as his views of Paris and Normandy beaches demonstrate.
In 1905 the artist experienced a major revelation. At the Salon d'Automne he discovered the Cage aux Fauves *and Matisse's famous painting* Luxury, Calm and Voluptuousness. *This event marked the beginning of his Fauve period, characterized by bright colours. In 1908 it resulted in a technique similar to Cézanne's before leading, after a brief Cubist period, to a definitive style after the first world war. The artist's lively curiosity spurred him on to probe the various forms of art, which explains his abundant output of ceramics, fabrics, tapestries, lithographs, watercolours, book illustrations and ballet sets. The range of these works demonstrates the scope of his creativity.*

In 1906 Raoul Dufy returned to the Normandy coast, which he had already visited in 1902, 1903 and 1905, to spend the summer with Albert Marquet in Sainte-Adresse, whose beach he painted. Raoul Dufy and Albert Marquet were such close friends that they planted their easels side-by-side to paint the same subjects. Some of the views of Le Havre and Trouville are so similar that it is sometimes difficult to tell whether they were painted by one or the other.
Sainte-Adresse is a little seaside resort on the English Channel that had already been immortalized by Boudin, Monet, Jongkind and Friesz. Dufy was sensitive to the atmosphere there, which could be found only in Normandy, the cradle of Impressionism. He was impressed by the wet skies and shimmering light. The artist conveyed the ephemerality of a moment with a spontaneous drawing style and bright colours. He described his evolution himself: "Around 1905–1906, I was painting on the beach at Sainte-Adresse. Until then, I painted the beaches the way the Impressionists had done, and had reached the saturation point. I understood that using nature as my model would lead me to infinity, all the way to its twists and turns and smallest, most fleeting details. I remained outside the painting [...]. I set up my easel and started looking at my tubes of paint and my brushes. How, with that, could I manage to render not what I saw, but what is, what exists for me, my reality ? [...] From that day on, it was impossible for me to go back to my sterile battle with the elements that offered themselves to my sight."
The moment Raoul Dufy distanced himself from reality, his work was no longer an imitation of nature but the sensitive expression of the emotions he felt. The colours in the *Beach at Saint-Adresse* are no longer limited to the ones he actually saw. They have become autonomous in relation to the line, as the foreground demonstrates. Raymond Cogniat recalled, "one day he noticed that the sensation of shape is independent of the sensation of colour. A little girl wearing a red dress and playing on a green lawn leaves behind a trace, a sensation in red, when she moves." Dufy did not base his choice of colour range on a reality, but rather on the value of the tones that surrounded him. Therefore it was not the lifelikeness of the details that interested him, but the intensity of the whole. He based his painting's organization on reds, greens, blues, oranges and violets backed up by deep blacks. However, the colours in

these "moving images" are enhanced only by their relationship to light. In the *Beach at Sainte-Adresse*, shadows no longer exist. Black, which is used as a real colour, does not darken the painting but, on the contrary, brightens it. The light's intensity is rendered not by whites but by blacks, which accentuate the burst of pure tones from the artist's palette.
This work sums up Dufy's temperament and basic trademarks. He was obsessed by light and used harsh colours to render it. Moreover, the line describes an expressive, arabesque drawing style. The brushstrokes capture movement and provide the composition with rhythm. An apparent lightness and spontaneity emanate from this painting. This is partly due to the bright, fresh palette, but in fact it is also the end result of many preparatory studies. Dufy tirelessly filled his sketchbooks with various silhouettes until he captured the expressive line, then filled in his canvas with a speed that has an air of controlled improvisation about it.
However, this painting's grace and cheerfulness are based on a sound organization of space, which is stabilized by the line of the landing stage. An airy, dynamic technique breathes live into the beach. Raoul Dufy was nothing less than an enchanter. In the Rau collection painting his lively, joyful style, featuring incisive strokes, bright tones and a supple drawing technique, conveys the transparency of air, the vibration of light, the movement of colour and the calm instability of the sea.
F. K.

99

Kees van Dongen (Cornelis Theodurus Marie van Dongen, known as Kees van Dongen, 1877–1968)
Little Girl with Sailor Collar or *Dolly van Dongen*, 1912

Oil on canvas.
H: 55 cm; W: 55 cm.
Barely visible signature, upper right: *van Dongen*.
GR 1.801

History:
Marly-le-Roi, private collection; Paris, Madame van Dongen's collection; London, Sotheby's, July 3, 1979, no. 96.

Exhibitions:
Liège, Salon triennal, *Van Dongen*, 1921; Saint-Germain-en-Laye, salons de l'Hôtel de Ville, *Chefs-d'œuvre de collections privées de Gauguin à Kupka*, February 14 – March 8, 1967, no. 93; Paris, Musée National d'Art Moderne, *Van Dongen*, October-November 1967, no. 83; Rotterdam, Museum Boymans-van Beuningen, *Van Dongen*, December 1967 – January 1968, no. 83; Tucson, University of Arizona Museum, *Van Dongen*, 1971, no. 75, repr.; Warsaw-Katowice, *Les salons d'automne à Paris*, April-May 1973; Geneva, Musée de l'Athénée, *Van Dongen*, July-October 1976, no. 33; Paris, Musée Jacquemart-André, *La Ruche, l'Ecole de Paris à Montparnasse, 1910–1930*, 1978, no. 52; Ingelheim am Rhein, Altes Rathaus, *Die Explosion der Farbe. Fauvismus und Expressionismus 1905–1911*, Internationale Tage Ingelheim, Boehringer Ingelheim GmbH, 1998.

Kees van Dongen (Delfshaven, 1877 – Monaco, 1968) was twenty years old when he arrived in Paris in July 1897. At first, he led a poverty-stricken, bohemian life. In 1905, he took part in the Salon d'Automne in Paris. Since his painting was hung next to one by Matisse in the Cage aux Fauves *(room VII), he was considered a member of the Fauve movement from the outset. He was very close to André Derain and Maurice de Vlaminck, extolling pure colours and rejecting the academic values of perspective, space and light in an Impressionistic naturalism.*
In 1908, van Dongen's friendship with Max Pechstein led him to take part in the exhibitions of the Die Brücke Berlin group. His painting revealed definite affinities with the German Expressionists. He was increasingly successful, obtaining a contract with the Galerie Bernheim-Jeune in Paris in 1909. His growing fame would make him a privileged witness to Parisian life.

When van Dongen painted this portrait of his daughter in Paris in 1912, he had just left his apartment at 6 Rue Saulnier in the Nouvelle Athènes neighbourhood for 33 Rue Denfert-Rochereau in the Montparnasse quarter. This move marked the beginning of a lifestyle change that can be seen in his work. He organized big parties in the new studio and increasingly moved in fashionable circles. The next year, 1913, he exhibited *Le Tableau* at the Salon d'Automne in Paris. This painting was a nude for which his wife, Guss, had posed. There was an immediate scandal and the painting was taken down by the police, which consequently made it famous.
The abundant, harsh colours van Dongen had been using a few years earlier (*Acrobat with Bare Breast*, 1907–1908; Paris, Musée National d'Art Moderne; *At the Bois de Boulogne*, 1907–1908; Le Havre, Musée des Beaux-Arts) are softened in this portrait of a child. Stylization and schematization give way to refined, elegant lines. This new technique is clearly evident in this picture of his only daughter, Augusta, affectionately nicknamed Dolly. She was eight years old when she posed for this portrait, which, as usual, shows her wearing a bow in her hair (*My Daughter with the Teddy-bear*, 1911; *My Daughter*, 1912; *Dolly en costume marin*, 1914). Dolly was the object of no less than a cult on the part of her father. She sat for him many times until 1914. Edmond des Courrières, a critic and van Dongen's friend, expressed the artist's affection for children: "Because he loved them, van Dongen painted children the way they really are, little animals barely tainted by civilization. With a few subtleties, he has rendered their clumsy or graceful poses, their wise airs of big dolls."
Here, a knowing, mischievous sensuality radiates from the child's face. As a confirmed colourist, the painter was already evoking what would become posterity's vision of twentieth-century femininity. The eyes are made bigger by khol, the lips are full and the face is fringed with green shadows. The turquoise touch of the bow in the hair, red of the lips and virginal white of the shirt front are so many chromatic foils that lighten the painting's dark blue, almost black background and highlight the model's flamboyant hair. The crimson line on the sleeve stresses the navy blue collar's intensity. This bold colour harmony is one of French Fauvism's and German Expressionism's contributions to van Dongen's style.
F. K.

100

André Derain (1880–1954)
Cypresses, 1907

Oil on cardboard panel.
H: 24 cm; W: 33 cm.
Signed in blue on back:
a. Derain.
GR 1.911

History:
Paris, sale at Derain's studio, 1907, bought by Kahnweiler Gallery; Paris, Galerie Simon; Paris, Galerie Louise Leiris; Paris, Bellier's collection, 1932; Paris, sale at Drouot's; London, Sotheby's, June 30, 1981, no. 30.

Exhibitions:
Los Angeles-New York-London, *The Fauve Landscape*, 1990, p. 290, fig. 304, repr.; Marseille, Hôtel de la Région – Paris, Palais du Luxembourg – Lisbon, Fundação Arpad Szenes Viera da Silva, *Peintres de la couleur en Provence 1875–1920*, 1995, p. 275, repr.; Ingelheim am Rhein, Altes Rathaus, *Die Explosion der Farbe. Fauvismus und Expressionismus 1905–1911*, Internationale Tage Ingelheim, Boehringer Ingelheim GmbH, 1998.

Bibliography:
G. Hilaire, *Derain*, Geneva, 1959, fig. 60; M. Kellermann, *Catalogue raisonné de l'œuvre de Derain*, being prepared.

During his military service in Commercy (Meuse) from 1901 to 1904, André Derain (Chatou, 1880 – Chambourcy, 1954) spent three years away from Maurice de Vlaminck, who had been his best friend since 1900. Upon his return to the Chatou studio, he was back in touch with his elder, Henri Matisse. They had been sharing the same pictorial interests since 1899. Their common appreciation of Mediterranean light brought them even closer together. From the summer of 1905 on, they both worked on the motif at Collioure. An intense friendship followed.

Matisse joined Derain in Cassis during the summer of 1907. It was in this region that the younger artist painted this version of the *Cypresses*, among others. This tortured theme evokes Vincent van Gogh's paintings (*Wheat Field and Cypresses*, 1889, Amsterdam, Rijksmuseum Vincent van Gogh; *The Yellow Wheat*, 1889, London, National Gallery; *The Road with Cypresses*, 1890, Otterlo, Rijksmuseum Kröller-Müller). At the time, Derain willingly cast aside the pure colours he had so vehemently advocated beforehand (*Barges at Le Pecq*, 1904; Paris, Musée National d'Art Moderne). He preferred graphically structuring his painting rather than studying the effects of colour intensity. Here he grasps a new conception of light by stressing the contrast between light and shadow. "Shadow then becomes a world of brightness and luminosity that contrasts with sunlight" (letter to de Vlaminck quoted by J. Leymarie, *Le Fauvisme*, Geneva, 1987, p. 56).
This work makes it possible to pinpoint Matisse's influence on Derain. It brings to mind the older master's painting, *Ajaccio* (1898; Birmingham, Mrs. Philip N. Lilienthal collection). By 1907, André Derain's Fauve period – which he would call "the ordeal by fire" – was over for good. It was followed by what at the time could have been called his "Cézannian" or "gothic" period. André Derain's contacts with his Fauve friends, Maurice de Vlaminck, Kees van Dongen and Emile-Othon Friesz, spurred him on to experiment with colour and free himself from all the constraints of chromatic harmony. This emancipation gave the Fauve period works a new balance.
The Rau collection landscape sketch reveals the sureness of the artist's hand. He ordered his composition according to coloured divisions delimiting fields, trees and sky, creating a harmonious readability. Broad, squarish strokes, again bringing Matisse's technique to mind, reveal the pigments' thickness and intensity. The flattened brushwork clearly appears in the juxtaposition of tones. It never overlaps the neighbouring colour, and sometimes even lets the grey cardboard panel show, for example in the lower right and on the left. The painter's sense of colours allowed him to invent a pale green sky, a pinkish-ochre ground and an orange meadow without chromatic clashing. This technique is the end result of a long hesitation between colour and line.
Until 1910, Derain would give his paintings increasingly strong structure without giving up the pigments from which he knew how to draw the most intense effects nor completely joining the nascent Cubist movement. The Cassis landscapes (Troyes, Musée d'Art Moderne, Donation Pierre Levy) are examples of this period.
F. K.

Expressionism

As a reaction to Impressionism, Expressionism appeared at the start of the twentieth century, alongside Fauvism. Under the impetus of such artists as Grünewald, Goya, El Greco, and later on van Gogh and Munch, the Expressionist artists wanted to express their emotions and their subjectivity by condemning the urban and industrial society of their times, and by creating a world filled with lyricism. The anguish, and even sometimes the violence, found in their paintings were visually expressed by the use of a contrasted and outrageous chromatic scale, a simplified composition and heavy brushstrokes. This movement spread throughout Europe among different groups of artists. It found its most illustrious representatives in Germany with, among others, Heckel, Schmidt-Rottluff, Kirchner, Nolde and Pechstein, who gathered in a group entitled "Die Brücke" (The Bridge). Other artists such as Kandinsky, Marc, Jawlensky and Macke joined up in Munich in the movement "Blaue Reiter" (The Blue Horseman). Like the Fauves, their palettes were brighter and more contrasted than those of Die Brücke. Their themes were less emotive and their interior vision sometimes veered – particularly with Kandinsky – towards Abstraction.

In Austria the movement was represented by Egon Schiele and Kokoschka. The chosen subjects appear like anguished and introverted characters, with their emaciated limbs, and they seem almost an echo of the tragic fates of many Expressionist painters.

*101

Edvard Munch (1863–1944)
Portrait of Madame von Hoffmann, 1927

Oil on canvas.
H: 92 cm; W: 73 cm.
Signed and dated upper left: *Edv Munch 1929*. On the back: *Munchmuseet Oslo*.
GR 1.101

History:
Hamburg, Senator Hudtwalcker's collection; Geneva, sale at Galerie Motte, December 8, 1970, no. 81, repr.

Edvard Munch (Loetgen, Norway, 1863 – Ekely, Norway, 1944) lived in Christiania from 1864 and began technical college in 1879. He worked with Julius Middelthun at the National Arts and Crafts School in 1881, and the following year with Christian Krogh. After a first trip to Paris in 1885, he returned in 1889 to work with Léon Bonnat and exhibited at the Salon des Indépendants and Salon de l'Art Nouveau in 1895. His work was increasingly acclaimed throughout Europe and he travelled to Germany in 1893, Italy in 1899 and Prague in 1905. In 1908–1909 he was treated for psychological disorders. The same year he was made a Knight of the Royal Order of Saint Olaf. Pursuing his career, he exhibited in Cologne in 1912 and Berlin in 1927, and began working on the decoration of the Oslo Town Hall in 1928. In 1936 he exhibited in London and the following year eighty-two of his works were confiscated in Hitler's Germany. He died in 1944 near Oslo in the house he had bought in 1916.

This painting, entitled *Woman in Green* in the Galerie Motte catalogue of 1879, is a real portrait. As has sometimes been thought, it is not that of Maria Agatha Hudtwalcker, wife of the Hamburg collector who owned this work, but of Ludwig von Hoffmann's wife. Munch painted this portrait in September 1927, not in 1929 as he himself indicated on the canvas, when the couple came to visit him at Ekely. It has been proven that Munch sometimes signed and dated his works several years after he painted them, without adding anything else to the picture. The date of 1927 is all the more plausible because a photograph was published in the Norwegian newspaper *Aftenposten* on September 3, 1927, showing Munch and Mr. and Mrs. Hoffmann standing round the sketch, presently in the Munch Museum collection in Oslo, for the portrait.
A work from his mature period, this richly coloured painting demonstrates Renoir's influence on Munch. The extremely simple composition shows the frontal, half-length figure sitting behind a table. Halfway between Impressionism and Expressionism, the painting's intense luminosity is the first thing that strikes the eye. The forms, for example the hands, are but colours, barely delineated by a contour line. Munch goes further into modernity, demonstrating a certain boldness by leaving some parts of the hat white, uncovered by paint.
Munch's work is also surprising in the face's colours, which are a sort of tonal inversion. The forehead and eyes are in light tones, the cheeks in darker hues, evoking the radiance of a beautiful summer day. This impression is reinforced by the violet of the clothing, which expresses the reflection of light in the blue jacket. The green background is of an intensely powerful expressiveness which suggests a full garden. A few vertical brown lines represent tree trunks and visible brushstrokes depict the foliage. The technique creates a green ambience that entirely permeates the sitter by colouring the shadows of her white blouse and her face a pale green.
Ph. L.

102

Alexej von Jawlensky (1864–1941)
Maria II, 1901

Oil on canvas.
H: 74.8 cm; W: 62.8 cm.
Signed upper left: *A. Jawlensky*;
inscription on the back: *A. Jawlensky / "Maria" II.1901.*
GR 1.39

History:
Munich, Galerie Gunzenhauser, December 1971, no. 1.

Exhibition:
Dortmund, Museum am Ostwall, *Alexej von Jawlensky, Reisen-Freunde-Wandlungen 1893–1937*, 1998.

Bibliography:
C. Weiler, *Alexei Jawlensky: Köpfe, Gesichte, Meditationen*, Hanau, 1970, p. 149; "Jawlensky bei Gunzenhauser", in *Artis*, December 12, 1971, p. 40, repr.; "Jawlensky zum Gedächtnis", in *Die Kunst*, December 12, 1971, p. 722, repr.; J.-J. Lévêque, *Les années de la Belle Epoque, 1890–1914*, Paris, 1991, p. 417, repr.; *Catalogue raisonné de l'œuvre peint de Jawlensky*, London, 1991, p. 48, no. 23, repr.

Alexej von Jawlensky (Tver, Russia, 1864 – Wiesbaden, 1941) went to secondary school in Moscow from 1874 to 1882. Refusing a military career, he trained at the Academy of Fine Arts in Saint Petersburg in 1889, then in Munich in 1896, where he was the student of Anton Azbé until 1899 and met Kandinsky. In 1903 he travelled to Paris and Normandy, and in 1905 met Henri Matisse. In 1909 he founded the New Association of Munich Artists with Kandinsky and the Blaue Reiter in 1911. From 1912 on he frequented Emil Nolde and Paul Klee, creating the Blauen Vier with Klee, Feininger and Kandinsky in 1924. In 1934 he began to paint his Meditations.

Jawlensky's training in Saint Petersburg and with Anton Azbé in Munich had provided him with a sound technique. His early works were heavily marked by realism before being influenced by van Gogh and Neo-Impressionism.
Jawlensky painted this portrait in 1901, as the inscription made on the back of the painting by the artist's son indicates. The painter showed his model half-length and turned to the left, with a flower-bedecked hat on her head. Maria was the sister of Jawlensky's wife, Helen. The artist painted her a first time in *Maria I* (private collection; *Catalogue raisonné*, 1991, no. 22, repr.). The young woman, seen frontally in a less expressive pose, is wearing a similar hat with flowers. More importantly, the technique suggests that the two versions were painted at a brief interval.
The surprise aroused by the Rau collection work, whose style is rather unusual for Jawlensky, stems from its sketchy technique, which is achieved with broad brushstrokes that catch the light. The face is more detailed, delicately rendering the figure's personality traits but without really seeking to depict an expression, which gives the painting its Impressionistic character. Throughout his life Jawlensky painted the female figure, which constitutes the major part of his oeuvre. From 1908 to 1913 he painted the *Expressive Heads*, a series of wide, abstract, brightly coloured and almost square-shaped faces. In 1917 he began the *Abstract Mystic Heads* series, where the outline is pronounced and the colours still very lively. Finally, from 1934 to 1937 the *Meditations* series presented small figures. In 1906 Jawlensky painted other half-length female figures, seated in a chair. Examples are the *Young Woman in a Yellow Apron* and *Young Woman in a Pink Dress*, both in private collections (*Alexei Jawlensky vom Abbild zum Urbild*, 1979, nos. 13, 14). These works serve as pretexts for spatial constructions. They are studies in composition in which the figurative subject as such is no longer very important. The artist's expressiveness was already leaning towards the abstract, his style being linked more to the structure of forms than to their perception. The strong outline in these paintings underscores the structure of the face.
Ph. L.

103

August Macke (1887–1914)
Clown in a Green Costume

Oil on canvas.
H: 121.5 cm; W: 72 cm.
GR 1.658

History:
Hamburg, sale by Dr Ernst Hauswedel, June 8–10, 1972, no. 1426, repr.; Cologne, Lempertz's.

Bibliography:
Vriesen, p. 326, no. 327, repr.

August Macke (Meschede, 1887 – Perthes, 1914) spent his childhood in Cologne and Bonn. He took classes at the Art Academy and School of Decorative Arts in Dusseldorf from 1904 to 1906. He travelled to Paris in 1907 and became a student of Lovis Corinth in Berlin from 1907 to 1908. The collector Bernard Koehler encouraged him to go back to Paris in 1908. He joined the Blaue Reiter after meeting Franz Marc and Kandinsky in Munich in January 1910, but settled in Bonn in the month of October. In April 1914 he left for Tunisia with Paul Klee, returning to die on the front of Champagne at the beginning of the First World War.

In his catalogue, Vriesen dates the *Clown in a Green Costume* from 1912, when Macke lived in Bonn and was a member of the Blaue Reiter, the first pictorial movement in Germany to head towards abstraction. However, this date does not correspond to the painting's style. At the time, Macke's innovations were taking the course mapped out by Picasso's and Braque's Cubism as well as Italian Futurism. In the work of this period, Macke translated space into a rigid construction of oblique lines, and coloured his pictures with vivid hues. From then on the subjects' movements became the true basis of his experimentation. Vriesen dated the *Clown in a Green Costume* to 1912 by comparing it with other works which were painted the same year and have a similar theme.
Macke loved the theatre, circus and shows of any kind. Walter Gerhardt, one of his friends, relates that he often went to the Appollotheater in Bonn, and that he drew while the performance was in progress. In October 1912 Macke saw Diaghilev's Russian Ballets in Cologne. He was particularly impressed by the *Carnival* ballet, in which Waclaw Nijinsky and Tamara Karsawina danced to the music of Robert Schumann. He made some sketches of it on the spot, which today are in the Bremen Kunsthalle, and executed several pictures on this theme. The first, the *Russian Ballet I*, depicts the most important scene of the performance, when Harlequin and Colombine dance while Pierrot finds himself alone, in a melancholy mood. The second, *Ballet Russe II: Nijinsky and Karsawina*, was destroyed. In 1913 Macke reworked this theme in *Pierrot* (Bielefeld, Kunsthalle) by organizing the space whose linear structure, bright colours and geometric forms place the accent on the figure's solitude. A black chalk drawing done the same year depicts *A Clown and a Woman Riding a Horse*. The composition of the scene, which takes place in a circus ring, is more reminiscent of Seurat's *Le Cirque* than of *Clown in a Green Costume*. Despite the thematic similarity, Macke's stylistic development points to an earlier date for this last piece, that is to say around 1909–1910. In the *Clown in a Green Costume* the apple green suit contrasts with the blue-green background. Macke did not yet experiment much with turning forms and space into geometric shapes. In reality, this painting is stylistically more similar to works such as the *Self-portrait in Litewka* of 1909.
The artist is shown full-length and the same simplification of forms can once more be seen, particularly in the hands whose fingers are not defined. Also characteristic of Macke's work around 1910 is the emphasis upon contour lines, which lend his figures a very particular, almost melancholic expression.
Ph. L.

104

Emmanuel Mané-Katz (1894–1962)
The Rabbi, 1925

Oil on canvas.
H: 60 cm; W: 67 cm.
Signed and dated upper right: *Mané-Katz 25.*
GR 1.515

History:
Geneva, sale at Galerie Motte, November 2, 1971; Paris, Drouant collection.

Bibliography:
R. S. Aries, *Mané-Katz. The Complete Works*, London, 1970, vol. I, p. 40, no. 125 repr. (no signature, no date).

Emmanuel Mané-Katz (Krementchuk, Ukraine, 1894 – Haifa, 1962) was completely immersed in the Jewish tradition during his childhood. His father, director of conscience (schamesch) *at the Krementchuk synagogue, brought him up in accordance with the precepts of orthodox Judaism, planning for him to become a rabbi. The young Emmanuel broke the Mosaic law forbidding the representation of images, and learned to draw in secret. He left his hometown's ghetto for the first time to study at the School of Fine Arts in Vilna, but knew nothing of lay life and quickly returned home. Soon afterwards, an artist from Odessa encouraged him to enroll in the School of Fine Arts in Kiev, where he was introduced to European culture.*

He arrived in Paris in 1913 at the age of nineteen and tried joining the Foreign Legion at the outbreak of war, but was turned down because of his small size. He then travelled to London, Marseille, Athens, Sofia, Bucharest and Krementchuk, visiting museums where he became familiar with the works of the old masters, especially Rembrandt. He also discovered works by his contemporaries, including André Derain, who had a decisive influence on him.

After nine years since his first trip to France, Mané-Kats returned to Paris in 1921. In the meantime, he had forged a style in which traditional Judeo-Slav themes were his main source of inspiration. He gradually became known as one of the painters of the Jewish soul alongside his elders, Amedeo Modigliani and Chaim Soutine. Mané-Katz painted this *Rabbi* in 1925. The very assertive technique and intimist character suggest that this may be one of his earliest paintings of a live model. This spiritual father inspires intellectual and moral respect.

The painting, which is outstanding for its powerful composition, demonstrates André Derain's influence, especially in the use of pure colours. The crimson of the long beard focuses the viewer's attention, while the background nuanced with small, light, luminous strokes ranging from red on the right to blue on the left makes it stand out against a field dominated by scarlet tones. The artist did not pick these tones by accident. The choice powerfully and brilliantly asserts his religious identity. Mané-Katz sought to keep the Torah's culture alive in his art.

His itinerary in the Paris School and the Montparnasse group was much more "orthodox" than Chagall's, for example. Mané-Katz came to the foreground as one of the diaspora's greatest painters. He was a witness to the scattering of the people of Israel, Judeo-Slav folklore and Yiddish literature. In his exile, he demonstrated loyalty to the tradition in which he was born.
F. K.

MANÉ-KATZ
25

After 1940

105

Marie Laurencin (1883–1956)
Three Young Girls and Two Dogs, 1940

Oil on cardboard-lined canvas.
H: 38 cm; W: 46 cm.
Signed in ink, upper right: *Marie Laurencin*.
GR 1.179

History:
Silvano Lodi's collection.

Bibliography:
D. Marchesseau, *Catalogue raisonné de l'œuvre peint par Marie Laurencin*, supplement being prepared.

The young Marie Laurencin (Paris, 1883 – Paris, 1956) was surrounded by poets, including Guillaume Apollinaire and Max Jacob, and artists, such as Picasso and Braque. By 1905, she was already moving in a circle of innovative artists, gradually finding her identity, the feminine mystique. Her stormy affair with Guillaume Apollinaire and the twists and turns of her love life were in the news. Each of her works can be viewed as one of the pages of a diary where the self-portrait and alter ego appear side by side. The legendary grace in each of Marie Laurencin's paintings reveals her personal vision of woman.

These *Three Young Girls and Two Dogs* seem to have been painted during the 1940s, as other versions demonstrate (*Three Young Girls and Two Dogs*; *Catalogue raisonné*, 1986, no. 834).
Marie Laurencin painted many variations on the same composition, especially during the last fifteen years of her life. As usual, she used a palette of lemon yellow, fuchsia pink, delicate blues and greens that are thinned down with turpentine. She explained, "I didn't like all colours. So why should I use the ones I didn't like? Stubbornly, I put them aside. I used only blue, pink, green, white and black. As I grew older, I accepted yellow and red" (*Conferencia*, August 15, 1934).
These colours, which are painted in light strokes, and the creamy, smooth paste, loaded with ceruse white, express the figures' sensuality. The discreet, nearly flat modelling gives importance to the texture. Some structural particularities – the ribbons in the hair, the arabesque yellow scarf and the fabrics' diaphanous aspect – demonstrate the painter's concern with finding a balance. This construction in space places the figures in a playlet. Big black eyes and small, full mouths accentuate the mischievous character of these impish, roguish little girls. The looks on their faces are almost the same, yet reflect different moods. Their slender, sinuously bending bodies evoke both a farandole and part of a blind man's bluff, with two rapidly sketched dogs. The artist's inner world is conveyed between the dream and reality, the freshness and fragility of these actresses. Marie Laurencin's work contributed the grace and ambiguous softness of her feminine world to twentieth-century art.
F. K.

106

Giorgio Morandi (1890–1964)
Still Life with Bottle and Glasses, 1945–1955

Oil on canvas.
H: 30.3 cm; W: 45 cm.
Signed lower left: *Morandi*.
GR 1.678

History:
Geneva, Galerie Motte, circa 1973.

Giorgio Morandi (Bologna, 1890 – Bologna, 1964) was the son of a cultivated Bologna family. In 1907 he began taking classes at his native city's Academy of Fine Arts. He remained there for the rest of his life, as a teacher of drawing from 1914 to 1930 and printmaking from 1930 to 1956. The only time he left Italy, it was to see a major Cézanne exhibition in Zurich in 1956. However, at a very young age he had already travelled the length and breadth of his native country. He discovered works by Cézanne in 1909, Renoir, Giotto, Masaccio and Monet in 1910 and Matisse in 1914. Seurat and Corot also strongly influenced his oeuvre.

Morandi deliberately chose to spend most of his time in Bologna, but he was not isolated from the artistic world. He took part in the Futurist movement in 1914, the metaphysical Valori Plastici in 1918 and the Novecento Italiano in 1926. His paintings would always be shown at the greatest international exhibitions.

Morandi stands out radically from his contemporaries because of his work's unclassifiable nature. His oeuvre, which is essentially composed of landscapes and still lives, is based on a powerful, modernist yet timeless discipline and thematic obsession.

Giorgio Morandi created a highly personal, thought-provoking iconography by taking up the traditional genre of the still life. The artist intelligently laid the humblest objects, such as bottles, vases, pitchers, cruets and ewers, out on his studio table and recreated their colour in the painting's imaginary space. All of these simple, lifeless, traditional and familiar vessels have a soul. Morandi's resolutely mature simplicity enabled him to compose an organization similar to a landscape's, with its special, meaningful reliefs in the organization of the composition.

Each of his paintings is ordered according to an intensely rigourous architecture that is always imbued with singularity. The artist paid particular attention to his choice of objects, painting some of them beforehand. This demonstrates the acuity of his eye as well as the extreme sensibility of his temperament. Each painting constitutes the perpetual renewal of an eternal scene. Whatever the number, shape, colour, position or lighting of each of the items the painter shows, the subject's obsessional nature responds to his endless quest.

The composition of the Rau collection's *Still Life with Bottle and Glasses* suggests that it must have been painted between 1945 and 1955. Four perfectly simple, cylindrical objects are lined up on a grey-ochre table. There is a white jar with beige edges, a straw-yellow bottle containing a pink-ochre liquid, a white cup with grey edges and a dark green jar. The vessels stand out against a light beige background painted with broad strokes that let the canvas show through in spots. The delicate, limited colour range attests to an extreme economy of means. Perhaps in this way Giorgio Morandi's work evokes that of Chardin and Corot.

At the centre of the artist's intense, meditative approach to painting is his contemplation of nature and the silent world of objects. Colour and texture are not important in his work. Here, as in each of his many other paintings in the still life genre, which he endlessly renewed, he probed the subtle, inexpressible relationships between shapes and volumes. These objects are imposing because of the simple power of their intimate presence. They alone justify the painting's urgent necessity.

Morandi's quest to capture the sense of the eternity of things transforms the simplest still life into meditative, sensitive painting. Jean Leymarie summed it up well when he wrote, "Morandi renews a genre that marks his work with pure moments of grace [...] his work is a reflection of modern anxiety, the split between being and appearing. His miracle is having managed to strike [...] the difficult balance between bursting reality and controlling reason, between objectivity which is hidden and subjectivity which is hurrying" (*Giorgio Morandi*, 1971).
F. K.

Appendixes

List of Illustrations

Anonymous painter,
Italy / Lombardy-Piedmont
(end of seventeenth –
beginning of eighteenth
century)
Portrait of Maddalena del Grande (1634–1713)
(cat. no. 10)

Fra Angelico
Saint Michael
(cat. no. 2)
Saint Nicholas of Bari
(cat. no. 1)

Frédéric Bazille
Fisherman with a Net
(cat. no. 54)

Bernardo Bellotto
The Tower of Marghera
(cat. no. 12)

Pierre Bonnard
Saint-Tropez Bay
(cat. no. 88)
Window Opened at Uriage
(cat. no. 89)

François Boucher
The Flute Lesson
(cat. no. 38)

Eugène Boudin
The Beach at Trouville
(cat. no. 53)

Gustave Caillebotte
The Snow-covered Rooftops
(cat. no. 74)

Canaletto
Saint Mark's Square
(cat. no. 11)

Giovanni Battista Caracciolo
Joseph and the Wife of Potiphar
(cat. no. 7)

Mary Cassatt
Louise Feeding Her Child
(cat. no. 75)

Paul Cézanne
The Sea at L'Estaque
(cat. no. 55)

Philippe de Champaigne
Portrait of Doctor Boüin
(cat. no. 34)

Chevalier Volaire
Still Waters, Fishermen
(cat. no. 41)

Jean-Baptiste Camille Corot
Algerian Woman
(cat. no. 51)
Path Leading Towards a House in the Country
(cat. no. 50)

Colyn de Coter
Saint Veronica
(cat. no. 14)

Gustave Courbet
Bacchante
(cat. no. 52)

Lucas Cranach the Elder
Judith
(cat. no. 29)
Triptych
(cat. no. 28)

Vittore Crivelli
Christ of Pity or *Pietà*
(cat. no. 3)

Edgar Degas
Self-portrait
(cat. no. 58)
Two Young Girls Looking at an Album
(cat. no. 57)

Maurice Denis
July
(cat. no. 94)
Mother and Child on a Yellow Bed
(cat. no. 95)

André Derain
Cypresses
(cat. no. 100)

Carlo Dolci
Saint John the Evangelist
(cat. no. 8)

Gerard Dou
The Cook
(cat. no. 22)

Raoul Dufy
The Beach at Sainte-Adresse
(cat. no. 98)

Jean-Honoré Fragonard
Portrait of François-Henri, Duke of Harcourt
(cat. no. 42)

Thomas Gainsborough
Portrait of Mrs. Gainsborough
(cat. no. 49)

Anton Graff
Portrait of a Gentleman
(cat. no. 32)

El Greco
Saint Dominic in Prayer
(cat. no. 45)

Jean-Baptiste Greuze
Portrait of a Young Woman
(cat. no. 40)

Ferdinand Hodler
Portrait of a Lady
(cat. no. 84)

Alexej von Jawlensky
Maria II
(cat. no. 102)

Gustav Klimt
Old Woman
(cat. no. 85)

Nicolas de Largillière
Portrait of a Woman with Carnation
(cat. no. 36)

Maurice-Quentin de La Tour
Portrait of Charles-Jacques Colin
(cat. no. 39)

Marie Laurencin
Three Young Girls and Two Dogs
(cat. no. 105)

Judith Leyster
Young Girl with a Straw Hat
(cat. no. 20)

Max Liebermann
Playtime at the Amsterdam Orphanage
(cat. no. 76)

Jacques Linard
Vanitas with Candle
(cat. no. 33)

Bernardino Luini
Portrait of a Young Woman
(cat. no. 4)

August Macke
Clown in a Green Costume
(cat. no. 103)

Jan Mandyn
Temptation of Saint Anthony
(cat. no. 15)

Emmanuel Mané-Katz
The Rabbi
(cat. no. 104)

Edouard Manet
Woman with a Black Hat
(cat. no. 56)

Albert Marquet
The Old Marseille Harbour
(cat. no. 96)

Master of the Life of Mary
Last Judgement
(cat. no. 27)

Jean-François Millet
Heroic Landscape
(cat. no. 35)

Claude Monet
Flood, W 642
(cat. no. 62)
Houses in the Snow in Norway, W 1395
(cat. no. 64)
The Port-Coton Pyramids, W 1087
(cat. no. 63)
View of Amsterdam, W 303
(cat. no. 61)
The Wooden Bridge, W 195
(cat. no. 60)
Woods and Undergrowth, W 58
(cat. no. 59)

Giorgio Morandi
Still Life with Bottle and Glasses
(cat. no. 105)

Edvard Munch
Portrait of Madame von Hoffmann
(cat. no. 101)

Jean-Baptiste Pater
Stopping at an Inn
(cat. no. 37)

Camille Pissarro
The Courthouse at Pontoise
(cat. no. 69)
Portrait of Jeanne
(cat. no. 70)
The Road from Saint-Germain to Louveciennes
(cat. no. 68)
View of L'Hermitage, Jallais Hill in Pontoise, 1867
(cat. no. 67)

Frans Post
The Episcopal Church of Olinda
(cat. no. 21)

Frans Pourbus the Younger
Portrait of Guillaume Duvair
(cat. no. 16)

Odilon Redon
Apollo's Chariot
(cat. no. 83)
Rose in a Vase
(cat. no. 82)

Guido Reni
David Decapitating Goliath
(cat. no. 6)

Auguste Renoir
Head of a Woman or Woman with a Rose
(cat. no. 65)
Portrait of Henry Lerolle
(cat. no. 66)

Joshua Reynolds
Portrait of Rebecca Watson
(cat. no. 48)

José de Ribera
Saint Jerome
(cat. no. 46)

Hubert Robert
Monumental Staircase
(cat. no. 43)

Paul Sérusier
Spring at Pouldu
(cat. no. 86)

Gino Severini
Landscape at Civray
(cat. no. 81)

Jan Siberechts
The Art Lover's Cabinet
(cat. no. 26)

Paul Signac
The Sea. Saint-Briac. The Guérin Guard. Saint-Lunaire. Opus 211
(cat. no. 77)

Elisabetta Sirani
Allegory of Music
(cat. no. 9)

Alfred Sisley
Effect of Snow at Marly
(cat. no. 71)
Saint-Mammès, la Croix-blanche
(cat. no. 73)
The Small Meadow at By
(cat. no. 72)

Max Slevogt
Portrait of Sada Yakko and a Japanese Child
(cat. no. 80)

Antonio Solario
Virgin and Child
(cat. no. 5)

Jakob Strüb
Saint Acacius and the Ten Thousand Martyrs
(cat. no. 30)

Gerard Ter Borch
Portrait of a Gentleman
(cat. no. 24)

Hendrick Ter Brugghen
Backgammon Players
(cat. no. 17)

Giandomenico Tiepolo
Allegorical Portrait of a Young Woman with Flowers
(cat. no. 13)

Henri de Toulouse-Lautrec
Gabrielle the Dancer
(cat. no. 78)

Félix Vallotton
Max Rodrigues-Henriques in the Studio of His Stepfather, Félix Vallotton
(cat. no. 87)

Willem van Aelst
Still Life with Herring's Head
(cat. no. 25)

Kees van Dongen
Little Girl with Sailor Collar or *Dolly van Dongen*
(cat. no. 99)

Jan van Goyen
Storm
(cat. no. 18)

Salomon van Ruisdael
River Landscape
(cat. no. 19)

Jeremias van Winghe
Servant in a Kitchen
(cat. no. 31)

Elisabeth-Louise Vigée-Le Brun
Portrait of Charlotte Ritt
(cat. no. 44)

Maurice de Vlaminck
Fauve Landscape near Chatou
(cat. no. 97)

Edouard Vuillard
The Chestnut Trees, Rue Truffaut
(cat. no. 91)
Portrait of Monsieur André Bénac
(cat. no. 93)
Self-portrait, 1889
(cat. no. 90)
Self-portrait, 1906
(cat. no. 92)

Emmanuel de Witte
Interior of the Oude Kerk, Amsterdam
(cat. no. 23)

John Michael Wright
Portrait of Sir Hugh Wyndham
(cat. no. 47)

Ignacio Zuloaga y Zabaleta
Portrait of the Picador "El Coriano"
(cat. no. 79)

Timeline

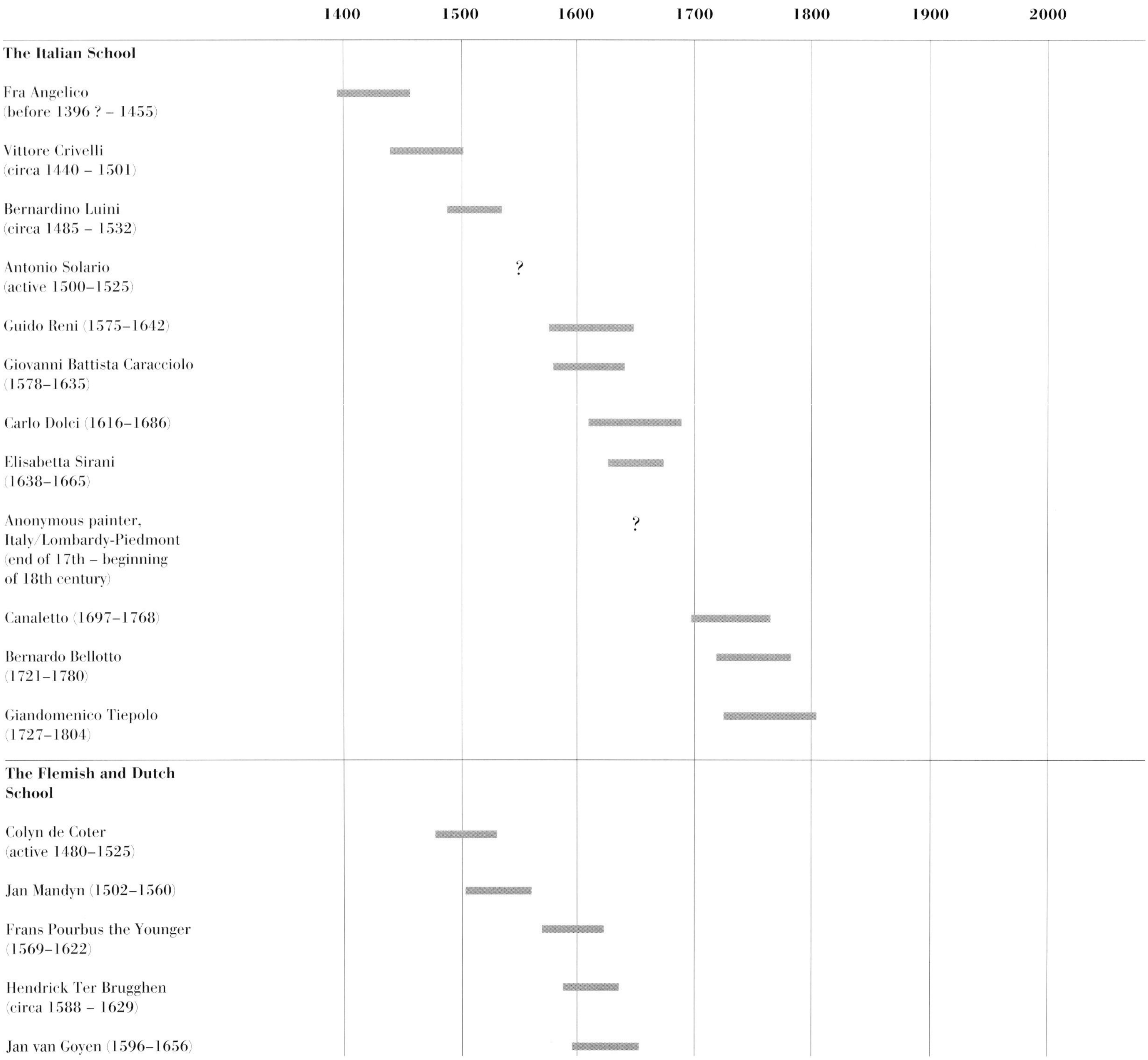
1400
1500
1600
1700
1800
1900
2000
The Italian School
Fra Angelico
(before 1396 ? – 1455)
Vittore Crivelli
(circa 1440 – 1501)
Bernardino Luini
(circa 1485 – 1532)
Antonio Solario
(active 1500–1525)
?
Guido Reni (1575–1642)
Giovanni Battista Caracciolo
(1578–1635)
Carlo Dolci (1616–1686)
Elisabetta Sirani
(1638–1665)
Anonymous painter,
Italy/Lombardy-Piedmont
(end of 17th – beginning
of 18th century)
?
Canaletto (1697–1768)
Bernardo Bellotto
(1721–1780)
Giandomenico Tiepolo
(1727–1804)
The Flemish and Dutch
School
Colyn de Coter
(active 1480–1525)
Jan Mandyn (1502–1560)
Frans Pourbus the Younger
(1569–1622)
Hendrick Ter Brugghen
(circa 1588 – 1629)
Jan van Goyen (1596–1656)

	1400	1500	1600	1700	1800	1900	2000
Salomon van Ruisdael (after 1600 – 1670)							
Judith Leyster (1609–1660)							
Frans Post (1612–1680)							
Gerard Dou (1613–1675)							
Emmanuel de Witte (1615/1617–1691/1692)							
Gerard Ter Borch (1617–1681)							
Willem van Aelst (circa 1626 – after 1683)							
Jan Siberechts (1627–1703)							
The German School							
Master of the Life of Mary (active 1460–1490)							
Lucas Cranach the Elder (1472–1553)							
Jakob Strüb (active in the early 16th century)		?					
Jeremias van Winghe (1578–1645)							
Anton Graff (1736–1813)							
The French School							
Jacques Linard (circa 1600 – 1645)							
Philippe de Champaigne (1602–1674)							
Jean-François Millet (1642–1679)							
Nicolas de Largillière (1656–1746)							
Jean-Baptiste Pater (1695–1736)							
François Boucher (1703–1770)							

1400 1500 1600 1700 1800 1900 2000

Maurice-Quentin de La Tour (1704–1788)

Jean-Baptiste Greuze (1725–1805)

Chevalier Volaire (1729 – before 1802 or 1790)

Jean-Honoré Fragonard (1732–1806)

Hubert Robert (1733–1808)

Elisabeth-Louise Vigée-Le Brun (1755–1842)

The Spanish School

El Greco (1541–1614)

José de Ribera (1591–1652)

The English School

John Michael Wright (1617–1694)

Joshua Reynolds (1723-1792)

Thomas Gainsborough (1727–1788)

The Impressionist Revolution

Jean-Baptiste Camille Corot (1796–1875)

Gustave Courbet (1819–1877)

Eugène Boudin (1824–1898)

Frédéric Bazille (1841–1870)

Paul Cézanne (1839–1906)

Edouard Manet (1832–1883)

Edgar Degas (1834–1917)

Claude Monet (1840–1926)

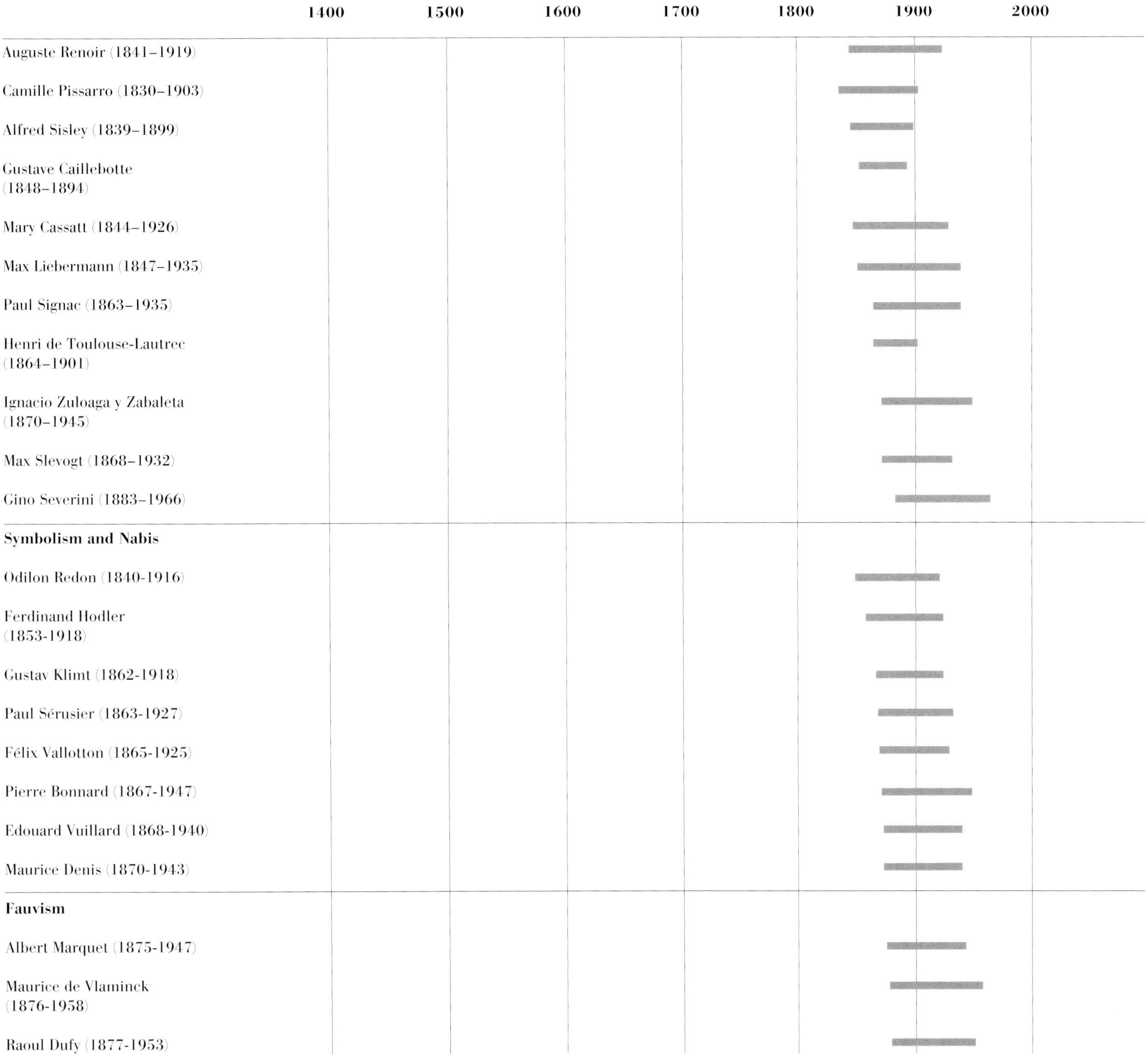
1400
1500
1600
1700
1800
1900
2000
Auguste Renoir (1841–1919)
Camille Pissarro (1830–1903)
Alfred Sisley (1839–1899)
Gustave Caillebotte (1848–1894)
Mary Cassatt (1844–1926)
Max Liebermann (1847–1935)
Paul Signac (1863–1935)
Henri de Toulouse-Lautrec (1864–1901)
Ignacio Zuloaga y Zabaleta (1870–1945)
Max Slevogt (1868–1932)
Gino Severini (1883–1966)
Symbolism and Nabis
Odilon Redon (1840-1916)
Ferdinand Hodler (1853-1918)
Gustav Klimt (1862-1918)
Paul Sérusier (1863-1927)
Félix Vallotton (1865-1925)
Pierre Bonnard (1867-1947)
Edouard Vuillard (1868-1940)
Maurice Denis (1870-1943)
Fauvism
Albert Marquet (1875-1947)
Maurice de Vlaminck (1876-1958)
Raoul Dufy (1877-1953)

	1400	1500	1600	1700	1800	1900	2000
Kees van Dongen (1877–1968)							
André Derain (1880–1954)							
Expressionism							
Edvard Munch (1863–1944)							
Alexej von Jawlensky (1864–1941)							
August Macke (1887–1914)							
Emmanuel Mané-Katz (1894–1962)							
After 1940							
Marie Laurencin (1883–1956)							
Giorgio Morandi (1890–1964)							